Praise for *H*

"*Hidden Light* is essential for anyone interested in contemporary Israeli cinema. Bringing deep theoretical and historical knowledge to bear on the 'Judaic turn,' Chyutin presents new ways of thinking about religion on-screen and ideas of spiritual transcendence endemic to the concept of 'the cinematic' since the art form's birth."

—Kyle Stevens, editor of *The Oxford Handbook of Film Theory*

"Dan Chyutin's timely study brings the 'Judaic turn' to bear upon a rich and engaging analysis of Israeli cinema. It does so by paying attention to cinematic appeals to the Judaic New Age, or what some scholars have recently termed the 'Jew Age.' *Hidden Light* is an important contribution that, through its Jew Age analyses, brings into question simplistic binary thinking regarding the Israeli secular-religious divide in favor of a more complex reading of Judaism's relationship to Israeli notions of identity."

—Brian Ogren, Anna Smith Fine Professor of Judaic Studies and Religion Department Chair at Rice University

"*Hidden Light* makes a singular contribution to the study of Israeli cinema, exploring and delineating one of the most important developments in Israeli cinema over the past three decades: the emergence of religious-themed Israeli films. Chyutin's analysis of films is meticulous and enlightening, as he expands and challenges our perceptions of the Israeli cinematic canon."

—Eran Kaplan, author of *Projecting the Nation: History and Ideology on the Israeli Screen*

"*Hidden Light* analyzes the 'Judaic turn' in Israeli cinema beginning during the 2000s in riveting and rigorous detail. But that is only one of this book's many impressive achievements. Chyutin grapples with nothing less than film theory's links to religious and mystical concepts, building new bridges between film studies, Jewish studies, and religious studies."

—Adam Lowenstein, University of Pittsburgh,
author of *Horror Film and Otherness*

"*Hidden Light* is an act of reclamation. Moving beyond a seeming dichotomy between a text-driven legal tradition and the visual poetics of cinema, Chyutin brilliantly illustrates how the recent wave of religiously inflected Israeli cinema is deeply rooted in Jewish traditions of longing, prayer, and transcendence."

—Shayna Weiss, associate director of the Schusterman
Center for Israel Studies at Brandeis University

Hidden Light

Contemporary Approaches to Film and Media Series

A complete listing of the books in this series can
be found online at wsupress.wayne.edu.

GENERAL EDITOR

Barry Keith Grant
Brock University

Hidden Light

Judaism and Mystical Experience in Israeli Cinema

Dan Chyutin

WAYNE STATE UNIVERSITY PRESS

DETROIT

ISBN 9780814350676 (paperback)
ISBN 9780814350683 (hardcover)
ISBN 9780814350690 (e-book)

Library of Congress Control Number: 2023930387

On cover: Haim-Aaron trying to find his way in the fog in *Tikkun* (2015), directed by Avishai Sivan, cinematography by Shai Goldman. Used by permission of Avishai Sivan. Cover design by Will Brown.

Wayne State University Press rests on Waawiyaataanong, also referred to as Detroit, the ancestral and contemporary homeland of the Three Fires Confederacy. These sovereign lands were granted by the Ojibwe, Odawa, Potawatomi, and Wyandot Nations, in 1807, through the Treaty of Detroit. Wayne State University Press affirms Indigenous sovereignty and honors all tribes with a connection to Detroit. With our Native neighbors, the press works to advance educational equity and promote a better future for the earth and all people.

Wayne State University Press
Leonard N. Simons Building
4809 Woodward Avenue
Detroit, Michigan 48201-1309

Visit us online at wsupress.wayne.edu.

To my father, Michael Chyutin z"l, and my mother,
Bracha Chyutin, for being who they are

CONTENTS

ACKNOWLEDGMENTS

This book project began when I was a graduate student at the University of Pittsburgh's Film Studies Program. I would like to acknowledge the support given to me by various faculty members during this period, and especially Professor Adam Lowenstein, Professor Neepa Majumdar, and Professor Adam Shear. My deepest appreciation goes to Professor Lucy Fischer, whose generous guidance and advice as dissertation committee chair greatly affected my thinking process.

Also invaluable are colleagues who offered assistance and encouragement over the years, and especially Dr. Ali Patterson, Dr. Ohad Landesman, Dr. Ori Levin, Dr. Boaz Hagin, Professor Yvonne Kozlovsky-Golan, Professor Yaron Peleg, and Professor Raz Yosef. Professor Rachel S. Harris has been a particularly fierce advocate of my scholarship, and several of the ideas present in this volume came to me as a result of our fruitful conversations. Formal and informal discussions with students at Tel Aviv University's Steve Tisch School of Film and Television have proved incredibly helpful as well, pushing me to revise and nuance my arguments.

The first and second chapters are partially based on the following published essays (used by permission from their respective publishers): "Negotiating Judaism in Contemporary Israeli Cinema: The Spiritual Style of *My Father, My Lord*," in *Israeli Cinema: Identities in Motion*, ed. Yaron Peleg and Miri Talmon, 2011, 201–12, published through University of Texas Press; "'Lifting the Veil': Judaic-Themed Israeli Cinema and Spiritual Aesthetics," *Jewish Film and New Media* 3, no. 1 (Spring 2015), 39–58, published through Johns Hopkins University Press; and "'The King's Daughter Is All Glorious Within': Female Modesty in Judaic-Themed Israeli Cinema," *Journal of Jewish Identities* 9, no. 1 (Spring 2016),

25–47, published through Wayne State University Press. I am profoundly indebted to the readers of this preliminary work for their insightful comments, which aided me in developing it into the more complete and refined form present herein. I also wish to recognize the important feedback provided by the readers and editorial staff of Wayne State University Press, who were instrumental in making my book better.

Finally, I wish to single out the patience and kindness of those closest to me. To my friends in Israel, Iris Ozer, Nadav Noah, and Yael Mazor—you are my emotional bedrock, without which I would not have been able to face the challenges of writing. To my mother, Bracha Chyutin, and my late father, Dr. Michael Chyutin (z"l)—thank you for believing that there are no limits to what I can do in life. Though I do not always share this belief, it nevertheless exists as a bright light within me.

INTRODUCTION

Judaism and Cinema in an Israeli Context

In 2013, Israel's leading daily newspaper *Yediot Acharonot* asked ten local "cultural figures" to determine "who was their favorite God-fearing character on the Israeli screen."[1] The answers were diverse not only in their pick of character but also in the type of claims made about it. Among the accounts, respondents noted the merits of characters who honestly and painfully confront religion's strict edicts and mores, who arrest the flow of narrative action to approach God and ask for providence,[2] who exhibit "seriousness" and "contemplation" or rather "simplicity" and "naivete," who capture with authenticity the details of religious life or alternatively embody its value system without adhering to all of its codes. Such a myriad of responses not only testifies to the presence of many "God-fearing characters" in Israeli films, but also to the recognition that this presence carries with it a measure of significance that deserves our attention.

It may nevertheless come as a surprise to some that until recently this type of discussion was very rare. For the better part of its history, Israeli cinema paid little to no attention to the religious dimension of Jewish identity—that is, to Judaism.[3] Judaic characters were few and far between, turning Judaism into a largely repressed presence within Israel's cinematic landscape. Over the past twenty years, however, this landscape has seen the release of an unprecedented number of films that deal explicitly with Judaic life and the challenges around its integration within an avowedly secular Jewish-Israeli culture. As such, this "Judaic turn" marks a meaningful stage in the development of filmmaking in

Israel—one with which scholars and laypersons alike are still coming to terms.

Yet this shift toward a preoccupation with Judaism is not exclusive to Israeli cinema but part of a wider cultural phenomenon taking place in Israel of the new millennium. While during the state's first decades the dominance of Zionism's militant secularist ideology meant that Judaic life would be allowed to exist as a marginal phenomenon, the last two decades have seen Judaism being admitted and legitimized as part of Israeli dominant identity. This shift did not only—or even primarily—manifest itself in the growth of Israel's recognizable observant sectors—the ultra-Orthodox (Haredi), the Religious Zionists (Zionut Datit), and the traditionalists (Masortim)—but also in the opening up of a broader web of engagements with Judaism that, in a sense, blurred the boundaries between these communities and Israel's supposedly secular center. Of such engagements, perhaps the most groundbreaking have been permutations of the Judaic New Age—or "Jew Age"—which profess an inclusive vision of religiosity over and against fundamentalism's sectorial philosophy.

This book is dedicated to exploring Judaism's ascent in Israeli society through its reflection in cinema, focusing primarily on how films appeal to New Age–inflected Jewish mysticism in order to negotiate the ambivalences surrounding this sociocultural shift. Israeli cinema scholarship only recently began to address Judaic themes, after years of collapsing them into other categories (ethnicity, gender, sexuality, and such) that were deemed more significant. And as valuable as these current Judaic-centered scholarly interventions are, there is still much ground to cover with regard to the evolving Judaic turn.[4] In particular, the intersection with Jewish mystical aesthetics and experience, a staple of Jew Age priorities, has not been given sufficient attention in this context, causing scholarship to rely too heavily on traditional sectorial categories.[5] Without dismissing the social relevance of these categories, it appears that Israeli cinema is less interested in being entrenched within them and the air of ghettoization they entail. Rather, the New Age appeal to mysticism is one way Judaic-themed Israeli films imagine the possibility of transcending denominational ghettoes toward a greater unity.

Looking at these films through the lens of Jew Age mysticism also allows us to reflect on broader questions regarding the nature of cinema aesthetics, experience, and even ontology. Underexplored not only in Israeli cinema scholarship but within the film studies discipline as a whole, a possible analogy between cinema "magic" and mystical "vision" should be taken seriously, especially in relating to what Jeffrey Pence termed "films' spiritual aspirations."[6] In this, I would argue that certain parts of Judaic themed Israeli filmmaking do not only relate to mystical thought by way of thematic reference but also foreground and attempt to capitalize on the medium's alleged ability to provoke mystical or quasi-mystical states through its particular attributes. As such, the significance of these filmic texts goes beyond local issues of cultural representation and touches at the heart of cinema's ability to induce in us a "suspension of disbelief."

Such claims are nevertheless made with awareness of the need to be tentative. The historical moment in which this study is produced has not yet seen the end of Israeli cinema's Judaic turn and therefore does not offer the writer the privilege of hindsight. Consequently, the present argument cannot foresee the path this turn will take, or even claim that the conclusions regarding what has already transpired on the Israeli screen will remain relevant to what will come in the future. Moreover, we should be aware of the dangers in which exegesis can sometimes turn into eisegesis—especially when one moves from specific to wider spheres of inquiry, such as those of medium specificity in light of the intersection of cinema and Jewish mysticism. While these limitations can be insurmountable, their effect may be mitigated through a careful consideration of the cultural and scholastic context in which both this study and its object operate, so as to position their relationship more fruitfully, and more candidly, for the discerning reader. Such contextualization is the task of this introduction.

Judaism in an Israeli Context

While there are many ways through which to describe the history and evolution of Judaic life in the Israeli context, all must inevitably contend with the modern crisis of Jewish identity in Europe. Jewish existence in the European diaspora had traditionally been one of imposed marginalization. De jure, Jews were considered lesser citizens and forced out of positions of influence within their Christian host cultures; de facto, these legal measures were supplanted by pervasive anti-Jewish sentiment that circumscribed and often threatened the very possibility of Jewish agency. This state of affairs, however, gradually changed as a result of Emancipation, which opened the way for Jews to assimilate into gentile society. Assimilation, in turn, brought about a profound challenge to traditional Jewish identity's association with Judaism, which appeared at odds with Enlightenment's secular values. Some Jews resisted this challenge and sought instead to seclude themselves into a life of extreme traditionalism. Many others, however, followed the path of secularization, to varying degrees, under the general heading of Jewish Enlightenment (*Haskalah*). Capturing the hearts and minds of these Maskilim with its vision of a national home away from European antisemitism, the Zionist movement soon became a focal point for secularized Jewish culture, overshadowing other voices of dissension vis-à-vis traditional Judaic life.

Zionism's initial relationship with Judaism was more varied than often recognized, with several voices attempting to maintain a measure of the Judaic in the Zionist. Yet as the Zionist project of nation building in Palestine became a pressing goal, such voices were increasingly sidelined by the political Zionism of David Ben Gurion, which leaned heavily into the ethos of secular nationalism. Central to this vein was the principle of "negating the diaspora" (*Shlilat Ha-Galut*), wherein diasporic existence is reduced to the traditional mode of Judaic living and then discarded in favor of a "superior" form of Jewishness more suitable for the construction of a homeland. Suitability was characterized by vigor and aligned with physical labor, as seen in its most enduring symbol—the Zionist pioneer (*Halutz*), and especially the Palestine/Israel-born Sabra pioneer. This New Jew cut a heroic figure, making it the proper secular replacement for the devout old-world Jew, whose bookishness appeared as origin and sign of irredeemable weakness.

Following the end of World War II and the establishment of statehood (1948), mass immigration waves to Israel created the foundation for a culturally diverse society. Amid such diversity, it became clear that a sizeable part of the population wished to remain affiliated with Judaism and not surrender to Zionism's New Jew ideal. Scholars tend to single out three major social constituencies within this section of Israel's populace,[7] based on their (variable) observance of a Judaic lifestyle.[8]

Of these, the ultra-Orthodox constituency was most commonly—and institutionally—regarded as "religious," its literal ("scripturalist") interpretation of Jewish law (*Halakha*) emerging as the standard in relation to which all other Judaic-Israeli identities are determined.⁹ Rising from the ashes of the Holocaust, *Harediut* carried over the isolationism of European Orthodoxy's major strands (Hasidim and Misnagdim/Litvak) into the Israeli context, challenging Zionism through its desire to create a "learners' society" devoted to Judaic study. The Zionist leadership acquiesced to this challenge through a "status-quo" agreement that preserved certain religious tenets within national law and provided a position of primacy to the ultra-Orthodox as arbiters on Israel's Judaic matters. While Ben Gurion hoped that ultra-Orthodoxy would eventually wither away, it in fact managed to survive under the protective conditions of its self-imposed ghettoization. Not only that, but Haredism also expanded its reach through incorporating young Mizrahim (Jews of Middle-Eastern descent) into its (Ashkenazi) institutions of higher religious learning. Partly due to ethnic bias on the side of the Haredi Ashkenazi elite, Mizrahi Haredim gradually carved out a separate niche within Israeli ultra-Orthodoxy, marked by a "gentle Harediut" that is open to nonscripturalist forms of Judaism.¹⁰

Another "observant" community that came into its own during the state's founding period was Religious Zionism (or National Religious). In lieu of Haredism's oppositional stance, Religious Zionism wished to operate within the Zionist mainstream, supporting the nationalist project while infusing it with a Judaic-messianic message. This trajectory placed its followers in a difficult position: on the one hand, their adaptation to Zionist doctrines courted tension with Haredi-controlled rabbinical authorities, and consequently undermined their religious legitimacy; on the other hand, their Judaic affiliation situated them on the margins of a Zionist hegemony that rejected the tenets of religious life. Rather than consent to a definition that sees them as failing Judaism and Zionism alike, Religious Zionists attempted at all costs to show themselves as victorious on both fronts. Accordingly, they aimed to match secular Israelis in their commitment to Zionism but also to give no reason for devout Israelis to question their religiousness.

In contrast to Haredim and Religious Zionists, the third Judaic constituency—Masortim—is by and large seen as an offshoot of Mizrahi immigration during the early statehood years. The older generation of fresh Mizrahi immigrants found it difficult to adjust to the lay of the land, while their children assimilated with greater ease, mainly through the school system. This latter transformation entailed assimilating the nation's secular ethos while abandoning Judaic traditions that characterized the Middle Eastern Jewish diaspora for generations. Enthusiasm with secularity nevertheless transformed into disillusionment as years went by and the Ashkenazi-secular establishment's racial biases became more evident. Unable to identify with Israel's outer markers of religion (ultra-Orthodoxy) and secularity (Zionism), these young Mizrahim sought instead to recover their forefathers' flexible form of faith, which is characterized by a partial observance of religious edicts. Such "inconsistency" by the standards of strict scripturalism, in turn, was often used by non-Masorti Israelis to belittle Masotriut as a retrograde form of Judaism.

As long as secular Zionists held the demographic superiority, and more importantly the cultural hegemony, they were able to marginalize these religious identities and establish their own "civil religion" as norm. Following the Six Day War (1967), however, this position was no longer tenable. According to Anita Shapira, in the period leading up to the war, "it was suddenly felt as if the fate of the Jewish People had reached the shores of the Mediterranean, that the distinction between the fate of the Jewish people in the diaspora and that of the Jewish people in its homeland did not stand the test of history, that the state was no longer a guarantee against destruction."[11] Thus, rather than embodying a New Jew, many avowedly secular Israelis now saw themselves linked, albeit negatively, to their diasporic roots, and by implication, to the traditional lifestyle of Judaism that the diaspora came to signify in the Zionist mind. And while the strategic success of the Six Day War abated such anxious identification, the subsequent trauma of the Yom Kippur War (1973), which took Israel by surprise and nearly ended in military defeat, brought it back to the fore of public consciousness with greater fervor. Consequently, as Yair Auron explains, if in the pre-1967 period mainstream identity was commonly defined as "Israeli first and Jewish second," then in the aftermath of these two wars it was largely defined "Jewish first and Israeli second."[12]

As this transformation took place within mainstream culture, the marginalized religious minorities, which by then had grown considerably in size, found themselves able, for the first time in their history, to take on a more influential role in shaping Israeli society. In the 1970s and 1980s this process was most visible in the sphere of politics. Its beginnings are often traced back to the rise of the Gush Emunim settlement movement after the Yom Kippur War, which turned its Religious Zionist leadership into a major powerhouse in the Israeli political landscape. The 1977 elections marked another stage in religious empowerment, when after ending the Labor Party's thirty-year reign, right-wing Likud party head Menachem Begin asked the religious parties to join his coalition and gave their members important cabinet roles. In the 1980s a new Mizrahi Haredi party, Shas, emerged on the scene with astounding electoral successes, originating from its grassroots efforts in mobilizing Mizrahi resentment against the Ashkenazi-Zionist establishment. And in the 1990s especially, it became the practice of many top secular politicians to make highly publicized visits to local "holy personages" such as Rabbi Yitzhak Kaduri to receive their blessings and garner their and their constituency's support. As a result of these changes, the Judaic was no longer strictly articulated in relation to a bygone lifestyle that had been destroyed and then replaced by secular Zionism; rather, it was presented as a thriving contemporary force that could potentially replace a declining secular Zionist ethos and realize more fully Israel's nationhood.

The growth and rise of Israel's religious sector fueled, and was fueled by, a hardening of its positions toward Zionism's secular value system (as can be seen, for example, in the forceful discourse of messianism that has dominated certain precincts of Religious Zionism, or the increased Haredization of Israel's self-avowed religious constituencies, most notably through the Mizrahi Haredi enterprise of religious repentance [*Mifa'al Ha-Teshuva*]). A concomitant radicalization of antireligious tendencies within Israeli secular discourse has also taken place, especially in response to acts of "religious coercion" (*Kfiya Datit*) in the public sphere. The ensuing clashes have inevitably led to the impression that contemporary Israel is undergoing a veritable *kulturkampf* between its religious and secular dimensions.[13] While this claim rings true especially for the relationship between—in Eliezer Ravitsky's terminology—the nation's religious and secular "orthodoxies,"[14] which combat each other for influence, the lion's share of Israelis, who are not part of these extremes, take a less polarizing view.[15] Rather than deepen the religious-secular divide, this majority has yielded a complementary move toward greater open-ness and cooperation, whereby many in the religious sector appropri-ate elements of secular-liberal culture,[16] and many in the secular sector express an avid interest in Judaic texts and customs[17] (most prominently in the vein of "Jewish Renewal"—a loosely networked movement of pluralistic study halls [*Batei Midrash*], prayer communities, and activ-ist groups that, over the last few decades, has set out to build bridges between Jewish secularity and religiosity).[18]

A main driving force for bringing Israeli secularism and religious-ness in dialogue has been New Age spirituality, which has gained a significant foothold in both lowbrow[19] and highbrow[20] Israeli culture since the 1990s. Taking its lead from global trends, the Israeli New Age emerged as a fluid spiritual phenomenon, whose focus is more personal than communal, promising the individual a redemptive transformation, often through a supposed direct encounter with a higher power or truth that is more immanent than transcendent. Within this broad field of action, not all New Age–related manifestations have made use of Judaic elements, as may be gleaned from the local popularity of Eastern tra-ditions and techniques (especially in meditation and yoga). Yet many manifestations *do* exhibit a Judaic bent, motivated by the understanding that Judaism is central to Israelis' cultural identity and thus can act as a more potent catalyst for their spiritual journeys.[21] Accordingly, as Tomer Persico argues, in the twenty-first century not only has the Israeli New Age become more diversified, but also "more Jewish."[22]

Such "Jew Age"[23] spirituality inspires practices meant to deepen familiarity with Judaic tradition as well as those that use this tradition without feeling fully beholden to it. Examples include Judaic channeling, which may reference important Jewish figures of old as well as divine entities known from Jewish lore;[24] healing ceremonies that are integrated into Judaic rituals in more mystically inclined Jewish Renewal commu-nities;[25] women's circles, which often empower womanhood through veneration of such key feminine entities in Judaic cosmology as Lilith and the Shekhinah (the female side of the Divine);[26] neo-pagan, nature-based ritualistic celebration of key holidays on the Jewish calendar that mark the change of seasons;[27] syncretic teachings that combine Juda-ism with other spiritual traditions, such as Buddhism ("JuBu") and Reiki ("Jewish Reiki");[28] therapeutic methods that connect mental health with

Judaism's mysterious powers, such as the "Yemima Method," named after its founder Yemima Avital who counseled her followers through cryptic texts she received while in a state of trance;[29] and Judaic approaches to mental health and guidance, which are taught by gurus and in schools such as Elima—the College for Alternative Medicine in the Jewish Spirit and Kavana! Jewish Coaching for Results.[30] Though such phenomena seem to place the Jew Age outside of Israel's religious sector, others point to how this sector has been reshaped by a New Age mentality. These are found, for example, in New-Age-infused neo-Hasidic terminology used to "modernize" certain ultra-Orthodox constituencies;[31] in various shifts within the Religious Zionist value system, such as putting greater emphasis on a discourse of self as the bedrock for a language of faith;[32] and in the emergence of new "spiritual traditionalists" whose identity interweaves Mizrahi Masortiut and New Age culture, leading to increased investment in the latter's search for authentic selfhood, transformative experience, and immanent divinity.[33]

Of particular importance in this Israeli Jew Age phenomenon has been the increased reliance on the symbols and techniques of Kabbalah, Judaism's purported mystical tradition, which are adapted through the prism of New Age values.[34] Though an esoteric practice, Kabbalah now assumes a more central role in shaping spiritual belief not only within the confines of strictly religious populations but also in so-called secular ones, as indicated by the high profile of such institutions as Rabbi Philip Berg's The Kabbalah Centre and Rabbi Dr. Michael Laitman's Kabbalah for the People, whose avowed goal is to bring the teachings of Jewish mysticism to the (predominantly secular) masses. It is this very esotericism that appeals to many who wish to construct a Judaic spirituality unshackled from the constraints of mainline Judaism. For these spiritual seekers, certain Kabbalistic elements are found to be offering "an alternate theology and view of the cosmos" to that of "pure theism;"[35] "a nonliteral approach to scripture,"[36] which does not focus so much on the letter but on the deeper symbolic message of biblical words; "alternate forms of worship and understandings of religious practice" that connect between a personalized faith and "immanentist understandings of divinity;"[37] and a "positive, forward-thinking outlook" that frequently places within individual action the power to "advance the future repair (Tikkun) of the cosmos and the bridging of the chasm between the physical and spiritual realms."[38] The twenty-first-century revival of Kabbalah also brought about a revisiting of certain twentieth-century Jewish philosophers such as Martin Buber, Emmanuel Levinas, Walter Benjamin, and Gershom Scholem, whose work related directly or indirectly to Jewish mysticism. Evidence to this interest has been the republication of their books and the publication of studies about them—both of which have received coverage in the daily press.[39] As a result of such attention, the oeuvre of these thinkers revealed its relevance to the ongoing conversation on Israeli spirituality, offering means for particular social milieus to imagine a mystically infused challenge to the dogmas of Judaism and Enlightenment. Moreover, the present-day surfacing of these modern works also showed them to be important precursors to the contemporary, postmodern revisioning of Kabbalah and its role in Jewish life.[40]

Thus foreseen, it becomes clear that the growing presence of Israeli Judaism has had a profound impact on the nation's sociocultural makeup. On the one hand, it led to social divisiveness—an ever-widening gap between hardened versions of secularism and Judaism that seems to be splitting the country in half. On the other hand, it brought about attempts—such as New Age inflected appropriations of Jewish mysticism—meant to overcome this gap, conjoining Israeli secularity and Judaism into hybrid identities that redefine them both. The combination of these factors colors Israeli popular discourse with profound *ambivalence*, to use Sheleg's definition[41]—a constant push and pull around the question of where Judaism fits within a national ethos that once marginalized Judaic reality. This ambivalence reverberates through the various precincts of Israeli cultural creation, which, burdened by the knowledge of its importance, attempt to negotiate its effects in a variety of ways. Such negotiations, it is argued, stand at the heart of Judaic-themed Israeli cinema—a "filmic cycle" of sorts, that emerged as a direct result of Israel's Judaic turn and serves as a significant mode of commentary on it.

Judaic-Themed Israeli Cinema

Judaic reality—in the sense of the prevalent Israeli definition of an identity and lifestyle that place importance on Halakhic observance—were largely marginalized in Israeli cinema for most of its history. As such, by Ronie Parciack's count, only twenty fiction films out of over four hundred titles made during Israel's first fifty years had foregrounded elements of this reality.[42] This situation drastically changed in the 2000s, with an exponential rise in the number of Israeli filmic texts taking Judaism as their central object of interest. The radicalness of this shift may over-shadow preceding manifestations and disavowals of the Judaic within Israeli filmmaking, but it is only in relation to these that its particular characteristics and cultural significance can be fully appreciated.

Before independence and during early statehood, cinema made in Palestine/Israel was largely devoted to the enthusiastic celebration of Zionist ideology and iconography. Thus, early films from the 1920s until the 1940s tended to foreground the nation-building efforts of Jew-ish pioneers, who work the land and "make the desert bloom"; while after the War of Independence (1948), pioneering themes were comple-mented by a sharper focus on war and the protection of the fledgling state, in what came to be known as the dominant "Heroic-Nationalist genre" of the 1950s and 1960s. As a means of propaganda, cinematic output from both these periods tended to treat Judaism through the Zionist prism of "negation of the diaspora." Thus, religion was present mostly through reference to biblical symbols and quotations as well as the occasional religious artifact, which charged Zionist pioneering with a spiritual aura. On the other hand, recognizably religious char-acters were almost never shown on-screen, and when they were, their representation was reduced to Zionism's image of the diasporic Jew as passive, static, and defeatist.[43]

Although this paradigm of marginalized representation dominated Israeli cinema for subsequent decades, it did not altogether preclude the production of texts in which the Judaic theme was more pronounced. Starting in the mid-1960s, a cycle of Israeli films featuring Judaic figures and rituals came into being, arguably because of a decline in social com-mitment to the Zionist ethos and in the state's power to enforce it on its citizens.[44] The majority of these texts belong to the *Bourekas* genre of popular comedies, which was characterized through its focus—unusual for the time—on the lifestyles of Mizrahi-Israeli Jews. Bourekas films often used ethnic stereotypes to present the Mizrahi Jew as more vibrant and authentic than the Ashkenazi one, who no longer possesses

FIGURE 1. Sallah (Haim Topol), the emblematic Bourekas protagonist, prays to God with a demand for assistance. From *Sallah Shabati* (Ephraim Kishon, 1964).

the heroic stature of the Sabra pioneer. This carnivalesque reversal of social roles allowed for various scenes of humorous conflict that undercut claims for Ashkenazi supremacy; yet at the same time, its vision of Mizrahim also reduced them to being the butt of condescending jokes.[45] Such duality is clearly present in the strategy of certain Bourekas films to devote substantial screen time to exploring Mizrahi Jews' religious rituals. At times, the showcasing of rituals served to highlight the Mizrahi character's rootedness and commitment to tradition, over and against the Ashkenazi-Zionist model of rootlessness (at least in relation to diasporic culture).[46] On other occasions, however, the presentation can also mock religious rites, showing them up as signs of naivete or obvious shams attributed to Mizrahi "colorfulness."[47]

In tandem with Bourekas cinema there existed the much smaller, though still very popular, "gefilte fish" cycle of comedies featuring Israeli-Ashkenazi Haredi protagonists. These characters, according to Yaron Peleg, "rank far below"[48] their Mizrahi counterparts in Bourekas films.

While Bourekas protagonists are often depicted favorably, those of the gefilte fish cycle, as exemplified in the paradigmatic comedy *Kuni Lemel in Tel Aviv* (Yoel Silberg, 1976), are ridiculed and debased. This grotesque representation figured ultra-Orthodox society as socially irrelevant, while at the same time expressed a profound sense of anxiety and animosity, felt by Israel's Ashkenazi secular elites, toward Haredi fundamentalism and its effects on the Israeli public sphere.[49]

Interestingly, as this cultural hegemony focused its hostility against Israeli Haredim, it became more open to recuperating its diasporic roots in the form of Yiddish shtetl culture.[50] This openness led in the late 1960s to the emergence of a third group of films that foregrounded Judaic life: a brief cycle of cinematic adaptations to classic Yiddish literature, including *Two Kuni Lemel* (Israel Becker, 1966), *The Dybbuk* (Ilan Eldad and Shraga Friedman, 1968), *Tevye and His Seven Daughters* (Menachem Golan, 1968), and *Miracle in the Town* (Leo Filler, 1968). Judaism was depicted favorably in these texts, as part of a communal fabric marked

FIGURE 2. Kuni Lemel (Mike Burstein) being assailed by his fiancée Malka (Ronit Porat). From *Kuni Lemel in Tel Aviv* (Yoel Silberg, 1976).

by quaint authenticity, and which sadly no longer exists. Since religion is seen here as belonging to the past, it did not run the risk of arousing antireligious indignation.[51] Rather, through the use of anachronism, the cycle harnessed the powers of nostalgia in order to make Judaism more palatable to the nation's dominant Ashkenazi-Zionist tastes, even as those struggled with the growing presence of religious orthodoxy within the Israeli landscape.

Though the decline of the traditional secular Zionist ethos and the concomitant ascent of Jewish religion in the Israeli public sphere were in full swing during the 1980s, these transformations barely left a mark on Israeli cinema (as opposed to other cultural precincts like the visual arts, where Judaic themes grew to be more prevalent starting in the mid-1970s).[52] It was only during the 1990s, as Israeli films focused intently on various identities marginalized from Zionism's hegemonic ethos, that a shift toward greater filmic interest in Judaism became noticeable. As part of this transitionary period, three films—Daniel Wachsmann's *The Appointed* (1990), Hagai Levi's *Snow in August* (1993), and Yossi Zomer's *Forbidden Love* (1997)—presented tales of illicit romance between a Haredi and a non-Haredi, in which the ultra-Orthodox community was shown as an agent of violence and destruction. While such portrayals shared in the exoticizing tendencies of "gefilte fish" films, the shift from comedy to suspense signaled a heightening of secular fears toward an alleged Haredi "threat," yet also a newfound envy vis-à-vis Haredism's claim to spiritual power, over against the supposed spiritual bareness of Israeli secularity.[53] Also significant to this shift in filmic engagement is Shmuel Hasfari and Hanna Azoulai-Hasfari's *Shchur* (1994), which explored the largely positive role of "black magic" in the life of a Mizrahi Masorti family. According to Yosefa Loshitzky, the film's legitimization of magic as a spiritual force obliquely referenced the 1990s "manifestations of ethnic renewal [that] include the establishment of new sacred sites of Jewish saints; the nationalization of Jewish Moroccan celebrations (*Hilulut*) like the *Mimuna*; and the emergence of popular healers and practical kabbalists."[54] With that being said, the main goal in using magical tropes here was not to flesh out Mizrahi Judaism as a possible form of religious renewal, but much like Bourekas cinema before it, to turn this Judaic tradition into another marker of ethnic identity and contributor to an overall "ethnic renewal."

While limited in their scope of exploration, these 1990s films laid the groundwork for Israeli cinema's Judaic turn in the 2000s. The growth of this phenomenon was motivated by major changes in institutional infrastructure. Thus, the 1990s and 2000s saw the emergence of two filmmaking schools within the Religious Zionist sector—Maale and Torat Ha-Chaim—whose political and religious positions may differ somewhat[55] yet share the same goal of creating Judaic filmic texts for the general audience (including gentiles) and integrating their students into the largely secular film and television industry.[56] As a corollary to these educational developments, increased institutional support also became available for Judaic-themed film productions: either through government funds, which pursuant to the Israeli Cinema Act (2001), were asked to push for a more comprehensive manifestation of the pluralism of Israeli identities on the screen; or through US-funded NGOs like the Avi-Chai Foundation, whose mission was to encourage Israeli viewership to connect with its Jewishness. Such support undoubtedly helped legitimize the presence of Judaic life in Israeli cinema, yet without the continued success of Judaic-themed films with audiences, a veritable turn would not have come into being. Indeed, this success was felt even before the aforementioned institutional mechanisms took form, with the much touted release of *Kadosh* (Amos Gitai, 1999). Popular with viewers and critics alike, Gitai's cinematic exploration of Israel's Haredi society revealed the topicality of Judaism and sanctioned a "realistic"[57] rendering as the proper stylistic mode to engage this topic. In its aftermath, the floodgates were open to more and more "straight" fiction and documentary films about Israeli-Judaic realities, which have collectively constituted a meaningful attempt to think through the role Judaism plays in Israeli society of the present age.

In the span of two decades, these developments transformed the Israeli filmic landscape (as well as the televisual[58]) from one that sidelined Judaic themes to one that presents a rich and multivalent vision of Israeli-Judaic reality, authored by nonobservant and observant creators alike.[59] The representational diversity found in Judaic turn texts makes the task of creating a systematic overview extremely difficult to accomplish. Nevertheless, it is possible to locate a few recurring themes around which many of Judaic-themed Israeli films coalesce, and which this study touches on directly or tangentially in the following pages.

FIGURE 3. Meir (Yoram Hattab) talks to his wife Rivka (Yael Abecassis) before going to synagogue. From *Kadosh* (Amos Gitai, 1999).

One recurrent theme explores the impact of fundamentalist politics on the Israeli-Palestinian Conflict, and specifically on the development of the settlement enterprise. Fiction films such as *Time of Favor* (Joseph Cedar, 2000), *The Holy Land* (Eitan Gorlin, 2002), *Campfire* (Joseph Cedar, 2004), and *Ruth* (Keren Avitan, 2008) tended to view the enterprise critically. In contrast to other Israeli films about the conflict, which foreground the reality of occupied and disenfranchised Palestinians, these works center on the oppressors' motives in oppression, highlighting the militant and eschatological fanaticism of Religious Zionist settlers. Similar critical perspectives are found in documentary works such as *I Am G-D* (Rino Tzror, 2014), *Messengers of God* (Itzik Lerner, 2014), *The Settlers* (Shimon Dotan, 2016), and *Unsettled* (Iris Zaki, 2018). Yet compared to fiction filmmaking, the documentary field also shows a greater presence of filmic perspectives from within the settler community in support of continued occupation.[60]

Another recurring theme occupying Judaic-themed Israeli cinema has been the detrimental effects of religious androcentrism and modes of feminist resistance. Fiction films like *Kadosh*, *Bruriah* (Avraham Kushnir, 2008), *Fill the Void* (Rama Burstein, 2012), *Apples from the Desert* (Arik Lubetzky and Matti Harari, 2014), *Gett* (Ronit and Shlomi Elkabetz, 2014), *Mountain* (Yaelle Kayam, 2015), *Between Worlds* (Miya Hatav, 2016),

The Wedding Plan (Rama Burstein, 2016), and *The Women's Balcony* (Emil Ben-Shimon, 2016) as well as documentaries such as Anat Zuria's *Purity* (2002), *Sentenced to Marriage* (2004), and *Black Bus* (2009), all deal with the circumscription of religious women's agency by the patriarchal structures of Judaic community life. Inspired by a growing feminist awareness of the importance of corporeality and sexuality in defining women's place in Judaic regimes,[61] many of these films deal primarily with sexual "modesty" practices as a means of regulating women's bodies, and position their female protagonists as agents of resistance on a collision course with Judaism's power structures. While avowedly in support of the victims of Judaic androcentrism, these representations often occupy a secular feminist position that is not conversant with feminist perspectives held by women in the religious sector. In contrast, a few works, made mainly by religious women on the fringes of the mainstream market, have begun to pursue a middle ground of "devout resistance" between feminist ideals and religious edicts, which seeks to critique and transform Judaic androcentrism from within.[62]

Also related to Judaic sexual regulation is the theme of homosexuality within the Judaic world, which has been the focus of such fiction films as *The Secrets* (Avi Nesher, 2007), *Eyes Wide Open* (Haim Tabakman, 2008), *Thou Shalt Love* (Chaim Elbaum, 2008), and *Red Cow* (Tsivia Barkai, 2018) as well as documentaries like *Keep Not Silent: Ortho-Dykes* (Ilil Alexander, 2004), *Say Amen* (David Deri, 2005), *When I Measure the Distance* (Liat Daudi, 2016), *Rebbetzin Falsch* (Roy Goldman, 2019), and *Marry Me However* (Mordechai Vardi, 2020). The emphasis here is on how an unflinching commitment to heterosexuality leads the religious community to reject and oppress LGBTQ+ subjects in its midst.[63] Even if the twenty-first century has seen greater openness toward queer identity in these minority communities, as witnessed in the establishment of Judaic LGBTQ+ associations Hevrouta and Bat Kol, many of these films do not recognize such transformations. Rather, they position gay men and women as the perpetual prey of a traditionalist society that resists any sort of diversity in sexual practice and identification.

While the aforementioned films mostly deal with characters who are willingly or unwillingly entrenched within the confines of a Judaic community, other films partially or prominently explore Israeli Judaism in relation to its (relative) outsiders—the religious repentants (*Baali*

Teshuva). Fiction features like *Underwater* (Eitan Londner, 2002), *God's Neighbors* (Meni Yaish, 2012), *Magic Men* (Guy Nattiv and Erez Tadmor, 2014), *The Other Story* (Avi Nesher, 2018), and *Redemption* (Boaz Yehonatan Yaacov and Yossi Madmoni, 2018) as well as documentaries like *Seekers* (Yishai Oren, 2011), *The Holy Gathering* (Nahum Grinberg and Naamit Mor Haim, 2012), *The Big Leap* (Avner Ben Yair, 2013), *Returning Forward* (Dan Ben Chakon, 2013), *Zohar—The Return* (Yaniv Segalovich and Danny Rosenberg, 2018), and *Reflected Light* (Mordechai Vardi, 2018) tend not to offer a systematic analysis of the religious repentance enterprise. Rather, their attention is often given to the psychological process by which an individual finds his or her way toward greater religiosity and the tensions this process imposes on those who are caught "in-between" the secular and religious worlds. Through the pains of adjustment, these films frequently expose the intolerance that exists in both those worlds, whose inconsistencies religious repentants throw into sharp relief through their liminality. Yet on many occasions, protagonists are also positioned as potentially bridging the gap between believers and nonbelievers through their penitent emotionality—their profound and authentic love of God, which may be extended toward the multitude of His human creations.

Certain works—fiction films such as *Shofar* (Daniel Sirkin, 2001), *Slaves of the Lord* (Hadar Friedlich, 2003), *Ushpizin* (Gidi Dar and Shuli Rand, 2004), *Halakeh* (Abigail Sperber, 2008), *Shiva* (Ronit and Shlomi Elkabetz, 2008), *Shrouds* (Shalom Hager, 2010), *Encirclements* (Lee Gilat, 2015), and documentaries like *The Quest for the Missing Piece* (Oded Lotan, 2007), *Ponevezh Time* (Yehonatan Indursky, 2012), and *Sacred Sperm* (Or Yashar, 2014)—may also be grouped by their pronounced use of religious ritual as a central axis for their dramatic and ideological operation. Rituals in many of these texts become the prism through which the conflict between personhood and institutionalization, release and regulation, are explored and addressed. More often than not, this conflict is shown to be adversely affecting religious subjects, and as a result the coercive and constraining aspects of ritual are foregrounded without attention being given to its contribution to social cohesion and psychic integrity. On other, albeit rarer occasions, the redemptive dimensions of rituals are maintained, and characters face the challenge of adjusting to their demands in order to reap their rewards. In either case, whether positively or negatively portrayed, these films relate to rituals not just as praxis but also as an overarching metaphor on the nature of inhabiting a highly formalized and coded lifestyle. And in certain instances—such as those dealing with prayer—films also explore through ritual greater theological questions about the nature of God and the value of maintaining belief.

Finally, the presence of such questions, over and against Judaic-themed Israeli cinema's focus on religion as a sociocultural phenomenon, can lead to another form of grouping—a metaphysical one. Fiction titles whose theological interest equals or outweighs a social concern include *Ushpizin*, *My Father, My Lord* (David Volach, 2007), *The Wanderer* (Avishai Sivan, 2010), *Tehilim* (Raphaël Nadjari, 2007), *Tikkun* (Avishai Sivan, 2015), *Our Father* (Meni Yaish, 2016), and *Driver* (Yehonatan Indursky, 2017). These often use inconsistencies between personal wants or commonsensical perceptions and the strict demands of Halakhic edicts to question the Halakha's divine source of legitimacy. At times, when deploying a highly critical perspective, films raise doubts as to the existence of God, and even when conceding the possibility, declare divine nature to be fundamentally unknowable (and therefore untranslatable to human experience as the ground for an ethical-legal system like the Halakha). On other occasions, when the perspective is more affirmative toward religion, the nature of God is adjusted to bridge the chasm between the personal and the Halakhic, allowing a flexible take on Jewish theological tradition (a "religiosity" or even a "spirituality") to take form. Importantly, it is in this category that mystical revelation is often made present within Judaic-themed Israeli cinema, though usually via a moderate form that is not reminiscent of the Bible's spectacular miracles (as recreated by Hollywood productions such as *The Ten Commandments* [Cecil B. DeMille, 1956]). These apparitions, in turn, are used as a means of validating faith or of further deepening a sense of uncertainty toward theological axioms.

Judaism, Mystical Experience, and Israeli Cinema: Introductory Remarks and Initial Definitions

The recent advent of Israeli cinema's Judaic turn drew the attention of film scholarship, after a long period in which it neglected to confront the subject of religion.[64] To date, the most exhaustive engagement with this cinematic phenomenon has been Yaron Peleg's masterful volume, *Directed by God: Jewishness in Contemporary Israeli Film and Television* (2016). Peleg's study functions primarily on the level of symptomatic analysis, providing an account of how Israeli film and television's current interest in Judaism shows that Israel "is becoming increasingly more religious in many important ways."[65] As such, he structures his chapters along the traditional sociological division of Israel's religious sectors: ultra-Orthodox, (Mizrahi) traditionalist, and Religious Zionist. With the first category, Peleg asks to show how Haredi representation has shifted from images of an exotic Other to more "modern" portraits of "complex and loving humans." With the second category, his focus is on the integration of religion in representations of Mizrahi identity, which is figured as a way of situating Middle Eastern Jewry as the golden standard of Israel's new statist ethos. Finally, with the third category, the inquiry highlights contemporary cinema's critique of Religious Zionism's messianic investment in occupation and settlement.

These discussions offer insightful and important forays into the Judaic turn as a reflection of significant shifts within contemporary Israeli-Jewish society. At the same time, however, they also disclose a measure of conservativeness in their underlining assumptions. Peleg's reliance on the traditional tripartite model of Israeli-Judaic constituencies upholds a static definition of what constitutes as religious in Israel today, in spite of warnings against such essentializing categorizations put forward by sociological scholarship on Israeli religion. This, in turn, feeds into his emphasis on the notion of religious versus secular Kulturkampf in Israeli society, as can be gleaned from the volume's conclusion, which discusses the effects of Judaic fanaticism on Israel's policies in the Occupied Territories and the author's desire to see a different kind of religiosity that would be more liberal in character. While commendable, this vision also appears too prescriptive, and therefore restrictive, with relation to an evolving social phenomenon. For as Yossi Yonah and Yehuda Goodman remind us, "the dichotomous division between 'religious' and 'secular' in Israel did reflect [the latter's] complex social and ideological reality over the years. . . . Yet changes over the last two decades have acutely challenged such common notions about Israeli religiousness and secularity."[66]

An alternate model that takes these recent changes into account was offered by Merav Alush-Levron in her analysis of the Judaic-themed Israeli film *God's Neighbors* (2012). Through a detailed discussion of the "religious Mizrahi Hasidic" protagonist, Alush-Levron argues that the film "challenges the tension that exists in cinema between liberal secular and religious values,"[67] a position she describes as *postsecular*. This challenge is defined as an affirmation of religion over against its past marginalization, performed through "embrac[ing] the main character's religious experiment and validat[ing] it as genuine, that is, as stemming from a conscious state of repentance (*tikkun*)."[68] Importantly, such an embrace, in Alush-Levron's formulation, does not bridge the religious-secular chasm but rather reinforces its adversarial nature, through "casting the secular identity as a depressive or discriminatory force."[69] Accordingly, the restatement of traditional divides (of religiosity, overlaid on that of Ashkenazi versus Mizrahi ethnicity) articulates a narrow definition of postsecularity, one that ignores others that frame it as a mediating identity of "secular-believers."[70]

Like Peleg's and Alush-Levron's interventions, this volume aims to account for Judaic-themed cinema's relationship with the current state of Israeli Judaism. Yet it approaches this topic somewhat differently. While not ignoring the increased polarization of secular versus religious divides, the argument presented herein highlights a complementary impulse—one in which the categories of secularity and religion are brought together, both on and off the screen, into mutual recognition and even cooperation. As previously noted, Israeli efforts to construct a bridge between ostensibly irreconcilable religious and secular identities has resulted, more often than not, in a profound sense of cultural ambivalence. The following pages reveal just how this ambivalence reverberates through various Judaic-themed films, even when subsumed under a clear critique of one identity over another.[71] Its negotiation takes different forms and at times arrives at no clear resolution. Yet by being negotiations rather than one-sided rejections, these cinematic works ultimately gesture toward a possible overcoming of deadlocks through the dissolution of their seemingly inherent contradictions.

In referring to the partial breakdown of Israel's "secularity-religiosity dichotomy" into a "multifaced fluidity,"[72] this study positions Judaic-themed Israeli cinema within New Age culture's spheres of influence, and specifically in relation to their reliance on Kabbalah. As Jonathan Garb explains, "the dissemination of mystical-magical ideas and practices is one of the clearest characteristics of cultural life" in recent years, as part of the New Age's increased global reach.[73] "The world of Kabbalah," he further asserts, "plays a central role in this movement. [E]specially during the last decades, Kabbalistic motifs and imagery breached the boundaries of the Jewish Orthodox world and became common knowledge. . . . For many, 'Kabbalah' [now] emerged as a symbol for all that is hidden, wonderous, and magical."[74] The effects of this, both inside and outside of Israel, have been registered not only in everyday practices and beliefs but also in the fields of elitist and popular artistic creation. Accordingly, scholarship began of late to apply (and reshape) experiential and aesthetic elements of Kabbalah toward studying, for example, works of literature, poetry, or painting.[75] The ensuing argument performs a similar task in the context of film. As such, it aims to show how certain Judaic-themed Israeli films relate implicitly or explicitly to inflected Kabbalistic understandings, in support of the New Age project of "cutting through existent sectors" and creating "new forms of social organization."[76]

Following Garb's lead,[77] this argument is extensively grounded in a methodology more akin to cultural studies than to Kabbalah studies; as a result, it is less interested in the intricate evolution of Kabbalistic thought from the *Hekhalot* and *Merkavah* treatises of late antiquity until the eighteenth- to nineteenth-century Hasidic movement and beyond, than in its present-day uses within a particular cultural context. Motivating a cultural focus on contemporary applications of Kabbalah is the recognition that these "are no longer dependent on traditional Kabbalah in its contents and literary forms"; indeed, so distant can these applications be from traditional Kabbalah's firm commitment to Judaic doctrine that they often deserve the moniker "secular mysticism."[78] The origin of this dissonance may be found in the continued attempt, from the late nineteenth century until today, of reinventing Kabbalah as a mystical tradition that bypasses doctrinal demands so as to facilitate an immediate divine encounter. In order to support a discursive construction of Kabbalah as mysticism, scholars and laypersons alike became attached to the experiential/ecstatic facets of Kabbalistic literature at the expense of other dimensions that did not fit the mystical mold. What began as an effort by different neo-mystics—for example, Buber,

Scholem, Benjamin, and Levinas—to adapt Judaism to the demands of fin de siècle/early twentieth-century modernity, has achieved an "increased level of detachment from Judaism"[79] under the aegis of late twentieth- to early twenty-first-century postmodernity. According to Garb, "post-modern relativism" made it possible for contemporary popular Kabbalah to take on new forms through "the eclectic spirituality of 'the New Age,' which often does not need to be grounded in any specific tradition."[80] At the same time, Persico elucidates, this expansion was accompanied by a greater emphasis on the permutations of "inner self," to the extent that "the individual is ordered to center on his or her individual experience almost exclusively,"[81] and as a result, "those interested in spirituality are left with the religious experience, without the religion."[82]

Through this experiential focus, the present study will foreground two interrelated "states" attributed to the world of Kabbalah as well as other supposed traditions of mysticism, and which remain prominent within current Jew Age mysticality.[83] The first of these is the ineffable *trance* vision that confounds our basic categories of understanding the world. In his study of vision and imagination in Medieval Jewish mysticism, Elliot Wolfson argued that "while the experience related by Jewish mystics may involve other senses, including most importantly hearing, there is little question that the sense of sight assumes a certain epistemic priority, reflecting and building on those scriptural passages that affirm the visual nature of revelatory experience."[84] For mystics, Wolfson argues, sight is principally directed inward, to a supposed vision of God "that is contemplative or spiritual in nature rather than an actual physical vision of some aspect or entity within the spatio-temporal world."[85] Yet its acquisition also often involves using actual visual representations as perceptual aids and roadmaps. In the case of the internal vision, and especially in that of the external "guides," the act of mystical visualizing is theologically bound by the conflict between God's immanence and transcendence—by "standing before the face of God, yet being unable to describe or fathom it."[86] This conflict is assuaged at times through an appeal to visions that feature abstractness and diffusion, like a dazzling light or an all-enveloping darkness; on other occasions it leads to the compromise of "an *almost* tangible object,"[87] which even when anthropomorphic must nevertheless resist complete encapsulation by our categorical thinking. These negotiations, though theologically framed, also point to a basic phenomenological axiom: namely, that "human experience is such that the noetic content of consciousness is always tied to image and form—even if the goal is to experience (or not experience) the imageless and formless."[88] Yet what mystical visions also reveal is that an envisioning that seeks to transcend normative frames of understanding may not be only about form but also, and most importantly, about its *unraveling*.

The second of this study's experiential foci is a corollary posture of ekstasis—of being pulled out of one's normal sense of self—that yields a profound experience of interconnectedness, often described as a *unio mystica* where one integrates in the Divine. In spite of their supposed prevalence in non-Jewish mystical forms, it has been a common argument within Kabbalah scholarship that Jewish mysticism is lacking in states of *unio mystica*. For example, as Scholem stated in relation to mystical experiences in the Hekhalot and Merkavah period: "ecstasy there was . . . but we find no trace of a mystical union between soul and God. Throughout there remained an almost exaggerated consciousness of God's *otherness*, nor does the identity and individuality become blurred even at the height of ecstatic passion. The Creator and His creature remain apart, and nowhere is an attempt made to bridge the gulf between them or to blur the distinction."[89] In contrast to this and similar accounts, Moshe Idel has argued for the existence of unitive experiences in Jewish mysticism, especially among those mystics belonging to the branch he calls "Ecstatic Kabbalah."[90] According to him, such experiences "are as present [in Kabbalistic literature] as they are in non-Jewish mystical literature; and the imagery which kabbalists use is not so different from the most extreme forms of expression in other mystical types."[91] Tracing the appearance of *unio mystica* within major phases of ecstatic Kabbalah, Idel points to unitive experiences where mystics felt like they were being "assimilated into"[92] or "absorbed in"[93] or "swallowed by"[94] the Divine. Yet even when not experienced in such extreme forms of interconnectedness, Judaic *unio mystica* seems largely related to a visionary practice seeking to undermine mental concepts of coherence that describe the world as an assortment of discrete units.[95] The attraction to this experience has grown more popular in contemporary Jew Age culture, which like New Age culture as a whole, is invested in the idea of a unified source to all existence.

The main argument presented herein suggests that Judaic-themed Israeli cinema—as well as the immediate social milieu in which it is produced and consumed—prominently gestures toward these two interrelated experiential modes as a New Age response to the state of ambivalence plaguing Judaism's recent acceptance in the Israeli land-scape. Since ambivalence is provoked by the rootedness of secular ver-sus religious binarism, its resolution necessitates the dissolution of differences between religion and secularity so that the two supposed extremes would no longer seem inherently oppositional. A trance vision that unravels categorical forms and an ecstatic state of unity that ensues, in this respect, offer such means of dissolution, and hence become more appealing to the present age than other experiential elements within Kabbalah, which are not as able to the task. Under such terms of extreme indeterminacy, these specific mystical experiences can thus be easily co-opted away from their preexisting relationship with God and theology; at the same time, they may also be made to disclose their affinity with phenomenologically similar "peak experiences" that take place outside the scope of religion, within such diverse sites as love and sex, physi-cal exercise, engagement with nature, creative endeavors, and aesthetic appreciation.[96]

Film watching can also be deemed as one of those "peak experi-ences" with phenomenological proximity to mystical states of trance envisioning and ecstatic unification. Thus, from its earliest beginnings the cinematic medium was associated with the unique ability to cre-ate "magic"—to bring forth revelations that rival those described by the great mystics in transcending the boundaries of normal perception and facilitating integration with what exists beyond. Also like many mystical visions, those of cinema do not occur by mere happenstance but involve an active pursuit, one with important ritualistic (moviegoing) and aes-thetic (filmmaking) dimensions. Such similarities, for the Israeli New Age mindset, may appear sufficiently evocative to dissolve the differences between mystical and cinematic, allowing a narrow theistic faith in God to be subsumed or replaced by a broadly defined faith in the (cinematic) image—"perceptual faith," to use Maurice Merleau-Ponty's evocative ter-minology, which is a "belief in the veracity of perception, a belief 'that our vision goes to the things themselves.'"[97] Indeed, it will be stipulated that certain Israeli films not only refer thematically to *the idea* of these mystical states as a way of sketching out a potential route of escape from crippling ambivalence; they also attempt, via cinema's magical enlistment of perceptual faith, to have the audience undergo such experiences themselves—and be transformed by them as a result.

This stipulation, in turn, offers us ample opportunity to move past a cultural inquiry into the Israeli context and discuss the relevance of Judaic-themed Israeli cinema's mystical appeal to our theoretical understandings of cinema-as-medium. Discussions of this kind operate within the confines of "Religion and Film" scholarship[98] yet resist its dominant Christian focus by using New-Age-inflected Kabbalistic concepts to engage film's aesthetic, experiential, and ontological traits. At the same time, such elaborations also make inroads into general film theory, which, as previously mentioned, has been largely averse to using spiritual terminology due to its desire to function "empirically" and "scientifically." By surfacing links between Jewish mysticism and certain nonreligious yet quasi-mystical philosophies applied by film theory to elucidate its claims, the hope is that such aversion may be sufficiently overcome to revitalize interest in cinema's spiritual potentialities.

The volume's two main argumentative trajectories—cultural and medium-specific—intersect in a variety of ways throughout the subsequent chapters. The first chapter deals with the dominant "spiritual style" paradigm in film studies scholarship since the 1950s and explores its contemporary deployment primarily in relation to two Judaic-themed Israeli films—*My Father, My Lord* and *The Wanderer*. In these texts, it is argued, deployment is not meant to serve the spiritual style's avowed goal of affirming God. Rather, this style is seemingly used "against itself," casting considerable doubt on claims to divine existence. That it is articulated via spiritually inflected cinematic form nevertheless means doubt cannot amount to outright denial but instead devolves into a profound sense of ambivalence. Yet these films do not remain so mired in the ambivalent as to deny the possibility of its transcendence. Thus, through their oblique stylistic reference to Kabbalistic symbols (as in the Hebrew alphabet and the Sefirotic diagram), they attempt to appropriate symbolism's supposed mystical capacity to engender trance visions of transcendent unity. As a result, on-screen representation becomes irrevocably bound to the project of cosmic unification and repair (or Tikkun), which such symbols sought to realize, over and against human equivocation and its resultant social fracturing.

At the heart of the second chapter are films dealing with religious women who challenge their oppression in a Judaic-Israeli patriarchal context. Mirroring Israeli-secular public discourse on gender relations and feminism, these texts isolate modesty as *the* site where female oppression takes place and accordingly center their efforts on orchestrating scenes wherein sexual taboos are challenged. Yet in figuring feminist challenges only through the lens of modesty, these scenes also enact a "logic of striptease" whose aim is to lay bare the bodies of covered religious women for voyeuristic pleasure. This focus on modesty, then, reveals a basic ambivalence in the secular attitudes toward Israeli Judaism, figuring it as "other" in order to disguise shared patriarchal tendencies. Nevertheless, in the case of two cinematic texts—*The Secrets* and *Bruriah*—a path is offered out of this ambivalence. Drawing on Benjamin's notion of "now-time" and Levinas's concept of "unhinged time," this avenue is shown to support a Jewish mystical-messianic temporal structure that undermines common understandings of reality and the social categorization derived from them. By evoking mystical-messianic time, these works aim to create trance visions where the terms of social otherness are unraveled, thereby allowing secular spectators to face and own up to their kinship to Judaic androcentrism.

Moving the emphasis from vision to experience, the third chapter engages the relationship between religious ritual and film in two complementary ways. The first asks how the ritual of prayer has been articulated in several Judaic-themed films and what this says about the legitimacy of Judaism as a social and belief system. Thus framed, these films appear to have been influenced by the modern discourse on the "death of God" and its resulting crisis in prayer, with this influence revealing itself through their representation of prayer's two primary coordinates—the social (communion with a group) and the mystical (communion with God). Evaluated collectively, a shared representational pattern emerges—where to varying degrees the social dimension of prayer is devalued on-screen in order to expose Judaic society as an inflexible and often abusive collective, and where, as a counterforce, the need for individualized mystical communion with God is asserted, thereby promoting a mode of personal ekstasis that detaches the subject from its allegiances to Judaic collectivity. The second part of this discussion looks at "Religion and Film" scholarship's continued effort to analogize filmgoing and religious ritual participation, specifically in the context of seeing spectatorship as a form of prayer. The analysis herein strives to redefine and test the limits of this equivalence by focusing on its experiential dimensions—not its discursive ones. Drawing on Buber's Hasidic-inspired definition of prayer and Vivian Sobchack's phenomenological model of film viewing, it therefore figures both practices as "privileged experiences," where the subject is invited to "step out" of itself and contemplate the common structures of its being in the world. While elaborating on how ekstasis shapes the particular phenomenological and noetic features of "conventional" spectatorship and prayer, attention is lastly given to more extreme permutations—that is, to those states in which the subject not only recognizes being's common parameters of coherence but also undergoes their unraveling.

Such experiential unraveling, and the feeling of unity that it may induce, serve as the principal focus for the fourth chapter. These sites are first explored in reference to the role "credulity" plays in Judaic-themed Israeli cinema's adaptation of the Hasidic tale literary genre. Readings of this form of adaptation often argue that it incorporates Hasidic storytelling's supposed penchant for escapism to avoid confrontation with modern-secular standards of credulity. In contrast, the current discussion sees the Hasidic tale as incredulously adjusting Judaic worldviews to these standards and claims that this characteristic is what contemporary film adaptations tend to seek out. Looking closely at three such adaptations—*Ushpizin*, *The Wedding Plan*, and *Magic Men*—the tale's incredulity seems to reverberate through their direct engagement with social tensions, and through their proposed "miraculous" solutions, which stress plausibility over fantasy. As a result of these adjustments, the films appear to endorse Hasidic storytelling's flexible religiosity as a viable model for overcoming the ambivalences of Israel's secular-religious divide—a stance that is also embodied in the fluid devotional positioning of their repentant Hasid protagonists and is epitomized through their ecstatic experiences of divine revelation. These experiences subsequently inform the chapter's concluding discussion, which explores ecstatic "unitive states" in film viewing away from their common reduction to spectatorial "credulity." Through the philosophies of

Merleau-Ponty and Buber, this section proposes a theoretical grounding for the order of unity that such states potentially manifest—not for the purpose of asserting the order's veridical standing but only to entertain the possibility of it having a certain phenomenological-ontological truth value. Hence, in entertaining this possibility, the chapter's conclusion suggests a way to affirm the incredulity of ecstatic-unitive spectatorship, which may be said to divulge significant experiential knowledge in relation to a cinema that—in André Bazin's influential phrasing—"bears away our faith."

Finally, the volume's afterword recapitulates its central claim: that Judaic-themed Israeli cinema's New Age appeal to mysticism serves as a means of escaping the basic categories of religion and secularity that structure its profound sense of ambivalence; and that while this appeal often remains wedded to the overarching secular-religious categories and adds to the overall ambivalence that surrounds them, it also points to their potential dissolution in a transformative moment of unity—a potential arguably enhanced by cinema's ability to unravel conceptual separations and create unitive experiences. This vision of, to use Philip Wexler's term, a "global mystical society," may appear inherently compromised by a horizon of utopianism, for it turns the blind eye to the impossibility of fully transcending the discursive foundations of society. Yet the afterword also suggests that by following an impossible goal, Judaic-themed Israeli cinema does not necessarily invite its spectators to pursue an exercise in futility but rather directs them toward a (minor) liberation within impossibility itself—even if one that exists only through film magic, and vivified solely on the silver screen.

1

LIFTING THE VEIL

The Spiritual Style and
Judaic-Themed Israeli Cinema

There are moments in which, to use a Talmudic phrase, heaven
and earth kiss each other; in which there is a lifting of the veil at
the horizon of the known, opening a vision to what is eternal in
time.

— Abraham Joshua Heschel[1]

In the opening to his oft-quoted essay on film and theology, André
Bazin elegantly stated, without resorting to qualification, that "the cinema has always been interested in God."[2] What may be dismissed at first
glance as yet another example of the French theorist's notorious predi-
lection to bold generalization, does in fact hold true to the history of
cinema. Indeed, only two years after the first public screenings, a host
of Christian-themed cinematic works were produced for general consumption, their popular success prompting the nascent film industry
to draw heavily on biblical narratives; and since then, countless films
have tackled religious subject matter, with specific (though not exclusive) emphasis on its engagement with a metaphysical realm of being
and power. While this ongoing interest in that which transcends our
common understandings of reality may be explained through social and
cultural contingencies, for Bazin its roots run deeper and touch on the

nature of the medium itself. Cinema, he argues, is not only interested in God, but "is in itself already a kind of miracle,"[3] materializing a world through light where once only darkness prevailed. Accordingly, through its particular ontological nature, it can provide us with mystical visions that radically reshape our perspective of ontology: that reveal to us "the world both concretely and in its essence,"[4] as if seen through divine eyes.

In spite of its foundational contribution to the burgeoning discipline of film studies, Bazin's thesis on cinema's function—if not vocation—as a *spiritual aid for revelation* was largely marginalized in scholarship. As Jeffrey Pence notes, since its nascence in the 1960s, the scholarly study of cinema highlighted "the connections between film and historical reality in the interest of social understanding or progress,"[5] and their allegiances to an Enlightenment-inspired "critical method that privileges that which is already known—and hence the cognitive templates in which the already known is."[6] Within this mindset, academic research did little to engage "films' spiritual aspirations," which seemed anathema to its scholarly focus, and thus merited "suppression, or translation to secular terms." Avoiding these aspirations, Pence adds, came at a great cost, as it aligned film studies "with the worst features of modernity," whereby "a criticism that evades an open engagement with the limits of the knowable becomes instrumental; a criticism geared exclusively toward demystification ultimately produces reification."[7]

Over the past several decades, only a handful of film studies scholars challenged this mode of criticism by tackling cinema's "spiritual aspirations" in earnest. Prompted by Bazin's influential call to consider cinema not only as ontology but as also a language, their efforts were primarily preoccupied with an aesthetic consideration: namely, how may these aspirations be realized through the particular use of film form? While employing different theoretical categories, answers to this question often shared a common understanding of what constitutes a cinematic "spiritual style."[8] As found in the oeuvre of key cineasts Robert Bresson, Yasujirō Ozu, Carl Theodor Dreyer, and several others, this style is marked by uncompromising asceticism. It does not seek to capitalize on cinema's expressive power in order to create a robust image that entices in its splendor. Rather, spiritual stylistics seek to undermine such expressiveness, to rob the medium of its more extravagant tools, which are deemed detrimental to film's innate capacity for revelation. Only by adopting this kind of radical austerity, scholarship argued, can cinema free itself and its audience from the oppressiveness of classical film language, whose aim was not epiphany but dramatic engagement on the basis of comprehension and identification.

While retarding a multifaceted discussion of cinema's spiritual aesthetics, the spiritual style's dominance in film theory helped sustain its significance for film practice as well, thereby promoting the adaptation of its signature features by different contemporary "spiritually minded" filmmakers into diverse cultural contexts.[9] The present chapter attempts to trace this adaptation within contemporary Judaic-themed Israeli filmmaking and account for its implications in aesthetic and ideational terms. With two films—David Volach's *My Father, My Lord* (2007) and Avishai Sivan's *The Wanderer* (2010)—as key examples, the following argues that their use of the spiritual style is not geared toward an unreserved affirmation of basic theological truths, such as those attributed by scholarship to the religiously grounded work of Bresson and Ozu. If anything, Volach and Sivan go against such affirmation, wishing instead to cultivate a position of skepticism in relation to Judaic dogma. That this position is articulated from within the spiritual style—rather than from without—nevertheless delimits skepticism to the confines of this style's "theological" framework. As a result, these films never amount to a wholehearted negation of a divine sphere, but rather remain fraught with ambivalence as to the possibility and nature of its existence.

A Spiritual Style in Film

The film theorist most credited with having initiated the discourse on spiritual film aesthetics has been Bazin.[10] A practicing Catholic, he rarely made extensive and explicit connections between film and religious terminology, yet religion had a profound impact on his thought. This impact is most apparent in Bazin's account of cinema's revelatory capability, which is inexorably linked to his theory of filmic realism. A useful jumping-off point to unpacking this complex theory may be found in his article "Painting and Cinema" (1950), where he made his influential claim on the different relations to reality held by a picture frame and the edges of the screen. For Bazin, the frame serves to delineate that which appears in the painting's interior as a world unto its own—a microcosm distinct from the macrocosm of reality. The screen's edges, on the other hand, appear to mask a continuation between what appears in the image and the greater reality that exists beyond. Hence the painting draws the viewer inward, to its interior, while the film propels the viewer outward—or to use Bazin's terminology, "a frame is *centripetal*, the screen *centrifugal*."[11] That the former creates the painting's space as "contemplative"[12] seems to align this art form with a particular mindset that seeks to confine the universe to the limits of contemplation—to the "knowable" as a category of thought and rhetoric. In its centrifugal push, the screen defies these limits and exchanges a microcosm that can be known with a universe that is, at least to an extent, unknowable and indefinite.

These distinctions, in turn, relate to Bazin's argument, made in his foundational "The Ontology of the Photographic Image" (1945), about the revelatory power of photography and cinema. Here the critic notably aimed to show how these media come to satisfy the human "obsession with realism":[13] that is, with possessing a *faithful* reproduction of the world. Plastic arts such as painting have failed in their response to this desire, for the beholder cannot escape the impression that their realization is the product of human intervention. In contrast, the aura of objectivity associated with photographic (and cinematographic) technology overrides spectatorial doubt, allowing the viewer to believe in the faithful verisimilitude of the resultant image. Yet this belief does not only carry over to validating reality's surface details in their visible concreteness but also to affirming reality's supposed "essence,"[14] which is as infinite as it is unknowable. In this centrifugal action, according to Bert Cardullo, Bazin finds the "spiritual" goal of photographic imagery: "to bear witness to the beauty of the cosmos . . . to render the reality of the universe and, through its reality, its mystery-cum-musicality."[15]

For Bazin, the filmic potential of revealing the essence of the world can only be realized through a proper use of the medium's means. Yet, as much as this essence is vaguely conceived in Bazin's oeuvre, so is his articulation of these proper means, which is why Cardullo claims that with him "it would be more suitable to speak of filmic 'realisms' than of a single definitive realist mode."[16] Following his premature death in 1958, Bazin's openness was gradually traded in for a narrower definition of "spiritual film style," which represented one vein of his variegated thought: a preference for stylistic austerity whereby "sentimentality is eschewed in favor of filmic reality and transparence."[17] Through the pioneering efforts of Bazin collaborators Henri Agel and Amédée Ayfre in France and of occasional film critics Susan Sontag and Paul Schrader in the United States, by the 1970s this definition received its first consistent articulation.[18] Building on these foundations, in turn, subsequent scholarship further solidified the "spiritual style" paradigm, cemented its dominance, and expanded the canon of spiritual filmmakers included in its purview.[19]

What virtually all iterations of this paradigm share is the basic affirmation, drawn from Bazinian theory, of a mysterious hidden presence within the real, which may be sensed but not conceptualized. Thus, in an analysis of the revelation in Bresson's films, Ayfre argued that "we are dealing with immanent transcendence, or even, one might say, with radical invisibility. For the invisible world remains invisible, or rather appears only as invisible."[20] Alternatively, his compatriot Agel described this presence in different though no less immanent terms, as "a pure point, a *center of life* that neither degradation, nor despair, nor constraint ever completely consumes, whose homage man must assure and preserve, a point where he finds self-respect and the power to unceasingly regain strength."[21] For her foundational discussion of Bresson's "spiritual style," Sontag speaks of how it revealed the "physics . . . of souls."[22] And decades later, Nathaniel Dorsky described this hidden-yet-palpable essence as "the depths of our own reality" that provides us with "a fuller sense of ourselves and our world."[23] In either of its various characterizations, the search for reality's hidden face is figured as inherently beneficial and redeeming; in some accounts, it is even thought of as a necessary element of human existence and a manifestation of a fundamental human desire.[24] And while a theocentric perspective is often avoided, descriptions of this presence at times use terms drawn from modern theology and religious studies,[25] and in general disclose a commitment to ontotheological thinking.[26]

As such, purveyors of the "spiritual style" paradigm argue that cinema, by virtue of its intimate relationship with the real (Bazinian indexicality), is uniquely positioned to evoke a vision of reality's hidden essence. Religious scholar Mircea Eliade's term "hierophany" is occasionally used to articulate this inherent characteristic of the filmic medium, relating it to the category of ritualistic objects that, for the predisposed mind, reveal the Absolute within mundane reality. Thus, for example, in his formative *Transcendental Style in Film* (1972), Schrader argued for certain cinematic texts as being instances of "movie hierophany,"[27] equivalent to man-made works in noncinematic areas of sacred art—for example, Byzantine icons or Zen gardens—"which are more expressive of the Wholly Other than of their individual creators."[28] Writing a decade later, Michael Bird arrives at a similar conclusion in his attempt to cast film as hierophany. For him, film's innate rapport with reality enables it to present an image of "belief-ful realism" (theologian Paul Tillich's term): a vision that "is at once 'realistic' and 'self-transcending,' which in its seeking of the Unconditioned focuses upon the concretely finite, which perceives culture both as surface and as transparent to its religious depth."[29] Accordingly, cinema becomes a mediating tool wherein the material object on screen may allow spectatorial access to a broader "*Real* that underlies the *real*."[30]

This mediation may be rooted in cinema's medium-specific features, yet its realization is contingent on the deployment of a particular aesthetic approach—a specific style—which separates movie hierophanies from other types of film. As previously put forth, scholarship argued for a use of film form based on austerity—that is, on the subtraction of all those elements the medium adds to reality, thereby allowing, in Ayfre's words, to ask "things themselves . . . what they manifest through themselves."[31] Ayfre likened this stylistic operation to the phenomenological practice of "bracketing" (or *epoché*) advocated by Husserl, arguing that similarly certain films eliminate (as in bracket off) the various perspectives placed on reality so as to divulge a certain measure of its numinous core. Rather than be swayed by distractions, then, the disciplining of imaged reality through an "ascesis of means"[32] opens spectatorial consciousness to "a total apprehension which is sequentially complete like existence in time, or like human events in which the whole mystery of the Universe is co-present."[33] Along the same lines, Schrader speaks of a "stylization of . . . elimination rather than addition or assimilation,"[34] which characterizes all artistic hierophanies, including those of cinema. Films that rely on this approach—dubbed by Schrader "transcendental style"—display a temporal progression from "abundant" to "sparse"—beginning

with a familiar and plentiful image of the world to keep audience members interested, and gradually making it less and less embellished in
order to thwart identification and set up a new priority. This priority, for
Schrader, must arrive through an intense encounter with what he terms
"the everyday": a representation of reality that highlights the commonplace, inexpressive, even banal. For only by presenting a seemingly dull
rendition of everyday life can the spectator be primed—in spite of his
or her self—to witness the Transcendent intruding into the immanent.

Drawn to Robert Bresson's definition of proper filmmaking as one
aimed at cleansing film from those added elements—"screens"—that
interpose and deny direct access to the unknown in reality,[35] scholarship saw his work as epitomizing the spiritual style's asceticism. In this
framework, the filmmaker's choice to use nonprofessional actors, and his
demand that they do not attempt to "act," attracted particular attention.
In his discussion of Bresson's early films, Ayfre, for one, remarked on "an
increasing tendency towards inexpressiveness in the acting," whereby
"anything which could be constructed as direct communication through
facial expression or gesture . . . is avoided."[36] This inexpressiveness, especially in faces, seems to represent nothing; yet "by expressing nothing,"
Ayfre states, the actors "express precisely that which is beyond expression."[37] Schrader describes the behavior of Bresson's characters in similar terms: "given a selection of inflections, the choice is monotone; a
choice of sounds, the choice is silence; a choice of actions, the choice
is stillness."[38] The result of such shaping—whose effects are augmented
by an austere decor, inanimate or stubbornly slow camerawork, and flat
and frontal mise-en-scène—undercuts the medium's ability to produce
familiar visions of an "abundant" reality, presenting in their stead an
austere representation in the "sparse" aesthetic of Byzantine iconography, which favors the godly over the human. A like-minded account
appears in Sontag's reading of Bresson's mode of narration, though with
different inflections. She claimed that this mode places an emphasis on
the Word, particularly through a reliance on first-person narration that
doubles—rather than replaces—the action seen on-screen. One effect of
doubling action through words is the undercutting of suspense, which
in turn subverts the viewer's desire for emotional involvement. Sontag
sees Bresson as deliberately sidestepping suspense in order to make his
films more antimelodramatic, and, by implication, more "spiritual." This

antidramatic impulse, which prevents spectatorial involvement, also manifests itself in scenes being cut short before achieving any marked catharsis, in the elision of anecdotal information, and in the chaste and self-effacing nature of the cinematography. Most of all, for Sontag as for Ayfre and Schrader, it is in Bresson's method of directing performers that one finds him at his most antimelodramatic. She reminds her readers that Bresson undermines expressivity by having his nonprofessional actors speak the lines rather than act them out, and by systematically hiding their motivations or making them opaque to psychological analysis. As a result, the protagonists of his cinema seem isolated from, and transparent to, the world; lacking in psychological profundity, immersed in deliberate physical action, they become receptacles for divine grace.[39]

On these terms, it seems that the spiritual style aspires toward transparency, asking the viewer not to *look at* but rather *look through* the image.[40] Yet what is envisioned through this translucent screen? Common to many of these accounts is, again, the emphasis on a profound sense of mystery—a *mysterium tremendum*, to use Rudolf Otto's formative term, coined in reference to the encounter of phenomena that exceed our normative understanding of reality. While often described rather nebulously, the dimensions of this encounter are at times given a more concrete and detailed theorization. Most famous in this context is Schrader's transcendental style model, which draws heavily on Otto's work, and especially on its foregrounding of rupture vis-à-vis a sublime Wholly Other ("creature feeling"). As Schrader sees it, a transcendental filmmaker uses stylistic austerity to prevent the viewers from using their familiar modes of interpretation, forcing spectatorial recognition that there is something more than meets the eye in the humdrum representation of the everyday. Recognition culminates in a "decisive action": "an incredible event within the banal reality which must by and large be taken on faith . . . a nonobjective emotional event within a factual, emotionless environment."[41] The decisive action forces a decision on the spectator: either reject or accept this mysterious event as gesturing toward the Transcendent. With the former choice, the viewer gives up on the film's deeper truth, opting for yet another screen; with the latter choice, however, mystery is embraced, and as a result, the viewer undergoes a metamorphosis, transforming "empathy into aesthetic appreciation, experience into expression, emotions into form."[42]

The telos of the spiritual style is to create this conversion experience—to make the spectator have faith in the unbelievable through the power of the cinematic image. Indeed, faith (or belief[43]) is the operative term in spiritual style theory dating back to Bazin, who saw it as key to his edification of filmic realism. For him as for those who followed in his footsteps, cinema's miraculous power lies in making us believe—against all reason—that what is gone can actually be vivified at the present moment of projection. While this belief in vivification is a common effect of all films, it accrues a spiritual valence in those works that contextualize it in relation to a mysterious and Wholly Other presence within imaged reality. Spiritual style theory does not dismiss this valence as spectatorial fallacy (like those who critiqued Bazin's argument as "naive realism"). Rather, it affirms the position of spiritual belief as revelatory, and by implication (more than by explicit admission), validates ipso facto the possibility, if not probability, of an ineffable presence existing within our world. In this respect, the spiritual style's success is measured by its ability to proselytize; and by supporting this success, Bazin and many of his acolytes also saw themselves as proselytizers, whose cause is to resist readings that reason with cinema, rather than submit to its mystery.

Evangelical posturing has led, in turn, to the consistent rejection of aesthetic strategies that differ from the ascetic model, for being nonspiritual or not sufficiently spiritual (as in the case of Schrader's noted claim that Carl Theodor Dreyer's partial use of the transcendental style exposes his doubts about the Transcendent).[44] Nevertheless, in recent years several scholars have argued against the dogmatism and narrowness of the spiritual style discourse and have highlighted the significance of nonascetic styles to our understanding of cinema's spiritual functioning.[45] Subsequent chapters in this volume pick up on the thread of criticism and discuss films with spiritual, even mystical, aspirations that do not adopt stylistic austerity. In this chapter, however, the focus is on Judaic-themed Israeli films that *do* operate within the confines of the ascetic spiritual style. Contra conventional framings, the following discussion shows how these cinematic texts use this aesthetic approach to question rather than affirm a spiritual existence, defined along theological terms. Questioning here is ambivalent because its articulation through the spiritual style ultimately binds it to some form of theological or ontotheological framework and thus prevents it from denying the possibility of this existence altogether. Nevertheless, it is this very ambivalence that lends more potency and complexity to subversion, precisely because its impetus of subversion arrives from *within* the world of religion rather than from without.

My Father, My Lord: Searching for an Undesirable God

My Father, My Lord, David Volach's directorial debut, is a work of autobiography to a certain extent. Volach was born to a distinguished Litvak Haredi household in Jerusalem and spent his adolescent years as a member of the esteemed Ponevezh Yeshiva in the religious enclave of Bnei Brak. Though destined to follow in the path of his elders and become a distinguished figure in the community, he decided at the age of twenty-five to turn his back on the Judaic world and embrace secularity. This move came at a considerable cost, as his family refused to speak with him for many years; yet the greatest burden had been the shedding away of an entire way of life, a process that, according to him, has yet to be completed.[46] It is from such a profound state of "limbo" that Volach, a relatively inexperienced filmmaker, made his first feature. In this work, which focuses on the religious community of his origins, he attempts to forge a critique of Judaism that is more theological than sociological. The critique, understandably, touches on the most central of religious concerns: the existence of God and the value of devotion.

Commenting on *My Father, My Lord*, several critics noted the strong similarity of its formal language to the spiritual style of Bresson.[47] This similarity is most evident in the approach toward the function of narrative. As in many of Bresson's works, the basic tale this film depicts is very lean in nature: Jewish Haredi parents prepare to go with their only son Menachem on a trip to the Dead Sea; at the end of this trip, the child dies by drowning, thereby prompting the parents to experience a crisis of faith. In transporting this bare-boned story to the screen, its dramatic potentialities were not enhanced by adding action-oriented sequences; instead, this fiction was effectively stretched out over seventy minutes, thereby slowing down the pace of the film and allowing for spectatorial meditation on the texture of imaged reality and its hidden dimensions.

In a telling interview, Volach explained this narrative approach through a distinction between "story" and "plot." "What is plot?" he asked,

> In still images you get a story and you don't need any plot. You see wrinkles, you see eyes. Every image is a story. Why can't cinema be like that? . . . In cinema things need to happen to the character in order for the spectator to become interested in its story, because the character cannot reveal its story unless something happens to it. Plot is a condition, a tool for telling the story. But it should not be mistaken with the story itself.[48]

In this respect, like Bresson before him (though perhaps not to the same degree), Volach advocates a narrative strategy of elimination—or, in his words, a "skimping on plot so to flesh out the story."[49] This strategy is supported, in turn, by an ascetic use of stylistic means: meandering camerawork that lingers on character actions; a minimalistic mise-en-scène; a subdued color palette; and relatively nonanimated acting, which relies on inexpressiveness of gesture and long moments of silence. Through these stylistic features, *My Father, My Lord* emerges as a text that does not invite us to skim over the fabric of existence in a hurried race toward a cathartic ending; rather, we are given the opportunity to appreciate the countenance of the visible world, not only for its physical attributes but also for the "story" that hides behind them, the meaning that transcends them.

Stylized through elimination, imaged reality seemingly becomes transparent, and viewers are thus made to perceive it as pointing to something else—as being referential. But to what does it refer? Ostensibly, but not exclusively, to a set of interconnected theological debates, which form the basis of Jewish religious law. The film incorporates several scenes that overtly connote Halakhic discourses, thereby setting up the conceptual framework for the appreciation of the symbolism of the narrative at large. This choice seems to position *My Father, My Lord* squarely within the traditions of Judaism, or as Volach explains: "the whole religious world is a world of symbols. . . . A man eats a matzo in Passover as a symbol for the exodus from Egypt, and I, who am making a film about religion, will ignore symbolism?"[50] Yet there is one fundamental difference between Judaism's symbolic world and that which is shown in this cinematic work: in Judaism, religious discourses are referenced for the purpose of their wholehearted validation; in Volach's film—for their explicit de-legitimization.

One such discourse is that surrounding the hierarchy of creation. Midway through the film, we are shown a scene where the father of the family, a rabbi and representative of religious law, is giving a sermon on a common piece of Judaic wisdom: how only human beings have souls and enjoy God's providence, and how only human beings who spend their waking hours worshiping the Lord have superior souls and receive God's utmost attention. This axiom is then undermined through other moments in the film. For example, in one scene, Menachem is seen observing an old woman being carried into the back of an ambulance. He notices the old woman's dog attempting to climb into the ambulance, only to be unceremoniously thrown out by the paramedic. The dog's desire to stay at its master's side, contrasted with the paramedic's callous reaction, makes us question why the Halakha would define an animal as soulless, simply because it is nonhuman, and a human soulful, even when behaving heartlessly. In another sequence, Menachem is shown trading picture cards with a child who appears mentally disabled. In the Halakha, individuals with mental disabilities are considered lesser souls since they are unable to cope intellectually with the task of worshiping God; this understanding in part prompted Halakhic authorities to put in place certain protective restrictions, such as the prohibition against trading with the mentally disabled.[51] In the film, Menachem not only breaks this Halakhic law regarding trading but also treats his friend, not as a lesser soul, but as an equal partner. The same sense of equality is not found, however, within Menachem's family. The father is depicted as the dominant figure in the household, owing to his Halakha-sanctioned position of superiority; in comparison, the mother is shown to be subservient, accepting the position of inferiority bestowed on her by Judaic law. Yet while presenting this hierarchy as part of the Israeli-Judaic world, the film also clearly attempts to subvert it by portraying the mother as the favorable—and thus, morally superior—character, which counterbalances the father's reserved and occasionally uncaring attitude toward Menachem with acts of compassion and tender nurturing.

Another related Halakhic discourse *My Father, My Lord*'s narrative evokes is that regarding idolatry. When the father discovers that the card

Menachem obtained from his friend carries the image of a bare-chested African tribesman, he deems it an object of idolatry and demands that it be ripped up, reducing the child to tears as a result. The comparison between the strictness of the father's demand and Menachem's empathy-inducing misery, as well as the contrast between Menachem's innocence and his Halakhic definition as sinful, establish Judaic law as harsh and inhumane. This discourse is further evoked by the choice to stage Menachem's death at the Dead Sea—a site for purifying vessels of idolatry, as is written in the Talmud: "If one finds utensils upon which is the figure of the sun or moon or a dragon [i.e., idolatrous utensils], he casts them into the Dead Sea."[52] The film reveals the idolatry discourse's falseness by showing that Menachem, formerly associated with idolatry due to his involvement in the card incident, does not achieve redemption by entering the waters of the Dead Sea but rather forfeits his life. In this, the Dead Sea delivers on the ominous promise inherent to its name, which stands in opposition to its supposed function as an "enlivening" force of purification.

The Halakhic discourse on reward and punishment is also featured prominently within the film's symbolic world. This discourse appears through overt references to two noted stories within Jewish religious tradition. The first of these is the story of the Binding of Yitzhak (Isaac), which is explicitly referred to on two occasions in the film: initially, when, in a classroom (*Heder*), Menachem and his friends recite the story of the binding; and later, when in the same classroom, the children, Menachem included, pictorially recreate the binding scene on the blackboard. The second story is that of Elisha ben Abuya and the bird's nest. This reference is made evident in a sequence where the father is seen performing the task of *Shiluach Ha-Ken*, as is written in the Book of Deuteronomy: "If, along the road, you chance upon a bird's nest, in any tree or on the ground, with fledglings or eggs and the mother sitting over the fledglings or on the eggs, do not take the mother together with her young, let the mother go, and take only the young, in order that you may fare well and have a long life."[53] The Talmud tells us that the notorious heretic ben Abuya once walked by a tree with a bird's nest and met a man who, like the father in the film, was intent on performing the mitzvah spelled out in Deuteronomy. The man had sent his son up the tree and he, after expelling the mother bird, fell down and died. It was this

FIGURE 4. The father (Assi Dayan) performing the ritual of Shiluach Ha-Ken. From *My Father, My Lord* (David Volach, 2007).

event—in which following an important religious command resulted in punishment rather than reward—that persuaded ben Abuya, according to the Talmud, to commit to a life of heresy.[54]

Both these stories run parallel to the narrative of *My Father, My Lord* and illuminate its theological stance in significant ways. The binding story, in which Yitzhak's life was spared because of Abraham's uncompromising devotion, inspired the Halakhic maxim that those who trust in God and follow His law will be rewarded with divine protection. This form of providence, however, is absent in the film, where the father, a true believer, is not rewarded with the life of his son as in the case of Abraham.[55] Rather, what we find here is a rendition of the story of Elisha ben Abuya and the bird's nest, in which a father's desire to abide by the Halakha does not save him from suffering the worst punishment a parent can receive—the loss of a child. Accordingly, the film gives further credence to ben Abuya's perspective, which it wishes the audience to adopt: namely, that the Halakha is wrong and therefore should be rejected. Yet it does not only lay blame on the Halakha's Almighty Father but also on the rabbi father who transferred his parental responsibilities onto Him. Thus, Menachem wandered off while being with his father, at the exact moment when the latter was too busy in praying to his

Father and in feeling "enveloped in the wings of divinity." By assuming divine providence, and by extension relying on Halakha's cosmological understanding of reality, the rabbi committed a crime of neglect, for he willingly let himself be cut off from the actual coordinates of existence. Importantly, this crime is not attributed to all devout subjects, but just to the male ones; in contradistinction, the film positions the protesting voices of women and specifically mothers as expressing recognition of the need to bypass Halakha laws and their (patriarchal) enforcement.[56] The father silences this voice twice during the film: first, during Shilu-ach Ha-Ken, by separating the offspring from the female bird; and second, by separating Menachem from his mother, with the claim that the child had "grown too old" to go to the women's section of the beach and must therefore accompany him to the men's section. In both cases, separation justified by religious edicts causes needless suffering. And while the female bird is not given room to protest against such measures, the mother does show a measure of defiance when, at the end of the film, she throws volumes of scripture from the women's gallery onto her husband's table on the synagogue's main floor below. It is in this wordless gesture that she shows her mistrust of Halakha's proclamations on the benevolent nature of God.

Some would define such mistrust of the Halakhic dogma as arguing against the existence of God. Yet this explanation arguably misses on the theological subtleties of *My Father, My Lord*. Thus, the film's quarrel seems to be with the interpretation of God and His desires by the Halakha; its critique is aimed at invalidating this interpretation, but not necessarily at invalidating the existence of a god that defies such an interpretation. In fact, it seems as if great effort is taken to allow room in this work for a possible envisioning of a hidden god. In making a vision of this kind manifest, we see the film's reliance on the spiritual style—as a signifying system for a sacred spiritual presence—come to its fruition. This style, as previously described, conditions the specta-tor to perceive the imaged reality as being both object and reference. Typically, *My Father, My Lord* situates this reality as referring to—and subsequently, invalidating—certain Halakhic discourses. Yet the film also contains a number of shots that escape an allegorical framework. These shots are beautifully crafted, poetic close-ups of commonplace objects, which appear so utterly irrelevant to the little drama taking place in the film that they cannot help but stick out as aberrant. Thus, for example, during an early scene we see Menachem at home with his father while he is studying. The rabbi has little time for his son as he works through the many books compiled on his desk. Consequently, the child becomes bored and distracted. At one aimless moment, he notices his father's teacup, its contents almost fully consumed. As he moves the cup on its saucer, we catch a glimpse at its bottom. The image is so close that the view becomes almost abstract. Every minute detail attracts our attention, from the glistening on the saucer's edge, to the effervescence where the cup meets the saucer, to the crepuscular hue of the background, to the water slowly consuming the surface of a piece of paper that once was part of the teabag. And after lingering on this vision for a while, the film returns to Menachem as he falls asleep and never revisits the teacup again. A similar moment occurs in a later scene, while Menachem's mother dresses him for school. Standing in the kitchen, Menachem shows his mother how he buttoned his shirt wrong. The two laugh, and the mother chastises the child's "naughtiness" in bemusing fashion. Then, as this exchange reaches its culmination, the film makes a surprising cutaway toward a low-angle view of the kitchen window. The vision is, again, abstract. Layers of depth permeate each other: painted tiles, a window frame, vertical bars overlaid on vertical banisters, horizontal ledges parallel horizontal stairs. Amid this static tableau, overwhelming in detail, is also a minor drama: a window curtain fluttering in a morning breeze, its gauzy texture catching the afterglow of morning sunlight. And as we take in this sight, it ends abruptly, cutting back to Menachem's face, his wide-open eyes bespeaking a measure of calm astonishment. What do these lyrical images mean? Their referential status is unclear. They seem to be speaking of "something," but its exact nature remains elusive, at least in relation to common Halakhic discourses.

A parallel phenomenon may be found in Ozu's works. As Schrader explains, Ozu tends to punctuate (and puncture) the dramatic flow of his films with seemingly irrelevant shots of everyday objects or outdoor landscapes. Each shot is paradoxically a disruption and an integrant of the natural order. It functions, according to Schrader, as a coda that "establishes an image of a second reality which can stand beside the ordinary reality; it represents *the Wholly Other*."[57] Dorsky had a similar

FIGURE 5. Focusing on a tea saucer. From *My Father, My Lord* (David Volach, 2007).

impression while looking at Ozu's codas. In referring to Ozu's first sound film, *The Only Son* (1936), he provides a lengthy description of how codas constitute and unravel dramatic scenarios in the Japanese master's oeuvre. An elderly mother arrives to visit her son, only to discover that his life, for which she sacrificed so much, is lackluster at best:

> We see the son and his mother settling down on an abandoned hill to talk. Below, not far in the distance, an incinerator billows smoke into the sky. Our characters, in a moment of vulnerability, finally open to one another with unguarded honesty and tenderness. He asks if she is disappointed in him and confesses to his own unhappiness. Perhaps he should never have left her. They sit and talk, and we feel the pain and the impossibility of their situation. Hearing the sound of a skylark, the son pauses and looks upward. Ozu cuts to a full-frame shot of the sky. We rest in this transparency and then cut to the mother sitting beside her son. Her head is lowered, weighted down by all that transpired. Then she too raises her gaze, and once more we cut to an open shot of the sky. We take in its lightness and then cut again. We see the incinerator, its large stacks spewing forth dark smoke. In a reverse angle, the mother and son walk away across the open field. There is no summation

to all these elements, only the direct experience of poetic mystery and the resonance of the self symbol.[58]

While in a conventional film, still life images are used as background to narrative drama and as a way of accentuating its affective force, in this and other Ozu scenes it is the narrative drama that serves as background to still life images, establishing them as the main focal point. With our attention focused on these "things," we enter a mode of discovery where the world is seen anew. For Dorsky, it is like the discovery of the magic of one's hand: "If you have ever looked at your hand and seen it freshly without concept, realized the simultaneity of its beauty, its efficiency, its detail, you are awed into appreciation. The total genius of your hand is more profound than anything you could have calculated with your intellect."[59]

Another filmmaker whose work deploys the still life codas in a comparable fashion is Krzysztof Kieślowski. As Vivian Sobchack notes, Kieślowski's films are filled with images of objects strewn through their dramatic scenarios: for example, a sugar cube touching the surface of an overflowing coffee cup in *Three Colors: Blue* (1993) or a country landscape inverted through a glass marble in *The Double Life of Véronique* (1991). These images, for her, "assert a signifying power and mysterious autonomy that emerge through the hyperbolic excess of ontic presence created by both the camera's close-up framing of them and its hyperempirical detailing of their material presentness."[60] Endowed with a sense of uncanniness and agency, such objects challenge the characters and spectators' normal vision by "looking back" at them. What emerges out of this challenge is a different perception of reality where materiality is expanded "beyond comprehension into the apprehension (and often apprehensiveness) of something more, something beyond, something other."[61] As a result, Kieślowski's oeuvre "articulates astonishment at the endless field of possibilities offered by being's ultimate exteriority, by its materialized thrown-ness into a world that it cannot fully comprehend."[62]

Comparable impressions are found in Joseph Kickasola's study dedicated to the "liminal cinema" of Kieślowski. Like Sobchack, Kickasola also singles out the on-screen presence of still life objects, arguing that their function is to reveal those thresholds within reality where the physical and metaphysical meet. Key to affecting this revelation, for him, is the great proximity through which the object is shown. By moving closer to things, the camera forces them to lose their known signification and acquire a mysterious appearance. The resultant abstraction, in turn, appeals to a primal level of human consciousness not overdetermined by reason, thereby opening the viewer up to a cosmic vision of reality "where time is timeless, and space is ever expansive and fluid."[63] Primed in such a way, the audience is thus made to feel that the metaphysical themes typical to a Kieślowski narrative are "at home" in the world on-screen, for they appear to emerge out of, and be validated by, the abstract image.

While Ozu and Kieślowski deploy their "codas" similarly, their approaches nevertheless differ on at least one major count: that is, in Ozu's films aesthetics seem to affirm the common metaphysical understandings prevalent in his culture,[64] while in Kieślowski's films aesthetics appear to question such understandings. A clear example for this questioning is *Dekalog One* (1988), which intersects with *My Father, My Lord* in important ways. In the first chapter of his *Dekalog* series, Kieślowski uses the relationship between a father, his son, and their sister/aunt, to take to task the two main explanatory models of existence: science and religion. Famously, the made-for-TV film shows the son as testing out the father's scientific mentality by skating on a layer of ice that the father, through his calculations, deemed "safe." The child's death by drowning (much like Menachem's) reveals this mentality as incapable and even erroneous in articulating a dominant order for our reality. At the same time, this death also challenges the ideas of providence and ethics that are espoused by the Catholic aunt—an affront to religion that is literalized in the concluding scene, where the father is seen destroying the altar of a neighborhood church. Yet even if *Dekalog One* goes against Christian tenets, it does not invalidate them completely. The codas dispersed through the film's narrative—a frozen milk bottle, a dead dog, a steaming coffee mug—seem to manifest a mysterious presence, which makes room for a trance vision of a hidden Spirit even as Catholicism's claims to truth are undercut. Kieślowski's film therefore exhibits "a sort of dialectic between metaphysical positions (the presence vs. absence of God)," lending support to Kickasola's claim that the filmmaker was not so much an atheist as "a 'hopeful agnostic' who vacillated on the issue of God's existence throughout his life but philosophically believed, for the most part, that 'an absolute reference point does exist.'"[65]

It may be said that like *Dekalog One*, *My Father, My Lord* also occupies an ambivalent position of doubt, rather than utter disbelief, in relation to the proposed reality of God. Yet it may also be argued that Volach's film is less agnostic in the sense that it allows for a more substantial theological framing of the mystery of the coda than one finds in the Kieślowski film. The justification for this claim is found, first and foremost, in their stylistic differences. While both deploy codas similarly, *Dekalog One* uses them outside of the framework of the "spiritual style." Indeed, as Kickasola explains, "this type of ascetic religious 'mode' throughout the form of a film cannot adequately describe the humanistic compassion and persistent vitality"[66] of Kieślowski's oeuvre as a whole. Accordingly, it seems that for the Polish cineast, a challenge against the systems of theological explanation could not arrive from within an aesthetic framework that is often interpreted as affirming them, especially within a religiously themed narrative; such a framework, deployed within a religiously themed narrative setting, would make mysteries seem too godly, too close to religion, for that criticism to seemingly achieve its aims. *My Father, My Lord*, on the other hand, operates firmly in the spiritual style, and as such, attempts to show how a critique of basic theological beliefs can come—and perhaps even *should* come—from within the world of religion, without negating theology altogether. Accordingly, the very force of style, which in Ozu's films turns codas into the climax of an ongoing project of affirmation, is employed here to present an almost unbearable equivocation on the question of God—which, if phrased differently, is tantamount to a simultaneous acknowledgment of godly existence *and* its inherent unfathomability.

In pushing for a theological contextualization of the film's mysteries, the choice to typically designate codas as Menachem's point-of-view shots gains particular importance. By doing so, *My Father, My Lord* again aligns itself with Elisha ben Abuya who, according to Jewish legend, believed that children stand closer to God since they have not yet been contaminated by years of studying religious law. Thus, the film seems to say, it is the child, and not the rabbi father, who can see this god to which the codas seem to refer (an understanding that is further underscored by the fact that the only point of view coda shot assigned to the father—during the film's final scene, when he looks up at a darkened synagogue ceiling in a state of mourning—conspicuously lacks the other codas' poetic beauty). And it is through Menachem's eyes, in turn, that the spectators are invited to envision a possible higher power in a manner unencumbered by the perspectives dictated by religious law. The question that remains largely open at the end of Volach's film, however, is whether the spectator should attempt to reach out to this unfathomable god, this mysterious being whose only true "miracle" and sign of agency in the context of the narrative is to bring about Menachem's drowning in the Dead Sea—a body of water whose famously high percentage of saline makes drowning almost impossible. In light of this human catastrophe, the film seems to say, perhaps it is better to ignore the existence of such an undesirable god than tackle the insurmountable task of understanding it.

The Wanderer: Verifying God through Pain and Violence

Unlike David Volach, experimental filmmaker Avishai Sivan did not come from the religious world, yet like Volach, he too chose this world as the setting of his directorial debut. The Wanderer emerged out of Sivan's fascination with the fierce devotional commitment of religious Jews, which he avowedly sought to emulate in making his own art.[67] The film, however, does not amount to a paean to religious life but rather levels a harsh critique against it. At the center of this work stands Yitzhak, an adolescent Haredi Jew, who lives with his parents, both religious repentants, in the ultra-Orthodox enclave of Bnei Brak. Forced out of the strict routine of Haredi life by a debilitating case of abdominal pains, Yitzhak acquires new awareness of the stifling nature of his surroundings. From this new position, he then embarks on a journey toward greater independence, which first takes the form of incessant wandering through metropolitan streets, and then transitions into raping an inebriated woman. Through this journey, the viewers are thus exposed to a vision of Judaic-Israeli life as one founded on repression and violence, specifically in relation to sexuality.

In depicting Yitzhak's tale, The Wanderer does not display the avant-garde techniques that served the filmmaker on previous projects,[68] but instead reflects the aesthetic influence of Robert Bresson, for whose work Sivan expressed admiration.[69] Accordingly, the film carries the staples of the spiritual style: the use of nonactors in order to foreground characters' "inexpressiveness"; the subversion of suspense to create an antimelodramatic narrative; the deployment of a subdued mise-en-scène and lethargic performances, captured through extended static shots that foreground their physical textures. These formal attributes support the aforementioned critical characterization of Haredi reality as fundamentally repressive. The inert and vacuous nature of the performance reveals repression to be ingrained within Haredi physicality, while the antimelodramatic structure and use of nonactors attribute "authenticity" to this impression. The choice to shoot both indoor and outdoor scenes from a stationary third-person camera perspective, in turn, further emphasizes the inhibited manner of Haredi corporeal behavior and implicates the frame—and by extension the viewing public—in the operation of Haredi panoptical surveillance.

This type of symptomatic reading of Yitzhak's journey, which situates narrative and formal choices in relation to a sociocultural context, is extremely valuable in illuminating the film's ideological operation.[70] Yet it would be a mistake to reduce *The Wanderer* to its social commentary. For as Haviva Pedaya explains in her study of the subject, Judaic wandering always transpires along two axes: horizontally, where the wanderer relates to societal demands, and vertically, where the wanderer relates to

Figure 6. Yitzhak (Omri Fuhrer) during his wanderings. From *The Wanderer* (Avishai Sivan, 2010).

God.[71] It is this vertical axis that is underrepresented in a strictly sociocultural reading of Yitzhak's narrative, yet it may be crucial for understanding the film's overall project, especially in connection with its use of the spiritual style. In exploring this trajectory, an obvious starting point may be the question—why must Yitzhak's journey be linked to pain and violence? A possible answer can instruct us on the relationship between the protagonist's corporeal development and the supposed nature of God's presence, as well as on the spiritual style's capacity to affirm or question certain essential theological maxims.

In her seminal study *The Body in Pain* (1985), Elaine Scarry sought to articulate through corporeal terms the interdependency between humans and their God. Looking at the Old Testament, Scarry returns to the traditional Hebraic equation of human with body and God with voice. Within this paradigm, "the physical and the verbal run side by side, one above the other, as two distinct or at least distinguishable horizontal ribbons of occurrence."[72] Here the presence of the Hebraic God in human life is not imagined via its materialization in bodily form; rather, the Scriptures render Him (problematically) visible only through the results of His commands, particularly in relation to two sites of human action: reproduction and wounding. The significance of this insight resides for Scarry in the fact that for both sites, the body in transformation serves to bridge the gap between the two ribbons of occurrence. Hence,

> the Word is never self-substantiating: it seeks its confirmation in a visible change in the realm of matter. The body of man is self-substantiating: iteration and repetition (the material re-assertion of the fact of their own existence) is the most elemental form of substantiating the thing (existence, presence, aliveness, realness) that is repeated. But the body is able not only to substantiate itself but to substantiate something beyond itself as well: . . . the existence, presence, aliveness, realness of God.[73]

While in the creation of the physical world one could find confirmation to the presence of God, it is in the continued reshaping of this world—and especially, in its human bodies—that His providence is supposedly made traceable. Of the two types of reshaping, Scarry asserts that violence, at least in the Old Testament, allows God's presence to be more palpable. "In the scenes of generation," she explains, "there is no fixed path imaging the passage from the upper to the lower ribbon: insofar as there is one, it must be improvised with each new instance of generative affirmation." Scenes of wounding, however, provide a more constant and "easily available form of conceptualization"—the image of the weapon—to connect the two ribbons.[74] The manifestations of God's presence as a weapon (fire, storm, whirlwind, rod, arrow, knife, sword, and such) often take place in scenes of doubt, where procreation ceases to satisfy humans as sufficient proof for divine presence. "Unable to apprehend God with conviction," Scarry adds, "they will—after the arrival of the plague or the disease-laden quail or the fire or the sword or the storm—apprehend him in the intensity of the pain in their own bodies, or in the visible alteration in the bodies of their fellows or in the bodies (in only slightly different circumstances) of their enemies." These passages of hurting are often figured through the vocabulary of punishment. Yet this vocabulary tends to describe "the event only from the divine perspective" and as a result, "obscures the use of the body to make experienceable the metaphysical abstraction whose remoteness has occasioned disbelief." Accordingly, the passages of punishment may be best understood, for Scarry, as "openly identify[ing] the human body as a source of *analogical verification*" and "specified forms of hurt . . . as demonstrations of His existence."[75]

Following this logic, the biblical primal scene that connects violence to the structures of doubt, verification, and belief, without reverting to the rhetoric of punishment, is that of the Binding of Yitzhak. Abraham is asked to sacrifice his son in order to prove his devotion. This proof, however, is not produced for the benefit of God; He already knows the believers from the nonbelievers by virtue of His omniscience. Rather, the proof is for Abraham, in order that he may extinguish those few remaining flames of doubt burning inside him. Appropriately, verification is offered through an undeniable physical alteration—the mutilation of the child, whose exposed entrails would overcome "the distance, dimness, and unreality of God" to make "the dimly apprehended incontestably present."[76] Before this cathartic climax is met, however, the scene ends abruptly, with God offering a ram as a substitute, thereby transferring substantiating violence from human to animal. Yet even with this dislocation, the impact of violent verification remains so pal-pable that it was enough to reinforce Abraham's belief in the existence of the Almighty.

But what of the young Yitzhak? Faced with the possibility of under-going the ultimate test of God's reality through his own flesh, was he left with no doubt as the blade moved from him to the sacrificial ram? Did he not secretly want further proof of his Maker? Since the Scripture hides the young boy from our sight, focalizing the narrative instead through his father, the question remains unresolved.[77] Yet it may be argued that this potential predicament, disavowed within the Old Testament, becomes a central concern for Yitzhak's namesake, the protagonist of *The Wanderer*. From the film's outset, the Haredi Yitzhak is shown to be questioning the reality of godly existence. This doubt, however, should not be confused with utter disbelief; if anything, by choosing to follow in the path of pain and wounding, Yitzhak does not attempt to assert the nonexistence of God but to locate sources of verification to His reality. Thus, his move-ment from suffering to inflicting pain may be seen as a way of overcoming doubt, of a gradual upping of the ante in terms of embodiment in order to respond to an ever-increasing suspicion that God does not exist. This process, however, ends in failure, since the moment of "presencing" God never arrives in the rape's aftermath. Consequently, the film's conclu-sion forces an understanding that substantiation through pain is a risky endeavor, not only on ethical grounds but also for the basic reason that the realms of God and humans are inherently distinct: since God may never be truly substantiated, analogical verification must be repetitive, obsessive, and—when violence becomes the means to an end—costly.

How does one avoid an endless cycle of verifying via violence? Per-haps this is what troubles Yitzhak's mind, as he stands tearful in front of his parents' apartment during the final moments of the film. God's oper-ation in the binding scene seems to suggest a possible solution, offering a sacrificial animal body so as to relieve the human corpus from the burden of verification. Another, less lethal solution to this problem, however, may be found in the category of artifact. Thus, artistic objects—especially, but not exclusively, figurative representations—can function as "a sub-stitute for man's body which was originally itself a substitute for God's body";[78] by their physical existence, subject to a process of initial cre-ation and continual alteration (additions, deteriorations), they facilitate "a materialization of God and a dematerialization of man."[79] This solution of an artificial intermediary may seem less appropriate for Judaism, read in light of the Second Commandment, than for Christianity, where the logic of transubstantiation engendered a rich visual culture centering on the figure of Christ, especially in relation to two major scenes of corporeal substantiation—birth (nativity) and death (the passion and crucifixion). This viewpoint, however, ignores the fact that the Second Commandment did not prevent Jews from creating an impressive material culture. As a product of this culture (though less committed to its religious tenets), *The Wanderer*, an artistic rendering of extreme embodiment, could be seen as engaging this role of artificial intermediary— of staging, if only fleetingly, the drama of making "the incontestable reality of the sensory world become the incontestable reality of a world invisible and unable to be touched."[80] But therein lies the rub. Scarry's arguments apply to graven images that have a material presence in our "incontestable reality." Yet a film does not have the same strong relationship to physical space that a sculpture, painting, or a theatrical piece have; unlike them, it is, in Christian Metz's words, "made present in the mode of absence."[81] Consequently, we are left to wonder: can cinema respond to a potential desire for analogical verification, facilitating a God-related trance vision at critical moments of doubt?

A possible key to answering this question may be found in film's relationship with the most final of bodily alternations—death. Bazin, for one, was adamant about the importance of this connection to understanding cinema's specificity. It is not coincidental that he often compares the film medium to objects with ties to demise: Egyptian mummies, burial statuettes, Turin's Shroud. This persistent analogy underlies his notion of cinema as existing in relation to the denial of mortality. Film can, if desired, present the moment of death only to transcend it again and again; it can allow us to "desecrate and show at will the only one of our possessions that is temporally inalienable: dead without a requiem, the eternal dead-again of the cinema!"[82] Yet what this assertion also makes clear is that the filmic process of cheating death is performed at the price of bringing spectatorial attention to death. And not only death per se but everything in film that, in the words of Serge Daney, "simulates death: the sexual act, metamorphosis. More generally, the main nodes of a story, the decisive moments when, under the impassive eye of the camera, something is unraveled, someone changes."[83] Even more broadly than these particular transformations, which seemingly relate to on-screen bodies, attention is diverted to the body of the film itself—that which sustains all represented bodies, and whose demise ("fin") marks their end.

Film can thus bring awareness to the passages and transformations of bodily modes, and as such may conceivably be used as a platform for the analogical verification of God. The measure of awareness is contingent on the choice of subject matter; hence, films that specifically deal with death, as Bazin's formative discussion (1950) of the documentary *The Bullfight* (Pierre Braunberger, 1949) clearly indicates,[84] may result in greater spectatorial engagement with bodily transformations than those that do not. Subject matter alone, however, is not enough to make a spectator cognizant of corporeal reality through film. Aesthetics can work to render this reality palpable—and hence amenable to use for overcoming doubt—or to dismiss it. For Bazin, Daney argues, the basic aesthetic rule was that "we must not glide over the precise moment of transformation. It must be seen and 'apprehended'; it must not be read or let itself be imagined in the back-and-forth movement of montage."[85] To refuse this aesthetic rule, then, is tantamount to making death, or any other form of bodily alteration, generalized and invisible.

The question of proper aesthetics subsequently affords us an occasion to return to *The Wanderer* and discuss the operation of its spiritual style. The decision to shoot the characters in extended uninterrupted shots, usually from a distance, allows bodies to maintain their integrity of action in full view. In addition, the uncanniness of "nonacting" draws attention to the minutia of physicality and its transformations, whose presence is also highlighted in contrast to the inertness and desolation of their surroundings. Finally, the insertion of gaps within the narrative, and the choice to exchange cuts-on-action for shots that function as "stand-alone scenes,"[86] undermine the film's linear flow, foreground the physical texture of the diegesis, and imbue it with mystery. Together, these characteristics function much like in a typical Robert Bresson film, which, according to Steven Shaviro, "exalts whatever it encounters, raising everything to its utmost level of carnal intensity, its highest possible degree of embodiment."[87] This description reminds us that the spiritual style is not merely a negation but also an affirmation—in phenomenological fashion—of "things . . . in their absolute, a signifying immanence, before they have been organized into stratified structures or organic wholes."[88] It therefore may acknowledge, as Shaviro contends, "the radical incompossibility of worldly and spiritual existence,"[89] but not at the price of eradicating their connection. Rather, with Bresson films as with *The Wanderer*, a vision that binds the physical and metaphysical is evoked, manifesting an enigmatic Spirit—one that in the context of a religiously themed narrative and in relation to common spiritual style theorizations, should be understood as godly.

Yet this aesthetic strategy also carries with it certain drawbacks in relation to the project of analogical verification. Shooting from a distance, for example, can sometimes block access to the particularities of imaged bodies. Similar distance is also created by the relative avoidance of cutting, which can prevent cinema from penetrating reality, to use Walter Benjamin's provocative metaphor, like a surgeon's scalpel into a patient's body.[90] And finally, the choice to fashion character movements as lethargic also alienates from corporeal experience by hiding the full range of bodily expression. As a result of these stylistic aspects, particular bodies occasionally dissolve into a generalized form; they stop acting as palpable effigies, helpful proxies for the viewers' physical body, and become imaginary and abstract, thereby undermining the promise of an experience of God's materialization established by other formal elements of the film. In presenting scenes of pain and violence through the spiritual style, *The Wanderer* thus ends up highlighting this style's inherent ambivalence vis-à-vis the (theological) prospect of materializing a supposed hidden divinity: a simultaneous push to locate God through the "things themselves" and pull away from these things in fear that such an operation would reduce Him into profane matter. Like the film's protagonist, this aesthetic strategy therefore seems at odds with itself, unable—or unwilling—to appease doubt completely.

Bresson scholars may have implicitly recognized this equivocation in the spiritual style—and in analogical verification as a whole—which *The Wanderer* emphasizes. It is for this reason, perhaps, that Schrader asserted the importance of a "decisive action," which countermands the style's proclivity toward absenting materiality by introducing an undeniable physical presence. Such an action, which allows corporeal transformation to be apprehended in its utmost intensity, arguably appears only once in *The Wanderer*. The moment in question, unique in its

stylistic rendering, takes place in the office of Yitzhak's doctor, following the operation. Yitzhak is seen watching the doctor, when suddenly,
he faints and falls to the floor. The collapse is shot from the general
direction of the physician and follows the transition into a loss of consciousness, only to cut after Yitzhak has fallen; concurrently, the frame,
centering on Yitzhak's upper body in medium range, begins to shake, as
if in identification with the protagonist's bodily transformation. Caught
off guard by this stylistic choice, the spectator is impelled to acknowledge the existence of two bodies. On the one hand, there is Yitzhak's
body, whose unraveling is made tangible by the camera shaking. Rather
than our usual removal from this body, we are now touched by it. On
the other hand, however, we are aware that the shaking frame looks
on Yitzhak rather than strictly represents his point of view, thereby
indicating the existence of another body: not the doctor's, but that of
the camera/film itself. Yitzhak's body then relies on the body of cinema
to survive; they are linked by an invisible umbilical cord. Accordingly,
each side is affected by the connection: as Yitzhak breaks down, so does
the film, and when the film ends, Yitzhak is no more.

"An editor's cut," Sivan once noted in an interview, "resembles the
guillotine—one has to know where to cut, and when to let the frame
breathe a while longer."[91] Nowhere is this statement more apropos than
in relation to the cut that follows Yitzhak's collapse. The awareness of
the two intertwined bodies—the represented Yitzhak and the film object
that contains and sustains it—unexpectedly makes them both appear
in the flesh; and as the cut arrives, the editor's blade goes deep. For an
instant, it may even feel for the viewers like the guillotine's reach can
extend as far as their own bodies, resulting in some discomfort. It is
in this moment of impact, where bodily transformation is affected on
and off the screen, that doubt could potentially find appeasement. Its
placement in a seemingly inconsequential section near the ending of
the film—as opposed to climactic "decisive actions" of Bresson and
Ozu—may work against this aim, and serve as a deliberate manifestation
of the filmmaker's aforementioned ambivalence regarding the possibility
and value of verification. In the diegetic world, at least, this instance does
not offer Yitzhak a pathway to deliverance, perhaps because it seems to
him insufficiently violent, inadequately corporeal; hence, he is impelled
to continue on wandering in search of other diegetic bodies whose pain

may help him overcome his misgivings. Yet for certain inclined audience members in search of verification, the reverberation (and amplification) of Yitzhak's pain through a body of film can still seem potent enough to provoke the comforting impression of divinity incarnate.

Spiritual Aesthetics, Judaism, and Israeli Film

Through careful unpacking of their narrative and thematic complexities, it becomes evidently clear that *My Father, My Lord* and *The Wanderer* aim to challenge Judaic dogma's basic coherence and ethical character: in the former, by figuring the Halakha as fundamentally erroneous in its understanding of reality, and as undermining the humanity of its adherents; in the latter, by arguing that the struggle to maintain Halakhic commitments leads to a disastrous preoccupation with suffering and inflicting pain. For all its potency, however, this critical stance is mitigated, and rendered more ambivalent, through the films' reliance on the "spiritual style" for the articulation of their claims. As a result of using recognizable spiritual aesthetics in the context of a religious discussion, these works cannot but create mysteries and affirm a need to interpret them theologically. To be sure, such theological interpretation—of the experience of this mystery as the trance vision of a hidden god (or its traces)—is not tantamount to an acceptance of conventional theologizing. Indeed, Volach's film appears to resist traditional interpretations by contrasting the hidden god with the one described by the Halakha, while Sivan's film performs a similar resistance by revealing tensions within Judaic theology itself as to the possibility of making a hidden god amenable to physical manifestation and human comprehension. Yet as a form of critique, these measures do not amount to a denial of divinity either. Instead, *My Father, My Lord* and *The Wanderer* seem committed to proving that an effective criticism of Judaic dogma can only grow from the bedrock of doubt, and not of disbelief—that only by not foreclosing on the possibility of God's existence can one avoid the reductive secular-religious binaries and truly come to grips with traditional theology and the social actions performed in its name.

Thus imagined, we may well ask, in light of the Second Commandment prohibition against making a graven image, whether the mere act of attempting to provoke an experience of a hidden god in these films does not still manifest an avowedly heretical stance? Does it seek to distance them completely from Judaic tradition? At the very least, Jewish history may offer some evidence to the contrary. The Second Commandment does seem to embody the biblical preference of the audible over the visual as a mode of divine revelation. Yet while this audible emphasis, in the words of Melissa Raphael, did not turn Judaism into "a markedly iconic tradition," it also did not lead to "a general and indiscriminate ban on visual images."[92] In actuality, the contemporary conception of Judaism as aniconic has been the result of nineteenth-century Christian anti-Semitic reformulation of Jewish culture as fundamentally inartistic and therefore inferior, which was then used by assimilationist Jews to assert their similarity to iconoclastic Christianity in a manner that made "virtues out of the vices attributed to them by the surrounding society."[93] In contrast, Judaic discourse on the Second Commandment since biblical times has been remarkably diversified and included many voices that were in favor of images, especially if these are not explicitly referenced as idols. As a result, though the prohibition of images has limited the output of Jewish artists in comparison to those of other cultures (at least in the pre-Emancipation era), it did not prevent Jews from developing an impressive visual culture that profoundly shaped Judaic thought and identity.[94]

If *The Wanderer* and *My Father, My Lord* are essentially compatible with a Judaic mindset that permits visual representations—even of God—then one also has to consider whether the representational strategy employed in their visual storytelling—the "spiritual style"—should be read as endemic to Judaism or rather as a foreign entity that is incorporated from outside of Judaism to "contaminate" it. Justification for the "contamination" reading may be found in the tendency of "spiritual style" discourse to ground itself in Christian ideas,[95] often as a result of its principal authors' particular denominational background (and in the case of Schrader and Ayfre, actual theological and clerical training). Does this mean, however, that the spiritual style is fundamentally anti-Judaic? Again, such an unequivocal assertion seems unwarranted, since the style's mélange of the material and immaterial appears to resonate with a certain Judaic approach to envisioning God. Contrary to common understandings, divine revelation in the Bible was not solely auditory, as the voice was often preceded by a visual manifestation that foreshadowed its appearance. This appearance of visual theophany, in turn, oscillated between presence and absence, masking and unmasking, in order to simultaneously maintain the sanctity of divine transcendence (God as spirit) *and* immanence (Man as made in God's image).[96] Much of Jewish visual culture maintained a similar oscillation, especially in relation to the representation of the human figure. In this respect, Judaic tradition resisted giving the represented figure a sense of fullness, because that would indicate an attempt to capture the completeness of God—which is futile—or to collapse it to materiality—which is blasphemous. At the same time, it also did not want to discard the phenomenal world, and in particular the human body and face, because these carry the traces of God's visage. The result of this was the acceptance of an aesthetic rule whereby, in the words of Lionel Kochan, "if any material entity is to symbolize God, it must be of such a nature as both to disguise and reveal this relationship."[97] Such was achieved by means of subtraction: by indicating in visual fashion that the represented object is somehow partial, and therefore removed from godly perfection.[98]

Various strains of Jewish mysticism have contributed to this Judaic aesthetic tradition by producing visual aids in support of the mystic's ritualistic "imagery techniques,"[99] whose end is the ascent to a supposed divine realm beyond normal sense experience. Of the various aids used in ritual, two deserve special mention, not only because of their centrality to historical Kabbalah but also because of their continued presence within Israel's New-Age-infused cultural landscape of spirituality. The first of these is the Hebrew alphabet. In discussing the problem of the Second Commandment's legacy in Judaism, Moshe Halbertal explained how words as a symbolic form came to be seen as an appropriate representation of God while pictorial representations were considered less so. "A picture," he explains, "is meant to capture the entire essence of what is being represented; it strives to create a full representation, leaving no gaps. Not so language: A verbal description is only partial, and the open spaces it leaves make language an appropriate medium for representing God."[100] Accordingly, compared to words, visual imagery is at greater risk of replacing the referent with its representation in the mind of the beholder—which, in the context of representing God, is also the risk of idolatry.

Language's partialness—and resulting ambivalence of meaning—seems to have been what motivated Jewish mystics to use the Hebrew alphabet as part of their meditative imagery techniques. A central practice in this context involved recombining the letters of God's name. Kabbalists had hundreds of such combinations at their disposal and were encouraged not only to articulate them repeatedly but also to use them as grounds for the creation of new alphabetic juxtapositions. These combinations were often described in great detail within mystical texts: for example, R. Eleazar of Worms (1176–1238) in his *Sefer Hashem* and R. Abraham Abulafia (1240–1291) in his *Sefer Or Hasechel* offered extensive tables of different modes of assemblage, to be put to meditative use with the aim of experiencing divine contact.[101] As J. H. Chajes explains, certain manuscripts even helped their readers in the onerous task of meditative assemblage by placing the letters on *"volvelles*—inscribed discs of parchment sewn to the page that revolved." During the Middle Ages, these became "perfect visual aids to the practitioner of Abulafian meditation who had to undertake such cognitively demanding work in states of excitement and ecstasy."[102]

Though Halbertal is right in recognizing the "partial" and "unfixed" nature of words, what these meditative engagements with *the alphabet* seem to highlight is the shortsightedness of his attempt to deny the word the status of a "visual representation." Such has also been the main thrust within mysticism scholarship, where the Hebrew letters have been conventionally interpreted more as signs than as images.[103] Yet Kabbalist literature does feature "graphic sermons" that discuss the visual shaping of fonts as part of the letter's mystical operation.[104] To relate to letters in this fashion, Leslie Atzmon argues, is to acknowledge that they function as forms of "figurative symbolism"[105] aimed at overcoming the Jewish proscription against graven images. The symbolic dimension of the letters is manifested through their anthropomorphic design, which provides them with "striking figurative qualities including a 'head,' 'body,' and 'feet.'" As Atzmon explains:

> These lines [of Hebrew letterheads] are organic rather than geometric—they are curved and shaped like two-dimensional renderings of fleshy creatures with torsos, arms and legs. Although there is a strong visual relationship among the letters—certain

curves and thick to thin strokes, for example—each letterform is very distinct and each has its own recognizable visual character. *Koph* . . . has a head on top of a lengthy spine, in contrast to *Lamed* . . . with its long neck that ends in a curvy body. Each letter has its own recognizable visual temperament as well. The letter *Bet* looks like a seated creature, stolid and stationary, while the letter *Gimel* perambulates, one fleshy foot placed in front of the other. Looking at the complete alphabet, one could almost imagine the letters interacting with each other—some letterforms reaching out to, and some shunning, other individuals. These visual characteristics of the letters—designed artefacts that assimilate human qualities—make them ideal candidates for anthropomorphic attribution.[106]

Since "the Hebrew alphabetic 'characters' look and act like living creatures,"[107] and since the Kabbalist was asked to "meditate on the visual qualities of the letterforms and carry out meditative rendering of the letters,"[108] it is important then to not read them solely as components of abstract words, but as potential corporeal-material thresholds onto the secret of hidden divinity. They are formed through subtraction, as in the "spiritual style," in order to assert their partialness (for theological reasons) and prevent the distractions of reality's plentiful image (on experiential grounds); yet even under the influence of a negative aesthetic, these letters serve to highlight the Judaic need for a palpable vision as a bridge toward an unfathomable mystery.

More figurative is the symbol of the *Sefirot*, which may be rightfully seen as "the clearest indication of a kabbalistic worldview and of a text's reliance on kabbalistic traditions and sources."[109] Though central to Kabbalah, the Sefirot system was never conceptualized in a unified way. It is often described as a collection of ten "potencies" that make up God and as a means of divine emanation, through which holy light flows from the Infinite God (*Ein-Sof*) and animates creation. Most importantly, it served as a palpable and concrete way through which to understand and reach God. For as Elliot Wolfson indicates, the Sefirot were viewed as "the projection of the imageless divine into an image," which in turn allowed the Kabbalists to study them as "an exercise in imaginary visualization" and experience through them God's revelation.[110]

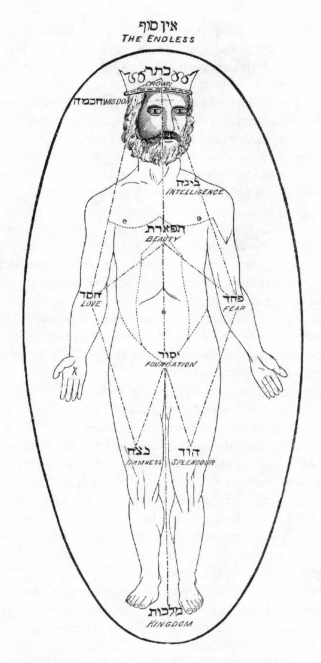

FIGURE 7. Sefirotic diagram as Adam Kadmon. From *The Kabbalah: Its Doctrines, Development, and Literature* (Christian D. Ginsburg, 1865).

This process of visualizing the hidden God through the Sefirot was not performed only as internal conceptualization, and was not left entirely to the vagaries of each Kabbalist's imagination. Rather, it was given form in the "Sefirotic diagram," which by the fourteenth century became the dominant way for representing God in Kabbalah tradition.[111] Seemingly following the principle of *harmonia mundi*—whereby God, cosmos, and nature are united by common structural elements—this diagram presents an abstract structure with visual correlations to "the bilaterally symmetrical human figure"[112] and "an inverted Tree of Life."[113] While avoiding full figuration, the diagrams deployed abstractness to varying degrees throughout their history. Thus, as Chajes and Eliezer Baumgarten explain, earlier examples "share an austere aesthetic," while many later works "added decorative elements . . . , including delicate floral motifs and animal iconography," as well as human features like "hair, moustache, and beard."[114] This variety manifests the paradox— and its attendant ambivalence—that undergirds the diagram, where pure abstractness insinuates the existence of a transcendental sphere of divinity removed from the world of finite forms, while the invocation of humanity and nature shows that our world and God's are nevertheless still linked, however tentatively.

This ambivalence helps animate the mystics' imagination as they interact with the diagram: by drawing iconic forms on single parchment or longer *rotuli* (vertical scrolls), and by "thinking with"[115] these material(ized) forms "to identify imaginatively with the divine in its emanatory unfolding—a meditative process that could be facilitated by the active scrolling"[116] of the multiple-parchment scrolls. As Chajes notes, such activity figured the diagram as not "merely a text to be studied, but something to be performed, irreducible to the sum of the inscribed information to be found within it." In this respect, diagrams "were like maps of divine topography. . . . Today's maps are commonly understood as navigational tools but the early modern map invited its observer to participate—almost in today's 'virtual' sense—in the landscape, on a journey, usually without leaving home. Contemplation of a map of the Holy Land was therefore a form of pilgrimage, contemplation of a map of God a form of divine encounter."[117]

Thus envisioned, the Sefirotic diagram and the Hebrew alphabet share with the "spiritual style" an aesthetic mélange of figuration and abstraction, which wears its ascetic partialness on its sleeve. Partiality here exposes ambivalences inherent to the image and offers no clear resolution. This, in turn, dissuades the viewer from settling on the image as a totality enclosed within its own frame and points him or her toward a greater totality that transcends the image, and where all ambivalences may potentially be resolved. As such, the trance vision that ideally comes into view in both graphic and cinematic traditions—to quote Chajes's description of the Sefirotic diagram—is a "fractal metonym, a prism through which [the] ungraspable whole might be refracted,"[118] and in the aftermath, affirmed along onto/theological lines. It may be argued that *My Father, My Lord* and *The Wanderer* are influenced by these traditions and hence are bound to their mystical project. Yet the two films do not reach for this project's set destination. Rather than affirm unity through transcending tensions between figuration and abstraction, they challenge unity by throwing ambivalences into an even sharper relief. This heretic challenge amounts to questioning the mystical framework, but not to its shattering. For as the fragile balance of partialness is maintained in these cinematic works, so is the horizon of an ungraspable divine whole—as a possibility more than unassailable reality.

Fragility is particularly noticeable when this balance is disturbed, as in the case of Sivan's 2015 feature, *Tikkun*. Like *The Wanderer*, *Tikkun* depicts the path of discovery of an ultra-Orthodox youth, which leads him away from the regimes of Haredi bodily regulation and toward a destination both tragic and perverse. Haim-Aron, the film's protagonist, finds himself troubled by his bridled lusts. Tension comes to a head early on, as he experiences arousal while showering, and then slips on his head. With injury proving fatal, and with EMT efforts ending in failure, Haim-Aron's father nevertheless manages to resuscitate his son and raise him from the dead. Yet what appears as a welcomed deliverance evolves into a continued nightmare. As soon as he is revived, Haim-Aron becomes defiant of his constrictive environment, both in the yeshiva and at home. Aberrance comes in similar forms as in *The Wanderer*: walking through desolate streets, lying on the sandy beach, propositioning a prostitute. These escalate to an even more horrific climax than the one found in the earlier film: walking through a landscape of mist, the protagonist stumbles on the body of a young female driver in the aftermath of a deadly car accident and proceeds to probe her genitals with his finger; then, on his return home, he enters his bed and bleeds out, while his parents observe him, this time doing nothing to stop their child's demise. Such dire fate—where the violator of Judaic law lies dead, and his father, in abidance with this law, does nothing—presses home an argument about the futility of Halakhic observance as a repressive and oppressive regime.

The body stands again at this argument's center, functioning as a site where opposing positions on devotion conjoin in ambivalence. This ambivalence is acknowledged explicitly when, during a conversation between Haim-Aron and a fellow yeshiva student, they ponder out loud how it may be possible to both love God and hate the body He created. For the most part, however, the film deals with corporeality's equivocal nature—as the paradoxical conjoining of sacred and profane—through tacit metaphor. Accordingly, the father's profession as butcher (*Shohet*) is used by Sivan to introduce scenes of animal slaughter and disembowelment, where body is reduced to perishable flesh. At the same time, the sterilized surroundings, shot at a distance with balanced and uncluttered composition, provide animal flesh with certain dignity, if not sublimity. Human corporeality is also manifested in similar fashion, especially in the climactic roadside sequence. Although this scene includes a dead cow—the cause and casualty of the aforementioned car accident—it is the driver's naked genitals that receive the most corporeal attention. The perversity of Haim-Aron's postmortem prodding, as well as the status of the body as corpse, push profanity to its limits. Concurrently and contrastingly, that the landscape of such a horrendous act is covered in thick mist, and that the deceased's pelvic area is rendered ephemeral through a delicate close-up, adds an air of sacredness—or even sacred rituality—to the scene. Caught between these *other* bodies, the protagonist finds in them mirrors to his own corporeal predicament. His body is a site of arousal and repression, of life and death; he cannot find a way to resolve these differences, and therefore lives out their resulting ambivalence as long as he can.

The stakes of ambivalence are raised through *Tikkun*'s reliance on an austere "spiritual style." Stylization of elimination is evident, first and foremost, in the choice to shoot the film entirely in black and white, as opposed to the use of color in *The Wanderer*. Other techniques of aesthetic austerity carry over from the earlier film, including relatively static camera work, long uninterrupted takes and avoidance of cut on action, absence of nondiegetic soundtrack, use of nonactors and downplaying of dramatic gesture, scarcity of dialogue, loose narrative structure with no clear causal and linear logic, and unusual emphasis on the dramatically inconsequential (for example, in extended close-ups of insects). By stripping reality bare, *Tikkun*, like *The Wanderer*, distills the body into its carnal kernel, while at the same time, by removing familiar contexts of interpretation (identity, psychology, culture, and such), propels it to the realm of the abstract. On this level, at least, the equivocation at the heart of the spiritual style—as well as of the Hebrew alphabet and Sefirotic diagram as meditative forms—is sustained, and with it, also the potential of transcendence toward a greater, divine unity.

Where *Tikkun* nevertheless departs from *The Wanderer*, or from *My Father, My Lord* for that matter, is in tipping the scales of ambivalence toward resolution in the form of what Sobchack calls "figural literalism"; that is, "making the content of transcendence and the transcendental intelligible by making it literally visible."[119] Figural literalism comes in the context of visions connected to the father, which carry explicit theological connotations. Like in *My Father, My Lord*, *Tikkun* evokes the Binding of Isaac myth; yet if in Volach's film, the father essentially sacrifices the son, but does not get a timely reprieve from God, in the case of Sivan's film, the father brings his child back from the dead, and then is rebuked by God for having usurped His authority. Divine wrath is presented in two oneiric scenes. In the first, the father jumps up from his toilet seat, as a crocodile emerges out of the drain, proclaiming Haim-Aron's resuscitation as an offense against God; then the father sees Haim-Aron lying in bed with a knife in his back, followed by the blade flying across the room to slice the patriarch's raised hand. In the second, the father carries the body of his younger son Yanke across the apartment hallway, reaching a precipice beyond which crocodiles lay waiting for a feast; with a knife in its back, the boy's body is laid to the floor, and a flying insect settles on it, after which a swarm of other insects attack the father. Through the literalization of the metaphysical in both scenes, a horizon of transcendence, made possible through the spiritual style's partialness, is effectively blocked. As a result, where the two earlier films previously discussed keep this horizon as an unaffirmed potential, in order to cultivate doubt, the reduction of the transcendent onto the immanent in *Tikkun* means to replace doubt with more outright dismissal. Not only is divinity demystified by its constraining in a knowable form but also by the choice of having this be a particularly profane form—the bleeding flesh, the reptilian and arthropodal. Such idolatrous visions take their inspiration less from the spiritual style canon than from the surreal films of Luis Buñuel (indeed, various moments in *Un Chien Andalou* [1929]—the famous slashing of the eye, or a hand exuding ants—seem to have particular resonance with *Tikkun*). And like the apparitions in these films serve to buttress an avowedly anticlerical message, so do the specters of *Tikkun* upset the spiritual style's delicate balance between figuration and ineffability, in order to sway the spectator in the direction of disbelief.

It is therefore somewhat ironic that the title of Sivan's film would evoke the widely popular, Kabbalistic concept of *Tikkun Olam*, which bespeaks of restoring all things to their rightful place in a unified cosmos.[120] As is elaborated on in the next chapter, Tikkun Olam provides a dimension of rectification to the experience of unio mystica, allowing the chasm between the tellurian and transcendent spheres to be mended. This restorative goal has been pursued through Hebrew alphabet and Sefirotic diagram related rituals,[121] whose aesthetic of austere partialness spur the mystic's imagination to "complete" what is hidden from view. The same trajectory is inherent to the spiritual style's operation, as a modern reiteration of these and other similar visual aids. To varying degrees, the three films discussed here challenge this trajectory; rather than activate ambivalence as a springboard toward transcendent unity,

FIGURE 8. Haim-Aron's father (Khalifa Natour) looking at crocodiles at the bottom of a precipice. From *Tikkun* (Avishai Sivan, 2015).

they use it as a bulwark against unbridled faith, casting doubt on the very existence of such unity. Yet however much ambivalence arises from this challenge, hope of transcendent resolution in the form of cosmic repair still remains, ingrained within a long-standing aesthetic tradition and cultural sensibility on which these cinematic works are based. Thus *My Father, My Lord*, *The Wanderer*, and *Tikkun* may pull the fragments of a broken reality in different directions, but they also inevitably gesture toward a unified whole shining through the cracks—a vision that is sustained by those viewers who seek to "lift the veil at the horizon of the known," and imagine what lies beyond.

2

"WHO CAN FIND A VIRTUOUS WOMAN?"

Female (Im)Modesty and Mystical-Messianic Time

> We know that the Jews were prohibited from investigating the
> future. The Torah and the prayers instruct them in remembrance,
> however. This stripped the future of its magic, to which all those
> succumb who turn to soothsayers for enlightenment. This does
> not imply, however, that for the Jews the future turned into homo-
> geneous, empty time. For every second of time was the strait gate
> through which the Messiah might enter.
>
> —Walter Benjamin[1]

As a nation shaped by the patriarchal logic of a militarist ethos, Israel
has been slow to adopt the lessons of global feminism. During the
1960s and 1970s, when second wave feminist movements were gaining
strength in the United States and Europe, Israeli women still accepted
their disenfranchisement as the order of things within a country fight-
ing for its very survival; picking up the feminist cause was considered a
luxury then, and therefore this path was only undertaken by a meager
number of (mostly Anglo-Saxon) activists on the fringes of Israeli society. Things slowly shifted during the 1980s and 1990s, as the impact of
the feminist revolution from decades before began to register on the
Israeli landscape, especially in areas of legislation; and it was only in

the 2000s that third wave feminism's call for diversity pushed Israeli feminist discourse away from a focus on the plight of Israel's hegemonic womanhood (white, Jewish, secular, heterosexual), and toward greater inclusivity of various female experiences under patriarchy.[2] As part of this development, Israeli Judaism's marginalization of women became a hotly debated issue, in response to increased media coverage of various Judaic exclusionary practices: for example, Israel Defense Forces (IDF) male soldiers purposefully leaving an official ceremony because it involved a female singing performance; women being harassed on "kosher buses" within religious settlements and neighborhoods for not observing gender separation by moving to the back; verbal and physical violence in public spaces against those who fail to abide by Judaic laws of propriety, even young girls; attempts to create gender-segregated classes for the purpose of integrating ultra-Orthodox students into public universities; instituting different bathing schedules for men and women in the waters of national parks; and denying observant women the right to take part in leadership roles within the major Haredi party, Agudat Israel. These and other similar instances provoked the ire of many Israelis, who drew from the insights of feminism in their protest against religion-based discrimination.

Much of this opposition understandably came from Israel's secular sector. Its adherents tend to stress the perspective that the Bible, as a text written by and for men, situates women as the quintessential Other, and thus acts as the condition for an institutional marginalization of womanhood that covers all spheres of Judaic life. With reference to this state of affairs, the Judaic demand for sexually based modesty (*Tzniut*), visible in the aforementioned incidents, has become particularly important for secular feminist critique. Judaism's modesty discourse reduces women to their naked bodies, understood as instigators of sin and therefore as needing to be hidden from sight. This understanding has resulted in a myriad of regulatory practices, which seek to segregate women and delimit their agency in different areas of life, such as dress and deportment, work and education, intimate relations and physical placement in public spheres. As a means of patriarchal domination aimed at protecting a supposed male vulnerability, these regulations therefore become obvious targets for the feminist appreciation of female subjectivity under Judaism.

Israel's Judaic community has certainly not been oblivious to this criticism, and while extensive parts of the rabbinical institution have reacted with conservative measures aimed at preserving the status quo, many observant women sought in turn to absorb some of feminism's tenets and challenge the religious system from within. These challenges have been most influential in different spheres of everyday Judaic life: for example, in revising ritualistic practices and synagogue spaces so as to represent a more egalitarian ethos; in increasing the scope of women's religious education, including the establishment of yeshiva-like all-women's educational institutions (Midrasha); in pushing for a more vigorous female presence in the public sphere, with religious women taking positions of greater authority in religious councils, in front of rabbinical courts, as teachers in schools, and even as rabbis; in demanding a more profound and explicit discussion of sexually related issues, especially surrounding the menstrual cycle, procreation, conjugal intimacy, and rape; and in reinterpreting Judaism's sacred literature in light of feminist values, with the intention of creating a new body of exegesis (Midrash) that would support gender equality.[3] Where these and other areas intersect with the question of female modesty, religious feminist discourse has tended not to dismiss the logic of Tzniut so much as refashion it: for example, by looking at modesty-regulated spaces as offering opportunities for women to "express and strengthen a self-conscious identity, out of which a sense of their own initiative and value commitments may develop,"[4] or by expanding the purview of modesty to the community as a whole in order to help people not "view themselves according to the images of each other that have been generated through generations of cagey anxiety and misguided notions, but in the far more forgiving gaze of the divine."[5]

For its part, Israeli secular feminism appears uninterested in accepting Judaic feminism's stance on the redemptive aspects of modesty-regulated spaces. Instead, it defines feminism and Judaism as fundamentally incompatible and therefore sees the abolishment of separations as the only proper response to violence perpetrated in the name of Tzniut. This position can be found not only on the pages of Israel's mainstream press but also in the proliferation Israeli films (and television programs[6]) in the secular media market whose aim, so it seems, has been to stage scenes with Judaic women transgressing the taboos of modesty in sexual and romantic contexts. As a cycle, these audiovisual texts collectively imagine religious women to not only be Israeli-Judaic reality's principal victims but also its primary challengers. Their challenge is imagined to emerge out of a desire for sexual exploration—a desire that is deemed natural and hence inherently in conflict with Judaism's artificial laws of sexual regulation. Accordingly, these texts place their characters on a collision course with Judaism's power structures, a process that ultimately necessitates that they abandon their religiosity or live in an unbearable tension with it.

The following pages evaluate this corpus of media texts in an effort to determine the nature of its feminist critique, and more importantly, to discuss this critique's underlying ambivalence as indicative of contemporary negotiations between Israeli Judaism and secularism. In this framework, the discussion accounts for Judaic-themed Israeli films' alignment with a secular perspective that imagines feminist resistance to religious patriarchal rule almost exclusively through the lens of sexual taboos. It is argued that this reduction facilitates a contradictory movement within many of these films: on the one hand, it surfaces dimensions of Judaic patriarchal oppression and provides a critical deconstruction of their operation; on the other hand, however, it fetishizes the Judaic as Other, and by extension, allows the secular viewer (or at least its male variety) to simultaneously repress a shared patriarchal ground with Israel's religious sector and indulge in the voyeuristic pleasures of seeing modest religious women in immodest situations. In delineating this model, the argument centers on two examples in particular—*The Secrets* (Avi Nesher, 2007) and *Bruriah* (Avraham Kushnir, 2008)—that attempt to countermand tendencies of reductive "othering" by addressing religious patriarchalism from within Judaism: a position of "devoted resistance"[7] that is akin to Judaic feminism. Thematically, these films expand the range of feminist engagements by exploring other sites of contemporary resistance (mainly through erudition) and by suggesting a new feminist midrash through intertextual references to female role models within Judaic tradition. In attempting to bridge the gap between religious and secular values, however, their critical stance ultimately succumbs to the dominant strategy of focusing on modesty, and to the intricate matrix of desire that it triggers by exposing women who are traditionally kept unexposed. While this level of narrative-thematic engagement unveils their conservative tendencies, the films' stylistic operation nevertheless poses a more radical challenge to the regimes of gendered and religious othering. This challenge, in turn, draws on the supposedly redemptive potential of Jewish mystical-messianic temporality, which has been the focus of various Jewish New Age phenomena, including those focused on questions of gender.[8]

Gazing at the Image of an "Immodest" Jewish Woman

As Judaism's formative text, the Bible pays relatively little attention to the Jewish woman. Its androcentric nature leads it to construct narratives almost exclusively around male figures. Women are often absent from these stories, or rather exist in their margins. The readers rarely gain access to their subjectivity, their feelings and desires, and their voices are seldom heard. What is privileged instead is the image of a Jewish woman as a male construct, a projection that caters to the Jewish man's fertile imagination. Consequently, woman is reduced to the various stereotypes that make up the Eternal Feminine: the dutiful mother, daughter, and slave, always subservient to the men in their lives; or the shrewish mistress and harlot, constantly forcing on men the actuality of sin.[9] Within this conceptual framework, biblical literature tends to foreground scenes of an "immodest" sexual nature, which play into patriarchal fantasies about seduction, intercourse, and rape. Following Laura Mulvey, biblical scholar J. Cheryl Exum argued that this positioning places the Jewish woman at the mercy of a penetrating scopophilic gaze. Exemplary of this ocular economy is the scene where David watches the bathing Bathsheba. Here Bathsheba is reduced to her physical features—to the fact that she is "very beautiful"[10]—and becomes an object of "to-be-looked-at-ness." As a result, viewing emerges as "one-sided, giving [David] the advantage and the position of power; he sees her but she does not see him."[11] The (male) reader, in turn, is more than "invited to take David's symbolic position as the focalizer of the gaze: he can look through David's eyes; he can fantasize himself in David's place. The woman is naked for his pleasure."[12] Such is the compromised position, Exum argues, of many other women inside Judaism's most sacred book.

For all their voyeurism, biblical descriptions of immodest Jewish women are often rather tame. Yet even in their unembellished state, these depictions succeeded in igniting the non-Jewish imagination with regard to the sexual qualities of "the Jewess." Of special import in this context is the trope of *la belle Juive*, which became prominent particularly in modern European public discourse as a way of relating to—and distancing—the Jewish Other. In modern occidental literature, the "beautiful Jewess" was "ubiquitously conflated with the Oriental woman, and recognized by her stylized sensual beauty: her large dark eyes, abundant hair, and languid expression."[13] Her beauty served as a marker of her purity, nobility, and loyalty, creating the image of an idealized Jew worthy of inclusion into civilized Western culture (for example, Rebecca in Walter Scott's *Ivanhoe* [1820]). Yet it also signaled danger to others, aligning her with the seductive femme fatale archetype (for example, Salomé in Oscar Wilde's eponymous play [1896]).[14]

The hypersexualization of the Jewess within non-Jewish culture is especially evident in Western pictorial tradition, which actualizes the Bible's voyeuristic gaze and heightens its effects. Exum notes, for example, that the story of Bathsheba and David provided "both theme and pretext for artistic representations of a naked woman."[15] In these paintings, Bathsheba is placed on display in a manner that asserts her exhibitionism. At the same time, the spectators "are invited to identify with David's perspective by means of the woman's body, which signifies his sexual arousal."[16] This visual strategy, which offered a way of controlling the threat of the Jewess to a susceptible patriarchy, was applied to the pictorial representation of not only biblical but also modern Jewish women and thus came to be the overarching model for visualizing Semitic femininity within Western-gentile cultural artifacts, including cinema.[17]

As opposed to the ideology of voyeuristic display, Judaic culture mobilized the Bible's tales of immodest women in order to support modesty's particular order of (in)visibility. Within Judaic thought, Melissa Raphael argues, a clear dichotomy is established along gender lines: man is considered spiritual, while woman is "essentially physical and sexual" and thus "lacks the ontological complexity of the male body."[18] In being more physical, the woman is also inherently more visible than the man. This visibility, in turn, marks her as a threat to Judaic manhood, since it is liable to draw men away from the infinite Divine and toward the finite human world. As a result, the real problem Judaism has with women seems less to do with "female sexuality as such, but the public *spectacle* of female sexuality,"[19] which brings them closer to the category of idol. Accordingly, in an effort to prevent the operation of idolatry, segregation is introduced to hide the Jewish woman from view.

This rule of segregation functions not only in the realm of everyday Judaic life, but in artistic representation as well. In contrast to the aforementioned Western paintings, Jewish art, especially before Jewish Emancipation, often denied women visibility. Consequently, according to Raphael, within Jewish paintings the frame has often been dominated by the presence of devout men, who function much like Christian icons, "defining the Jewish posture in relation to God and properly hypostasizing or summarizing the appearance of Jewish worship."[20] On the rare occasions when Jewish women were displayed during this period of relative paucity, their representation seemed detached from the Judaic world to which they belong. In the absence of a clear iconography, the Jewish woman emerged as "oddly un-Jewish" in assuming a blank expression and "an air of vacancy,"[21] as if she is "ordinary in relation to the specialness of the holy."[22] Even when visible in Jewish art, Raphael asserts, women remained a visual lack.[23]

The exclusion of women in this way seems to subvert the voyeuristic gaze, and indeed, religious apologetics have argued for the value of this invisibility as a protective measure against the harmful effects of female objectification. While this reasoning is not entirely specious, it nevertheless disavows the oppressive function of female invisibility within Judaism's patriarchal rule; namely, that by keeping them as absent, Jewish women are denied agency, which is hitherto reserved only for men. Furthermore, while the actual-ocular voyeuristic gaze is denied in Judaism, its textual equivalent, which may be traced back to the Bible's description of immodest women, continues to prevail. Thus, as Tova Hartman explains, the passionate and elaborate discussion of modesty within rabbinical literature "dismembers" women, constituting them solely "by the potential effects of their parts upon the spiritual lives of men."[24] Such methods not only allow Jewish men to reduce women into objects but also to release libidinal energy under the protective guise of modesty lawmaking.

It is in relation to this religious regime of invisibility and objectification that the operation of recent Israeli films on Judaic women may be best understood. These texts seek to provide observant women with visibility after being deprived of such during the long history of Jewish art. This visibility, in turn, underlines a statement on the necessity for such women to challenge the patriarchal regime that rejects their subjectivity and accords them the disparaging status of object. Yet what may be made with the choice present in many of these texts to *expose* their devout heroines almost exclusively in contexts of a romantic, sexual and/or erotic nature? Does this strategy not draw Israeli cinema closer to the non-Jewish pictorial tradition, which capitalized on the thrill of unveiling the hidden, presumably de-sexualized Jewish woman, in the process of breaking sacred taboos? Is this not fundamentally a matter of moving from a "religious" to a "western male gaze,"[25] with the major difference being that the former denies female agency by forcing women to be "modest," while the latter does so by forcing them to be "immodest"?

Religious Women in Judaic-Themed Israeli Film

Judaic-themed Israeli cinema has generally attempted to avoid a stereotypical representation of the Jewish woman as *belle Juive* and has rarely aligned itself in any explicit way with the matrix of desire and anxiety that this trope represents. Rather than reducing her to a misogynist symbol, this filmic corpus aims to provide a more elaborate, and affirmative, account of observant women as they confront the norms of traditional Judaism, particularly in the context of sexual comportment. Yet as already insinuated, these depictions also often tacitly implicate their viewers in the basic perspective underlying the *belle Juive* stereotype. In this context, images of immodest Jewish women—and particularly young women—become a key to unlocking these texts' broader commitments to the mindset of patriarchy, and by extension—the root of their ambivalence toward the relationship of Israeli secularism to Judaism. The following examples may serve to illustrate this point.[26]

Apples from the Desert (2014), Matti Harari and Arik Lubetzki's screen adaptation of noted Israeli author Savyon Liebrecht's eponymous short story, dramatizes Judaic female im(modesty) through the lens of matchmaking (*Shidduch*), which has been of popular use with other Israeli films dealing with this topic, and to similar ends. The film's protagonist, nineteen-year-old Rivka, is the only child of Victoria and Reuven, Haredi Mizrahi Jews residing in Jerusalem's ultra-Orthodox precincts. The father wishes his daughter to conform to the ways of her community, and the effect of this on Rivka is stifling. She tries to find release through clandestine participation in a folk-dance class. There she meets Kibbutz member Dov and, unbeknownst to her parents, begins to see him romantically. As it becomes clear that Rivka is transgressing community mores, Reuven attempts to drag her back to the fold through a lopsided betrothal with an older widower. While Victoria submits to her husband's plan, Rivka vehemently opposes it, opting instead to run away with Dov to his Kibbutz in the south of Israel. Though suffering the pains of adjustment, she ultimately finds happiness in Kibbutz secularity and life with Dov. Aided by her sister Sarah, until recently the family's foremost "black sheep," Victoria manages to track her daughter down and is made to see the good in Rivka's recent transformation. Thus, when Reuven suddenly appears in the Kibbutz at the heels of his wife, and forcibly attempts to take Rivka with him, Victoria sides with her daughter in opposition. The dejected husband leaves but is then appeased by a magnanimous Dov, ultimately joining his other family members for a meal in Rivka's new home.

To take "the short story's feminist agenda much further," the *Apples from the Desert* film, in Yaron Shemer's words, "involves at times the employment of trite tropes."[27] None is arguably triter than the Manichaean structuring of Haredi versus Kibbutz community. The Haredi landscape is rendered as stifling and oppressive. The streets of Rivka's ultra-Orthodox neighborhood appear in tight frames, which emphasize building facades over open skyline and hence create a distinct impression of cloistering. The family's apartment seems even more constrictive: it is consistently shot in low-key lighting and dominated by muted colors, even during daytime scenes, thereby creating a visual correlation to Rivka's depressive state; at the same time, shelves filled with religious literature and large portraits of well-known religious figures (Rabbi Ovadia Yosef and Baba Sali) hanging on the walls, like the printed warnings against breach of modesty placed on building facades (*Pashkevil*), point to the patriarchal-Judaic origin of this darkness. In contrast, the Kibbutz is imaged as a bright, open and spacious landscape, pervaded by nature. Particular emphasis is given to the uninhabited expanses of the desert as well as an imposing presence of clear blue skies. While the scenes of

Haredi streets and interiors seem to leave little space for the viewer to enter, those of the Kibbutz appear much more inviting to both characters and spectators. This visualized difference figures the Kibbutz as a site of social acceptance and therefore affirms both Dov's welcoming attitude toward Rivka and her successful assimilation into secular ways.

Along the lines of this binarism, Rivka's father is rendered emblematic of a Haredi logic of oppression. In comparison to the father in the original story, Reuven behaves far more fanatically and violently toward his wife and daughter.[28] Such negative characterization finds its stylistic correlative in visualizing the father as aligned with the darkness of his physical surroundings (throughout the film, Shemer notes, "his eyes are barely visible—they are sunken and dimly lit"). Subtending this alignment is Haredism's reduction to the dominant "paradigm in Israeli films of the oppressive Mizrahi male."[29] As a result, the film is able to lend more weight to a critical stance against religion by associating it with a prevalent, yet not always acknowledged, discourse of racially based vilification. Interestingly, Dov's father Zeev is also figured along reductive terms, as a stereotypical Kibbutznik weary of all things related to religion, including his son's new paramour. Thus imagined, this character primarily functions as a way of showing that Kibbutz society is also not devoid of narrowminded intolerance, in spite of its claim for a liberal outlook. The analogy is uneven, however, for Dov's father is a minor character in the film and occupies a fringe perspective within this society, while Rivka's father is a central character and appears representative of his community's dominant views. Hence, by positioning Zeev as an exception to the rule, and an anachronistic one at that, the Kibbutz's tolerance is ultimately affirmed, making for a starker contrast with the basic inequity of the religious world.

To the extent that the three main female figures resist this inequity, their challenge seems to operate primarily within the sphere of sexual modesty. Representing the old guard of Judaic womanhood, Victoria and Sarah are distinguished from one another according to their marital status: Victoria is socially affirmed by her standing as wife and mother, while Sarah is socially shunned due to her being unmarried. This difference dictates the measure by which each character flaunts her immodesty at the face of patriarchal regulation. For example, during an early scene, the two sisters talk about female sartorial deportment, with Victoria speaking for the necessity of a husband to "button up the dresses from behind," and Sarah responding that she "doesn't need a man for buttoning up," while adding that on hot days she alleviates her anguish by "not donning any socks, bra, or panties" underneath her dress. Their divergent positions on this matter reveal a more profound differential: that Victoria's responsibility toward her husband requires that she validate the masculine regimentation of bodily display (or lack thereof) for women, while Sarah's liminal state encourages her to test the limits of this regiment. Nevertheless, the two women's shared laughter over Sarah's "shocking" behavior indicates the possibility of an irreverent female bond, over and against Reuven's male authority. The feminist potentialities of this bond are realized later during the film's climactic scene, when the sisters stand by Rivka and her wayward choices in the face of Reuven's wrath. Yet this conclusion is built on precarious ground, for prior to her departure, Victoria chastises Rivka for "going too far" in her transgression, while Sarah, by keeping silent, abstains from coming to her niece's aid. Thus it appears that Rivka's flight is not only from the "law of the father" but also from its internalization by observant women, which drives a wedge between them, all but destroying their solidarity.

Without adequate support from the women in her life, the burden of Judaic regulation proves almost unbearable for Rivka—so much so that in the past, we are told, she had attempted suicide. In the diegetic present, however, Rivka acts out resistance through less drastic avenues, realizing her creative potential in drawing and dance. Though she professes a desire to study art at the film's denouement, this path of self-actualization—and its feminist implications—remain relatively unexplored. Instead, romance becomes for her the main site where religious edicts are contested. The film gives this contesting a sense of urgency through its opposition between the romantic liaison of Rivka and Dov, which appears to grow organically and reciprocally, and the Shidduch proposed by the father, whose aim is to maintain patriarchal rule over Rivka. Though matrimonial practices are slowly being liberalized in certain precincts of Israeli Judaism, here they are figured monolithically as coercive and oppressive, making Rivka's flight with Dov inevitable. As a result, female liberation becomes inexorably linked to romantic and (hetero)sexual experimentation.

FIGURE 9. Rivka (Moran Rosenblatt) receives an apple from her boyfriend Dov (Elisha Banai). From *Apples from the Desert* (Matti Harari and Arik Lubetzki, 2014).

Yet in contrast to certain like-minded films, *Apples from the Desert* does not wish to stack the deck against Judaism. Instead, through Rivka's particular brand of feminism-via-romance, the film strikes a delicate balance between secularity and religiousness, with religion being adapted in a way that makes it palatable for the secular mindset. As such, the path of exploration leads Rivka to encounter Yossi, a former yeshiva student, who now is busying himself with sexual conquests on Kibbutz grounds. Rivka is swayed by Yossi's laissez-faire attitude on romance, perhaps recognizing in it the drive toward liberation that carried both of them away from the religious world. Yet she doesn't follow through on hedonism as a radical form of release, opting instead to commit to her relationship with Dov and the heteronormative vision to which it conforms. While such a vision goes against many tenets of her religious upbringing, it also sustains one core "virtue" that is inherent to this background: the commitment to long-term monogamy and domesticity. By setting limits to her libidinal appetite through a socially acceptable form, the film not only accommodates Rivka's presence to secular society, but also uses Rivka's romantic position to normalize the presence of her religious family members as legitimate visitors to this society, with which they share certain values. In a diegetic reality where Yossi emerges as the menacing outlier, through his disruption of both religious and secular ideals, Rivka's role as a stabilizing center is to hold these ideals together and overcome the ambivalence of their wedding. For this to be achieved, however, she must exchange one form of forced confinement with another that is willingly accepted.

A similar dilemma of sexual awakening stands at the center of Tsivia Barkai-Yacov's semiautobiographical debut feature *Red Cow* (2018).[30] The film's protagonist is the teenager Beni (Binyamina), who lives with her Haredi-Nationalist father Yehoshua on a settlement in Jerusalem's vicinity. Yehoshua's religious-political views lean heavily toward extremism, and he devotes his (and his daughter's) life to furthering the messianic plan of erecting the Third Temple. As fate would have it, the existence of a red cow—a biological anomaly and supposed omen for the Temple's resurrection—comes to his attention, and he puts Beni in charge of the animal's well-being. For her part, Beni is dissatisfied with Yehoshua's fanaticism and seeks refuge in the company of girlfriends, smoking and reading poetry together. The arrival of a new girl—the slightly older Yael—changes the group's dynamic, with Beni developing romantic feelings toward her. As romance grows, so does tension in Beni's household, leading daughter and father to clash and become increasingly estranged. Yael, whose stay is sponsored by Yehoshua, feels it necessary to leave Jerusalem and her paramour behind, for fear of being ostracized. This leaves Beni without recourse but to abandon her father and community, to which she can no longer relate, and pursue an uncertain future in a secular city.

As some other like-minded Israeli Judaic-themed films,[31] *Red Cow* follows the thematic pattern of connecting Judaic fundamentalism's patriarchal oppression to its eschatological-messianic ideology, which has initiated and sustained the settlement enterprise within the Occupied Territories. The plot seems to insinuate that Yehoshua's growing fanaticism is a direct result of the absence of maternal figures in his household, with his wife apparently dying after a difficult birth, and his mother passing away only recently. Yehoshua's mother in particular appears to have had a curbing effect, and in her absence, Beni is left alone to fend off the father's desire that she play a part in his end-of-days plan. While this role provides Beni with unprecedented agency for a young religious woman, it also renders her desexualized—like when she lays tefillin "as a man would"—and even dehumanized—as when she is made to take care of the prized cow, whose enslavement symbolically parallels her own. The latter parallelism becomes more evident for Beni as the film progresses, especially after overhearing her father say that a baby who threatens the life of its mother must be sacrificed (*Din Rodef*).

Through her alarmed response, we are made to understand that such was the fate of Beni's mother, and that the father's inhuman logic would have his daughter—like the red cow—be killed for the greater good of a latter-day Israel. Not wishing it to suffer this fate, Beni attempts to release the cow from its pen, yet the animal would not leave, unwittingly acquiescing to the sacrificial role set forth. The protagonist's choice puts her in the opposite direction—neither an instrument nor a sacrifice, she would realize her own desires over against those of the patriarchal-apocalyptic framework in which she was raised.

The path leading to this choice is shaped mostly through acts of sexual discovery. Like *The Secrets* to be discussed further on, *Red Cow* sees this discovery as emerging from the agency of an alternative, all-female family cell. Without matriarchal figures in her life, Beni is drawn to the company of her girlfriends, who by virtue of their exclusion from places of import in religious society, can mildly transgress this community's patriarchal norms from the unchecked margins. Transgression comes in the form of clandestine smoking and reading of "secular" poetry, yet is most potently displayed when the girls decide to bathe together in a natural spring (*Mikveh*). Up until this scene, bathing is figured in two distinct ways. The first, anchored in Yehoshua's habitual visits to the municipal Mikveh, sees bathing as a means of *adding purity* to the male body, enhancing its ability to further God's plans for Israel. The second comes to the fore during an early scene that shows young girls, Beni included, receiving instruction on sexuality and purification rules (*Dinei Tahara*); here bathing is imagined as a means of *subtracting impurity* from the female body, especially in the context of menstruation (*Niddah*) as a locus of women's sinfulness. The group bathing of Beni and her friends does not submit to this negative definition and its regime of shame; rather, in defiance of male onlookers, the girls turn water submersion into a festive event of communal bonding and joy. Festiveness, in turn, sets this practice apart from Yehoshua's definition for ritualistic cleansing, which is marked by self-abnegation, and by contrast offers new ways to reclaim purification as a site of female empowerment and camaraderie.

To the background of such liberated and carefree female camaraderie, this bathing scene also allows Beni and Yael to share first moments of physical intimacy. In its aftermath, their relationship gradually

Figure 10. Beni (Avigayil Koevary, *right*) and Yael (Moran Rosenblatt, *left*) bathing together in the Mikveh. From *Red Cow* (Tsivia Barkai-Yacov, 2018).

takes on a sexual-romantic nature, featured through relatively explicit scenes of masturbation and intercourse. Again, transgression is para-doxically made possible as a result of women's marginalized position within Judaic reality: that is, due to their centrality in Judaism, men are considered responsible for the sacred duty of procreation, and therefore cannot engage in homosexual intercourse, for this would amount to a sinful waste of sperm; lesbian sex, on the other hand, does not involve the wasting of sperm, and hence is at worst a devia-tion from the norms of acceptable behavior rather than a mortal sin.[32] This difference exposes the true face of Yehoshua's stern objection to his daughter's romantic dealings: not buttressed by a resolute Judaic prohibition, it appears less to do with chastising abject physical behav-ior than with reasserting control over Beni's position as a participant of—and potential sacrifice within—the plan to erect the Temple once more. The father's successful attempt at pressuring Yael to leave the settlement makes clear the lengths to which he would go to forcefully keep Beni under his thumb. It therefore becomes painfully clear, for the protagonist as for the viewers, that escape is the only recourse for pre-serving Beni's right to develop her own identity as she sees fit. Thus, when she bathes in her father's favorite Mikveh before departing Jeru-salem, it is not out of respect to Yehoshua's messianic violence, nor to womanhood's allotted freedom on the margins of Judaic society. Rather, this act appears to be one of rebirth, from which Beni emerges as a new person, yet unformed.

The highlighting of sexuality—both thematically and visually—as the catalyst for Beni's rebirth finds resonance in two poems featured at prominent junctures in the film: Israeli poet Yona Wallach's "Yonatan" (1966), which is a topic of discussion during Beni and Yael's first intimate conversations; and Argentinian poet Alejandra Pizarnik's "Diana's Tree #13" (1962), which Beni hears recited at a poetry reading during the very last scene. Both poets led turbulent lives, including suffering from mental health problems, and met with an untimely death (Wallach of cancer at the age of forty-one; Pizarnik by suicide at the age of thirty-two). Their trials and tribulations were mirrored through shared thematic concerns, also present in the two poems just mentioned: loneliness, fear, madness, love, and sexuality. Much of the discourse around these poets was shaped by the theme of sexuality: through Wallach's sexually explicit verses, which reflect on a period of intense sexual exploration;[33] and Pizarnik's more tacit poetic treatment of her lesbian identity during a time in Argentinian history when lesbianism could not be acknowledged outright.[34] That both realized themselves as a sexual Other to traditional norms of womanhood, and were punished for being of a different ilk, is what makes them attractive for Beni, who has had similar experiences. Yet there is a profound divide that separates the film's protagonist from the two real-life poets: for while they all invest themselves in sexual exploration as a way of challenging patriarchal oppression, only Wallach and Pizarnik actively fused this exploration with poetic experimentation. Beni is but a passive recipient of poetry, not its active creator. And by reducing her quest to the confines of sexual discovery, she therefore misses out on the possibility of a different avenue for resistance—that which for Wallach and Pizarnik may have provided a more effective means of countermanding female marginalization and victimization. In this respect, the feminist challenge to Judaic androcentrism in *Red Cow* may be seen as trading complexity and multidimensionality for "sexiness."[35]

Yaelle Kayam's *Mountain* (2015) opts to discuss women's challenging position within Judaic society through a mother and wife protagonist rather than via an adolescent on the cusp of sexual awakening. Accordingly, the predicament here differs from that of the protagonists in the other two films, who fear their future submission to matrimonial regulation; *Mountain*'s lead character Zvia struggles with having already submitted to her assigned role, and what has been lost in the process. Living with her husband and four children in a brick house adjacent to Jerusalem's Mount of Olives cemetery, she is consigned to perform the labors of a dutiful homemaker—cleaning, cooking, and the like. Without a more enlivening outlet, she finds herself wandering the graveyard, reading poetry by the headstones or talking to those who pass by (most notably, the cemetery's Arab day laborer). Frustrated by the absence of physical intimacy between her husband and herself, the protagonist's nocturnal wanderings bring her into close contact, and even fraternization, with the pimps and prostitutes who conduct their affairs at the cemetery's edge. The intrigue and repulsion these encounters provoke end up radicalizing Zvia's discontentment with her supposedly stable family life. Ultimately, she finds no better resolution to her troubles than putting poison in her homemade food. While the ending is unclear on whether the family members, the pimps and prostitutes, or both are given the poisoned food, what remains clear is that the protagonist ingests some of the poison. The fatal outcome of Zvia's poisoning is not shown on-screen, thereby creating an open-ended focus on the act itself—and its attendant symbolic meanings.

Like *Red Cow*, *Mountain* foregrounds poetry as a means of elucidating the religious woman's aspirations toward freedom. In this context, an analogy is structured between the protagonist and her favorite writer: Israeli poet Zelda, who belonged to Hasidic aristocracy (her uncle was Chabad leader the Lubavitcher Rebbe) yet challenged its stringent norms, and who is buried in the Mount of Olives cemetery. This liminal positioning reverberates through the two poems featured in the film: "Drunk, Divided Will," where Zelda proclaims her dismay at wishing to open up to what lies outside her familiar surroundings, yet finding there a generation that "violently attempts (in a drunk, unbounded fury), to exploit the world's resources, whether material or spiritual";[36] and "I Stood in Jerusalem," which describes a moment both dark and blissful where the author communes with the dead, reflective of her desire to see death as balancing the "nothingness of a human life's ending and the resurgence of a different being in a different way."[37] Zvia faces similar dilemmas: she also wants to achieve agency vis-à-vis her assigned passivity, yet is inevitably confronted with a distasteful reality, in which men—the husband, the pimps—exploit material and spiritual resources at their will; and this dire situation, in turn, provokes her to court active communion with death as the ultimate countermeasure to passivity—a resurgence of a different order. As in "I Stood in Jerusalem," so in *Mountain*, transgression is rooted in the transgressive nature of the physical backdrop: a cemetery, where the living meet (and even reside with) the dead.

The parallelism between Zelda and the film's heroine nevertheless disguises a fundamental dissimilarity in their positions. Zelda's dilemmas were arguably articulated in mystical terms, whose proper destination was a transcendental experience of unity "beyond the conditions of reality," an "internal event that redeems the soul from the depths of spirit and returns it to its 'natural' state."[38] This is a state of *unio poetica*, to use Nitza Kann's term, for it is achieved mainly through the application of poetic language, breaking its boundaries "to touch the inner essence of things."[39] Not figured as a poet but as a reader, Zvia appears to have less access to poetry's mystical power to self-transcend. Accordingly, but not inevitably, her dilemmas and transgression are grounded in sexual terms with which Zelda would have probably been uncomfortable. More than Zelda's poetry, then, a different intertext seems to have shaped Kayam's film: the Talmudic stories of Judith, wife of Rabbi Hiyya. Uncharacteristic to the Talmud in questioning patriarchal assumptions,[40] these two extremely short stories focus on the plight of Judith, whose "suffering at childbirth" caused her "great sorrow" and prompted a desire to resist further demands on her fecundity. In both tales, the path of avoiding future pregnancy passes through an appeal to the esteemed Rabbi Hiyya for approval. Yet this path differs in form and result across the two stories. Thus with one narrative, Judith asks Rabbi Hiyya that he release her from matrimonial bonds, fabricating a lie about being promised to another at an early age; yet the husband refuses, stating that a former promise of betrothal does not justify a withdrawal from her obligations toward him. In contradistinction, with the second narrative, Judith disguises herself as a man and asks Rabbi Hiyya whether women are obligated by the decree of procreation, to which he responds that this is not the case; upon hearing this, to her husband's great chagrin, she drinks a sterilizing potion that would prevent future impregnation—an act whose measure of agency should not be underestimated. Apparently, this version—which stages a relatively successful challenge to patriarchy—is responsible for why the filmmaker, by her own admission, felt "especially drawn"[41] to the figure of Judith.

Attraction notwithstanding, Kayam reads Judith's tale differently than its articulation in the Talmudic text; namely, as a story about, to quote the filmmaker's gloss, "Rabbi Hiyya withdrawing from his wife, and the great frustration this causes her."[42] The director's (mis)interpretation permits her to reposition Judith as the antecedent of a filmic heroine whose plight is not so much the bodily suffering of repeated births as the absence of "proper" sexual intimacy within her family life. While both plights are lamentable, that of birth-related suffering—being a matter of physical survival—seems of greater urgency than that of sexual deprivation—being a matter of emotional well-being. Consequently, in order to give the film protagonist's desire for carnal intimacy the similar sense of urgency to that of Judith's predicament, *Mountain* establishes its diegetic world as torn by sexual opposites: on the one hand, the husband's "withdrawal" into abstinence (which distances him from his supposed predecessor, Rabbi Hiyya, who apparently did not abstain from sexual relations); and on the other hand, the prostitutes' sexual labor, which turns their bodies into currency within a strictly commercial transaction. In both cases, men decide whether sexuality would manifest itself and on what terms. And within a landscape governed by graves and tombstones—as by a visual scheme of stark contrasts, emulating the Baroque paintings of Caravaggio and Artemisia Gentileschi[43]—such decisions can only spell out a dire fate: one in which choosing life by

FIGURE 11. Zvia (Shani Klein) surrounded by a landscape of tombstones. From *Mountain* (Yaelle Kayam, 2015).

self-sterilization is no longer an option, and where the only comfort that remains is to dictate the terms of suicide.

Under these extreme conditions, *Mountain*'s protagonist is thereby rendered as—and reduced to—a (hyper)sexualized Judith, whose pursuit of physical warmth and libidinal release seems to encompass the entirety of her feminist challenge, excluding all other motivations or outlets. At the same time, through this pursuit, the film tacitly reduces sexuality and intimacy to the secular ideal of a romantic fusion between souls, at the exclusion of potentially viable Judaic ideals. By situating this secular ideal at the heart of *Mountain*, Kayam is able to realize her avowed ambition: "to tell not only my story, but to reach the worlds around me and get to know them and their modes of thinking. Then it all gets mixed together, my story and the story of those people I've met."[44] This mélange, in turn, permits the filmmaker to align the religious Zvia, not only with her own secular story, but also with a known cinematic character from a decidedly secular milieu—the eponymous heroine of Chantal Akerman's *Jeanne Dielman, 23 quai du Commerce, 1080 Bruxelles* (1975).[45] While undoubtedly evocative, the comparison between the two female characters nevertheless masks an important difference. Thus, Jeanne Dielman's double life as homemaker/sex worker and her final act of killing a client expose the hypocrisy of secularity's romantic ethos, as a means of preserving patriarchy's investments in exploiting women's bodies and sexual/reproductive labor. Zvia may also live through a duality and perform violence as a result, yet her goal is not to challenge this romantic ideal but those in the religious world (the husband) and the secular world (the pimps) who oppose it. Separate goals, in turn, spell out disparate renderings of women as sexual beings. In Akerman's film, Jeanne is not shown performing sexual acts in the nude, arguably because this would lead to her body's commodification, thereby implicating the film in the commodified logic it wishes to disclose at the core of romantic love. Contrastingly, in Kayam's film, the heroine is shown naked (from the back) during sex, with this nudity appearing as a visible sign of liberation from religious oppression; yet in setting secularization-via-sexualization as preferable over religious oppression, *Mountain*—like many other secular films that feature female nudity—denies the patriarchal oppressiveness inherent in secularity's sanctioned ideal of sexual romance.

Feminist Challenges from within Judaism: *The Secrets* and *Bruriah*

While the films just discussed, regardless of their creators' religious commitments (or lack thereof), occupy a largely secular feminist perspective on Judaic women, two other exemplary texts—*The Secrets* and *Bruriah*—highlight a more strenuous Judaic feminist stance of "devout resistance." The origin of this stance may not be attributable so much to the films' secular male directors as to their writer Hadar Galron, a self-avowed "woman of faith" who has sought to question the religious doctrines of her home community.[46] Such questioning is distinct from that of the other films by its interest in religious education for women as a significant arena of feminist resistance.[47] In foregrounding the importance of scholarly erudition in battling Judaic patriarchal regimes, these films also ground themselves in rereading Jewish religious literature against its (androcentric) grain so as to create a new Midrash.

The Secrets, Galron's collaboration with noted director of popular dramas Avi Nesher, unfolds the tale of Noemi, the erudite daughter of a yeshiva rabbi, who, after the untimely death of her mother, postpones her upcoming marriage to yeshiva scholar Michael in order to study in an ultra-Orthodox all-female Midrasha. There she meets Michelle (also known by her Jewish name Michal), a rebellious student who recently arrived from France. At first the two appear at odds with each other, but they later bond around a common cause: giving humanitarian aid to Anouk, a French-Christian woman residing in the city. In her past, Anouk served a prison term for killing her Jewish lover; now, while dying of cancer, she wishes to make peace with (the Jewish) God. Since the local rabbi refuses to provide assistance, Noemi, at Michelle's request, constructs a series of repair rituals (*Tikkunim*) in an effort to help Anouk achieve her goal. Their collaboration brings Michelle and Noemi closer together, and subsequently they develop a clandestine lesbian relationship. After word of the rituals gets out, the two students are reprimanded by the city rabbi and the Midrasha principal. This measure does not stop them, however, and following a last rite performed on Anouk's deathbed, they are expelled from the Midrasha. With their romance cut short, Michelle and Noemi make a pact that after a suitable cooling-off period, they would share a home together in Tel Aviv. Nevertheless, Michelle subsequently reneges on the promise, choosing instead to marry a klezmer musician named Yanki whom she met in Safed. Michelle's decision enrages Noemi, but she then decides to attend her former lover's wedding, and the scene ends with the two arriving at rapprochement while partaking in a festive dance.

The film takes as its background a relatively recent shift within the world of religious literacy, which has allowed devout women access to organized Judaic study, even in the traditionally masculine field of Talmud erudition.[48] The Midrasha principal describes this at one point as a "silent revolution" whose aim is to abrogate the continued marginalization of women from positions of power within the male-dominated Judaic public sphere. Evidence to this marginalization is provided on numerous occasions during *The Secrets*, particularly in the context of the androcentric religious discourse espoused by most of the film's male characters. Noemi's father, for example, sees female wisdom as only existent in relation to domestic concerns. Michael, the fiancé, also figures women's intellectual prowess as limited and defines their opinions through the derogatory term "female chatter." Both men reinforce standard gender divisions, which is why they are reluctant to allow Noemi to choose a path outside of marriage. Their position is therefore representative of institutional hostility toward attempts at crossing over, especially in terms of acquiring religious literacy. The revolution must be silent, the principal seems to argue, because the powers that be resist it. For this reason, the Midrasha is also framed by its staff as a matchmaking institution; rather than act as a site for acquiring knowledge, it becomes a tool for the containment of knowledge and for the preparation toward a better match.

At the outset, Noemi and Michelle arrive at this feminist revolution from different starting points. Michelle clearly stands at the margins of the religious world. She was sent to the Midrasha so that it would function as a correctional facility for her; it was supposed to bring her back to the fold, securing her a proper match. Yet she remains defiant, as is clear in her use of a cell phone in the classroom, her smoking, her initiative to help Anouk, and her active courting of Yanki. Noemi, on the other hand, seeks the path of strengthening connections with the religious world through scholarship. She feels stifled by a system that does not permit her to develop any intellectual faculties, and this difficulty is further aggravated on becoming a commodity in the male-centered practice of matchmaking—a gift to be given by the rabbi to his prized pupil. As her sister explains it at the film's opening, the road ahead for Noemi demands acquiescence: she is to become the wife of a yeshiva head, patiently waiting for him to return from study while rearing their three or four children. Noemi dreads this future, which she associates with her mother's personal tragedy—a woman who was reduced to the role of housewife and silently suffered through an unfulfilled life. Rather than escape this dire fate by departing the religious world, she seeks a different way of entering into it—of becoming, perhaps, the first Haredi female rabbi. Yet the trajectory of greater scholarship, Noemi seems to know intuitively, is likely to result in an impasse, since it raises awareness of Halakha's androcentrism.

The encounter with Anouk pushes this awareness to the fore, for both Noemi and Michelle. Though she committed adultery and possibly murder, Anouk is not figured as a negative character, the reason for this being that what she did, she did for love. Yet the religious institution refuses to treat her as anything but a negative character, not so much for her felonious actions, but first and foremost—because she is not Jewish. The conflict between Anouk and the Safed rabbi comes to represent, then, a conflict between love and the logic of bureaucracy. Bureaucratic mentality, *The Secrets* seems to say, dominates Judaism, and is the cause of victimization along gendered and religious lines. In face of this insight, Noemi is forced to reevaluate her position as a religious person. Her decision is ultimately to follow love, to do—as both Michelle and Yanki explain at different points—"what feels right," even if by some legalistic definitions it is the wrong thing to do. Yet the film appears to argue that such a direction, though inspired by a Christian woman, is not antithetical to the spirit of Judaism.[49] As a brief conversation in the first Midrasha lesson shows us, to treat God with love rather than fear reaps twice the reward. Jewish men seem to miss this insight, and their fear leads them toward an alienated form of observance—or as the Safed rabbi phrases it, he follows the letter of God's laws but does not think about His intentions. Yet women (and emasculated men such as Yanki, whose musical profession and overdependence on his mother render him symbolically castrated) can arrive closer to God's true intentions by following a Judaism of love rather than of impassionate bookkeeping—which in this case, as Noemi angrily explains to the principal in the end of the film, means not abandoning a dying woman, regardless of her specific denominational allegiances.

The way in which Noemi chooses to aid Anouk is significant in this context: rather than explore a solution outside of Judaism, she offers to perform a repair that would allow for Anouk's redemption from within the confines of religious tradition while transforming its legalistic-patriarchal meanings. As a Tikkun founded on a challenge to Halakhic patriarchy, it eventually encourages a bond of female solidarity. The spaces that are created between the women during the reparation ceremonies are founded on traditional symbols of femininity such as the circle and especially water. Most potent in this framework is the watery ritual where Noemi, Michelle, and Anouk bathe in the Mikveh as part of Anouk's process of purification. As previously mentioned, purification via immersion is associated with the Judaic perspective that equates femininity with impurity. By going after hours into an all-male Mikveh, the three women seek to challenge this perspective without abolishing the practice to which it is attached. They do so by appropriating the ritual for their own purposes, turning the Mikveh into a site where a new form of female freedom may be achieved.[50]

The female bond made possible through water enables Noemi and Michelle to explore new frontiers of physical intimacy: no longer inhibited by the fierce codes of religious conduct that regulate physical relations between genders, they find themselves free to express their homosexual desires. The discovery of their lesbian attraction deeply unsettles both characters, as it places them outside of ultra-Orthodoxy's societal norms. Noemi's response to this challenge is, again, typical of Judaic feminism: she studies rabbinical literature and finds justification that lesbian sex is not considered a mortal sin as it does not involve the wasting of sperm. While this provides some reassurance as to the legitimacy of their desires, the two women nevertheless remain strained at the prospect of removal from the cycle of matchmaking, which is a constant source of concern for many LGTBQ+ members of the Haredi community.

The realization of same-sex desire also serves to foreground an important biblical intertext within the film's search for proto-feminist precedents: the Book of Ruth. The name of the film's protagonist clearly

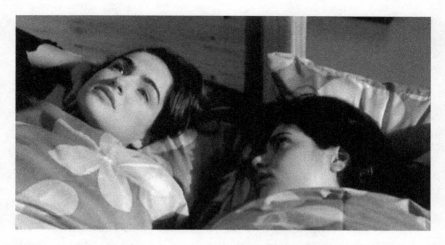

FIGURE 12. Noemi (Ania Bukstein, *left*) and Michelle (Michal Shtamler, *right*) sleeping together at Noemi's home. From *The Secrets* (Avi Nesher, 2007).

references Naomi, Ruth's mother-in-law, to whom she made a solemn vow of faithfulness: "Wherever you go, I shall go . . . if even death will separate me from you."[51] The Bible, and consequently traditional biblical scholarship, has interpreted this bond of female solidarity, where the foreigner Ruth follows Naomi into exile and takes on her faith, in essentially nonerotic and asexual terms. Yet as Exum explains, the

> language in the book suggests the intensity of [Ruth's] devotion to Naomi. Ruth "left [her] father and mother" (2.11) and "cleaved [*dabeqah*] to her" (1.14). This is the language used of the first couple in Eden: "Therefore a man leaves his father and his mother and cleaves (*dabaq*) to his wife" (Gen 2.24). The appearance of terminology commonly understood to represent the marriage bond and its use (whether deliberate or not) to describe a bond between women sets the stage for the appropriation of the book for same-sex relationships.[52]

In the face of a paucity of lesbian role models within Judaic tradition, Jewish lesbians have found inspiration in the intense commitment between Naomi and Ruth. As Rebecca Alpert notes, this kinship "point[s] to something greater than a relationship of loyalty and obligation between these two women"[53]—perhaps, to love. And though the Bible does not present any clear indication to the existence of sexual relations, according to Alpert, lesbians must "read between the lines of the text and imagine Ruth and Naomi as lovers."[54] For its part, *The Secrets* helps this interpretation by actualizing the lesbian relationship that was buried in the biblical text, and establishing a new Midrash as a result.

Ultimately, the occasion of Anouk's death and final reparation forces a turn of events in which Noemi and Michelle are separated and their lesbian romance comes to an end. Noemi chooses to follow her love to Michelle, and thus to separate herself from her father's company. Michelle, on the other hand, chooses to forgo with Noemi's affections and enter into matrimony with Yanki. At face value these paths seem to position the two characters on opposite sides of a great divide. Yet in the ideological framework of the film, this contrast is nonexistent, since both women seem to occupy a similar position toward both emotion and Halakha. Noemi has chosen to follow her heart, but still devotes herself to the Halakha; she does not want to depart the world of Halakhic Judaism but rather to redefine it from within. Similarly, Michelle has chosen to stay within Halakhic Judaism, but not succumb to its supposed tendency to eradicate emotion. Therefore, although following the dictums of proper behavior—that is, raising a family—she weds Yanki, who is aligned with the world of music—or emotion—rather than the categories of study and thought so valued within the ultra-Orthodox "learners' society." It is for this reason, the film seems to argue, that no real betrayal transpires between the protagonists, and they find their way to stay together in spite of everything. The ending, in which Noemi finally cries and the two women dance together, thus becomes a celebration of the possibility of retrieving an emotional, all-female space under Judaism's phallocentric rule.

Such an interpretation, however, seems to disregard the film's decisive withdrawal from positing a strong feminist stance. By forcing a dissolution of the lesbian relationship, *The Secrets* closes ranks behind Ruth's Old Testament narrative. Like her biblical namesake, the filmic Noemi gives up on her same-sex lover, sending her to the arms of a male protector (in the Bible, Boaz; in the film, Yanki). Since this is presented as a recuperable loss, *The Secrets* thus ultimately undercuts the radical potential of a lesbian reading of the Book of Ruth and legitimizes a narrative wherein female spaces must function only in solitude (Noemi) or under surveillance of sympathetic and understanding men (Michelle and Yanki). Not only this, but through the resolution, the film also provides a conservative reinterpretation of another biblical tale: that of Michal, daughter to King Saul and wife to King David. In the Bible, Michal is primarily referenced in relation to two key scenes: In Samuel 1:19, she tells David of Saul's plan to assassinate him and organizes his subsequent escape; in Samuel 2:6, now as David's wife, she emerges out of her room and angrily confronts her husband as he dances in front of the Ark of the Covenant during a public ceremony. Exum interprets the biblical character as looking "to assert her autonomy . . . by siding with her husband against her father in 1 Samuel 19 and by taking up the cause of her father's house against her husband in 2 Samuel 6."[55] In order to underplay the tension that arises from this woman's struggle to assert her autonomy within a system of heteronormative marriage that upholds patriarchal dominance, traditional biblical scholarship tended to paint Michal of Samuel 2:6 as the quintessential shrew and David as her perpetual victim. In *The Secrets*, however, a modern Michal/Michelle emerges as a female character who poses a legitimate challenge to patriarchal rule, and who is anything but a shrew. If the film recovers Michal as a positive figure, it does so, however, at the price of legitimizing the traditional institution of marriage. While the biblical Michal was the victim of domineering men who treated her like property, the filmic Michelle finds her way into a loving relationship with an "accepting" husband. In light of such a fitting match—much different than the tragic union of Michal and David—the possibility of an alternate lifestyle that does not involve marriage is therefore swept under the rug.

The Secrets' conservative agenda runs even deeper. Beyond its recuperation of heterosexual love and marriage, it also endorses an essentialist perspective on femininity as equated with emotionality and thus participates in the patriarchal project of disavowing the reality of women by subsuming it under the myth of Woman. In spite of attempts to the contrary, the film ultimately submits the female body to the ocular regime that reduces it to sexual categories and wishes it to be unveiled. In various instances, the film does shed light on the hatred that women, both religious and secular, feel toward their bodies: for example, in the continued references Noemi and Michelle's roommate Sheine makes to her overweight frame, and to how it will prevent her from becoming a wife and mother; or when, in the Mikveh, Anouk refuses at first to disrobe because in old age, the figure she was once so proud of has "betrayed her." The film's solution to this problem is to fashion safe spaces in which female intimacy and corporeal love could grow independently of the religious government's attempts to regulate women's bodies. Yet paradoxically, in those very scenes that depict homosocial intimacy, *The Secrets* finds opportunity to pursue, in Rachel Harris's words, an "obsession with the female body and nudity [that] undermines the more critical intellectual vision of this film."⁵⁶ Thus, when in one scene Noemi applies a rough textured fabric to her bare body as penance, the removal of this fabric allows for the revelation of Noemi's naked upper body—the same body she has sought to deny through a practice of self-punishment; and in the Mikveh, the camera scans the naked bodies of Michelle and Noemi from head to toe, while leaving the body of Anouk—the self-proclaimed "aging" and "diseased" body that seems of little interest to the traditional male gaze—in an unexposed state, barely hidden within the depths of purifying waters. The paradoxical nature of this exposure becomes explicit during a scene in which Anouk shows naked portraits of herself, painted by her late husband, to Noemi and Michelle. The two young women avert their eyes, proving just how much they have internalized the religious male edict that forbids gazing on the nude female. Slowly, however, they set their gaze on the painted nudity, becoming aware of the pleasure of exploring it in a physical setting where only women are to be found. This appears to be the film's self-reflexive comment on the possibilities of exposing naked bodies of women to women. But the scene, beyond its diegetic context, is not only viewed by female audiences, and could even be said to have been made for the benefit of a male viewership; consequently, its nudity is never simply nudity, but also spectacle.

Like *The Secrets*, Avraham Kushnir's *Bruriah* provides latter-day commentary on significant proto-feminist precedents within Judaic literature. Here, as may be evident from the title, the precedent in question is the Talmud's tale of Bruriah, daughter to the martyred Rabbi Hananyah ben Teradyon, and wife of Rabbi Meir, the great miracle worker of the Mishnaic era. The legendary Bruriah was described as a great scholar who bested her male peers and even schooled the great Rabbi Meir himself. As such, she represented an anomaly—a female sage in an all-male intellectual world. Her function within rabbinical literature, according to Rachel Adler, was to challenge the boundaries of the norm. In a context where women were thought of as inferior to men, the Talmud's male authors used the figure of Bruriah to investigate a crucial question to their belief system: "What if there were a woman who was just like us?"[57] Yet the potency of this challenge, so significant for modern feminists, was undercut in traditional literature's treatment of Bruriah's tragic end. Thus, enraged by his wife's claims to superior knowledge, Rabbi Meir sought to prove her frivolity by sending one of his students to seduce her. After frequent refusals, Bruriah finally yielded to the student's advances, and when the plot was revealed, she hanged herself. The sexual humiliation evident in this denouement permits the patriarchal Judaic institution to deny her any religious authority, since the matrix of rabbinical relationships on which authority is founded—of schoolmates, teacher and student—is fundamentally de-sexualized (although not entirely de-eroticized). In this way, Bruriah is transformed from a possible role model to a mere cautionary tale.

Picking up on these themes, the film focuses on a religious woman named Bruriah (portrayed by Galron), who lives with her Modern Orthodox family in contemporary Jerusalem. Thirty years before the diegetic present, her rabbi father wrote a book on the Talmud's Bruriah that raised controversy within the Haredi community and led to his ostracism and the public burning of his research. Haunted by this trauma, modern Bruriah dedicates her time to locating the last copy of this book in an effort to vindicate the family name and, perhaps, find a potent retort to Judaic misogyny. The husband Yaakov is upset by this obsessive search, which he sees as indicative of his wife's frivolity. Lacking in spousal support, Bruriah approaches Yosef, Yaakov's inquisitive colleague, in hopes that he may help her in this quest. When Yaakov discovers this relationship, however, he suspects the existence of an illicit affair. Subsequently, he procures the last copy of the book from his father, who was responsible for the original torching, and gives it to Yosef so that he may use it to seduce Bruriah. In their meeting, Bruriah seems tempted but retreats when Yosef tells her of Yaakov's attempt to recreate Rabbi Meir's morality test. She then dresses provocatively and traverses Jerusalem's Haredi precincts, eventually joining her husband at a spring on the city's outskirts, where they bathe naked and in a fond embrace.

Bruriah's challenge, like that of Noemi and Michelle, serves to high-light the continued presence of patriarchal tradition that traverses mil-lennia of Jewish culture. Perhaps too strongly, the film argues that the Talmud's legend of Bruriah was repressed within mainline Judaism for its explosive potential in empowering women—as is evident in the burning of the book written by the filmic Bruriah's father. Rather than explore this potential, contemporary Judaic institutions continue to rearticulate the Talmud's dictum that "women are flighty," as well as maintain its resulting discriminatory practices. The film provides several examples for such practices: for instance, when the protagonist helps her female friend battle the religious courts after being denied a divorce (*Gett*) by her husband; or when, during the school *Chumash* service of Yaakov and Bruriah's youngest daughter, a male audience member complains about the seven-year-old girl performing a song in defiance of the Talmudic pronouncement that "a woman's voice is sinful" (*Kol Beisha Ervah*).

Yaakov's response to these restrictive practices is ambivalent; he occasionally voices objection, yet his general behavior seems to embody a profound fear of destabilizing Halakhic tradition. Such trepidation arises primarily in relation to his eldest daughter and wife. Like *The Secrets'* Noemi, Yaakov's firstborn wishes to go to an all-girls Midrasha in hopes of becoming a great sage. This wish is rejected by the father, not for the child's lack of intellectual prowess, but because going to the Mid-rasha would disrupt a long-standing tradition and provoke communal sanctions, as was the case with the Talmudic Bruriah. The same logic is applied by Yaakov in relation to his wife's attempts at locating her father's book, which promise the acquisition of disruptive knowledge by women toward their liberation. As Harris accurately points out, the filmic Bru-riah's "intelligence is recognized not only by her husband—for example, he finds her working through a tractate of Talmud in her bedroom—but also by his friends, who welcome her contributions to their study ses-sions."[58] It thus stands to reason that she would cause anxiety as someone who is a viable candidate for spearheading a feminist educational shift in Judaism.

Like in the Talmudic tale, Yaakov's unease over his wife's intellectual faculties is transposed onto the threat of her putative sexual drives, and he subsequently develops an obsession about proving or disproving this threat through sexual manipulation. While accusing his wife of being "flighty" and driven by sexual desire, it nevertheless becomes evident the husband is the one who seems most sexually motivated. His manipulation appears therefore to be a twisted mode of sexual play within a context that dissociates masculinity from sexuality. Such play can only be justified by displacing responsibility onto the woman. As men, both Yaakov and Rabbi Meir are thus defined as susceptible to sexual urges, yet in their case these urges are implicitly regarded as necessary burdens that would be relieved through divine providence. In contrast, the stories of the legendary and filmic Bruriahs show that for Judaism, women are deemed culpable of whatever ill is associated with their sexuality and must actively pursue chastity and corporeal self-regulation in order to prove their worth.[59]

For her part, the contemporary Bruriah comes to inhabit the role assigned to her by Yaakov and Judaic tradition, and the film shows her to continuously transgress the laws of modesty. Bruriah's penchant for transgression first manifests when she exchanges her "appropriate" attire with her divorce-seeking friend's racy outfit to make the friend appear more respectable in court, and after that, visibly excited by the whole situation, calls Yaakov to entice him with a description of the sexy clothing. Her most provocative flirtation with sexuality, however, is in her relationship with Yosef. In a community that prohibits a man and a woman who are not married to each other to stay in the same room together unobserved, Yosef and Bruriah's proximity, although never explicitly sexual, is charged with eroticism. As a result, the filmic Bruriah's attempt to seek out Yosef figures her as a more active source of sin than the seduced Bruriah of the Talmud. Yet the film is not geared toward proving Bruriah as inherently sinful, by biological determination; rather, it shows her to be a victim of a context in which women have no choice but to collude in the act of their own annihilation, an operation that is literalized in the original Bruriah's decision to take her life.

The film's conclusion, however, does not recreate that of the Talmudic tale. Although close to being seduced, Bruriah nevertheless avoids falling into Yaakov's trap. Rather than follow in the legendary Bruriah's footsteps, and internalize the perspective of seductress, she appropriates the markers of seduction—the revealing dress, the heavy makeup—for her own purposes, exposing them as masks rather than essential characteristics. The masquerade that underlies Bruriah's final march through

Jerusalem's streets seems incompatible with Joan Reviere's formative articulation of the term: here the mask of womanliness is not worn as an "unconscious attempt to ward off the anxiety [of] reprisal" by "evoking friendly feelings towards her in the man,"[60] but as an act of defiance that forces religious men to avert their eyes and perhaps recognize their disavowed desires. In this respect, Bruriah's pageantry of womanliness seems closer to Mary Ann Doane's appropriation of Riviere's definition: rather than defensively camouflage and naturalize female challenge, masquerade for her is founded on "a hyperbolization of the accoutrements of femininity" that "confounds [the] masculine structure of the look" and "effects a defamiliarization of female iconography."[61] Doane's take on the masquerade, more than anything else, seems to resonate with the parodic operation of drag, as a means of revealing gender and sexual categories to be fundamentally performative. The lavish hyperbolic take on femininity in *Bruriah* connects with Judith Butler's claim that "hegemonic sexuality is itself a constant and repeated effort to imitate its own idealizations. That it must repeat this imitation, that it sets up pathologizing practices and normalizing sciences in order to produce and consecrate its own claim on originality and propriety." By imitating the signs of secular femininity, the protagonist's drag "is subversive to the extent that it reflects on the imitative structure by which the hegemonic gender is itself produced."[62]

In light of the challenge of Bruriah's drag to the act of heterosexual imitation and its naturalizing effect on the cultural definition of "natural woman," the final bathing scene seems particularly perplexing. On the one hand, Yaakov and Bruriah's choice to bathe together in the spring seems, like in *The Secrets'* Mikveh scene, a radical reinterpretation of Judaism's purification rites, which are founded on the separation of sexes.[63] Yet whatever feminist potentialities this reclaiming of ritual may inhere, they seem to be undercut by the way in which this bathing scene is realized cinematically. Thus, Bruriah's arrival at the spring is preceded by her husband's, and as she stands on the edge, visualized only through her exposed legs, the focus is on Yaakov, fully immersed in water, looking up at her. Her subsequent disrobement, shot through its reflection in the water, thus seems to be "only for him"—his exclusive right, activated by his gaze. In contradistinction to Bruriah's previous drag performance, this is an act that seeks male recognition. And this recognition comes by

FIGURE 13. Bruriah (Hadar Galron) dressing up provocatively. From *Bruriah* (Avraham Kushnir, 2008).

way of legitimizing her now fully naked body as the signifier of "natural womanliness"—that is, of her gender and sexuality as essential rather than performative. Consequently, through its denouement the film as a whole forecloses on the potency of legendary/filmic Bruriah's feminist challenge to Judaic patriarchy, affirming her reduction to sexuality and concomitant denial of her intellectual distinction—the very thing that, within Talmudic legend, marked "Bruriah's specialness"[64] in the first place.

Mystical-Messianic Time and Female Agency: Benjamin, Levinas, and Disjointed Temporality

Judged by their narrative elaborations, *Bruriah* and *The Secrets* explicitly mount a challenge to patriarchy from inside Judaic society. Yet for all their devout feminist resistance, the films ultimately align themselves with the overarching tendency of Judaic-themed Israeli cinema to surrender its female characters to a regime of sexual objectification. As a result, what one finds implicit in their accounts of women's plight under religious patriarchy is a fundamental equivocation vis-à-vis the actual necessity and value of the feminist project, not only in the Judaic-Israeli sector but also in Israeli society as a whole. However, while the films' plots exhibit conservative allegiances to patriarchal logic, their stylistic approach seems to unravel such inclinations and by extension open up new spaces for radical feminist criticism. This critical effort is made possible through the style's reliance on a disjointed temporality, which serves as the foundation for redeeming ethical encounters and the site of (utopian) hopes for female agency within Judaism. By transcending the known parameters of time, these cinematic texts also reveal their deference to age-old mystical-messianic temporal structures, which were translated to a modern idiom by Jewish philosophers Walter Benjamin and Emmanuel Levinas, in a manner that allowed for their recent popularization under the aegis of New Age priorities.

In an attempt to elucidate "the messianic idea" within Jewish religion, Gershom Scholem made the influential claim that rabbinic Judaism has been governed by three forces: conservative, restorative, and utopian. Conservativeness, whose emblematic expression is the world of religious law, directs itself "towards the preservation of that which exists and which, in the historical environment of Judaism, was always in danger." The other two forces, in contrast, are conditioned exactly on the unraveling of this law and on the redemption of the reality which it seeks to explain and regulate. Thus, the restorative impulse of Judaism is "directed to the return and recreation of . . . a condition pictured by the historical fantasy and the memory of the nation as circumstances of an ideal past," while the utopian impulse aims "at a state of things which has never existed."[65] Pace Judaism's conservativeness, these forces fuel radical Judaic-messianic aspirations and divert them toward a particular end: "the vision of a new content which is to be realized in a future that will in fact be nothing other than the recreation of what is ancient," yet an ancient that is not the actual past but "a past transformed and transfigured in a dream brightened by the rays of utopianism."[66]

As a complex temporal vision that looks simultaneously toward an immemorial past and a paradisiacal future, the messianic idea is also a fundamental intrusion into our known present. In this respect it is intimately connected to the twofold signification of the term "apocalypse": on the one hand, the common sense of an apocalyptic event, of a "transcendence breaking in," which in the messianic context is understood as an upheaval that destroys the prevailing order and establishes in its stead a new-old/utopian-restorative reality; on the other hand, there is the literal translation of the Greek word *Apocálypsis* as "revelation," understood in this framework as "disclosures of God's hidden knowledge of the End,"[67] to which only certain persons—a prophet or the actual Messiah—can gain access.

The presence of apocalyptic messianism was largely marginalized in the first millennium of Jewish history; during that period, the emphasis was placed rather on the conservative impulse of Judaism, in an effort to come closer to God in the living world and be awarded divine favor in the afterlife. The situation changed drastically in the aftermath of the Spanish Expulsion (1492), which introduced the mindset of exile (*Galut*) together with imposing visions of an end to all things and the sense of immanent redemption.[68] While the contemporaneous engagements with messianism were multiple and diverse, none has arguably been more influential on future generations, and on the modern/New Age reclamation of messianism in particular, than that of sixteenth-century rabbi-mystic Isaac Luria and the Safed school of Kabbalah. According to Scholem, Luria's engagement with messianism spearheaded a process wherein "the messianic theme became a productive element in the speculations of the mystics themselves,"[69] and underwent important transformations as a result. One major change was the legitimization of the viewpoint that saw messianism as being an integral part of history. "The Messianic ideal of the prophets of the Bible and other classical Jewish sources," per Scholem, saw "the world unredeemed and the world in the process of redemption [as] separated by an abyss. History was not a *development* toward any goal. History would reach its terminus, and the new state that ensued would be the result of a totally new manifestation of the divine."[70] These tendencies, Joseph Dan argues, were still largely preserved in early Kabbalah, which "conceived the prelapsarian divinity as perfection, and wanted to return to it while turning the proverbial mystical back to history"; Luria's Kabbalah, however, "marched with history towards the apocalyptic End where perfection, both divine and earthly, would be attained."[71] Thus, Luria argued against the traditional Judaic wisdom by stipulating that divinity had a basic flaw that emerged during a pre-creation catastrophe and caused all beings to be in a state of exile.[72] As such, human reality is seen as an expression of divine reality, their fates irrevocably linked. Yet even as Galut emerges as the condition of universal existence, there is also the possibility of Tikkun, which is "the Lurianic synonym for history—the ongoing process for achieving perfection, the reparation of the catastrophe and the realization of the world's *raison d'être*."[73] Transposing messianism onto history, Luria consequently imagines the Spanish Expulsion of his recent past as an important indication that the messianic age is upon him—as a decisive catastrophe that will undoubtedly bring about the denouement of history and the arrival of redemption.[74] It seemed, for the mystic, that a divine unity from a primordial past could emerge at any given moment, eclipsing former imperfections and establishing a harmonious cosmos where everything is where it should be.[75]

From this, another revolutionary change that Luria's messianic mysticism legitimized was the important role of human agency in facilitating redemption. In the Bible, messianism is figured as independent of human action;[76] for Luria, on the other hand, humanity's struggle to redeem itself was an integral part of messianism's goal of redeeming divinity.[77] Accordingly, redemption starts by individual effort of self-perfection, whereby the person who observes a commandment is engaged in the amendment of something greater, universal.[78] It continues, however, with taking ethical responsibility for other members of the community, who must also be made to abide by commandments in order to afford the generation's rectification, and by extension—the achievement of deliverance.[79] For Dan, this means that reparation is "democratic in the sense that the scholar and the ignorant, the Lurianic mystic and the unschooled laborer participate in it and share the responsibility."[80] Nevertheless, it would seem that the mystic *does* occupy a privileged position within this process, since he alone is able to experience a revelation of God's totality and the means by which it will be restored. Like a true apocalyptic, he finds himself at any given moment on "an intersection from which a vision of the past and of the future can be observed"; consequently, it is for him, rather than anyone else, to mediate this complex vision to the masses and inspire them into action as a result. The significance of collective redemption, in turn, prevents the mystic from becoming a Messiah. Indeed, because of its "democratic" inclinations, Lurianic mystical-messianism is only messianic in a limited capacity—the Messiah plays a minor role, for

He only "comes *as a result* of redemption, crowns it, and certifies its achievement."[81]

It follows that the constitutive role of apocalyptic upheaval is also transformed within Luria's doctrines. Luria related catastrophe to a divine reality in a permanent state of Galut whose reverberation can be sensed in the Spanish Expulsion. Yet as an expression of apocalypse, the Spanish Expulsion remains the background to a reparation process that does not facilitate redemption through upheaval but via human acts of improvement. "This conception of redemption," for Scholem, is "no longer catastrophic: when [human] duty has been fulfilled the son of David, the Messiah, will come of himself, for his appearance at the End of Days is only a symbol for the completion of a process. . . . Thus it becomes possible to avoid the 'travails of the Messiah.' The transition from the state of imperfection to the state of perfection (which may still be very difficult) will nevertheless take place without revolution and disaster and great affliction."[82] The absence of a final disaster testifies to Luria's belief that the redemptive End has an organic connection with human reality. The novel order that emerges within the human world does not demolish the old because it is fundamentally—and intimately—part of that "old." Seen in this way, apocalypse is never entirely external to worldly existence, and therefore its decisive appearance is never a replacement—only a transition.

Because of their positioning as a means of working through collective trauma, Lurianic teachings had a profound influence on a generation of Western European Jews who had to face the traumatic challenges of early twentieth-century Jewish existence. The failures of Emancipation forced these Jews to confront the lingering presence of anti-Semitism in their Christian-dominated surroundings. Concurrently, the advent of World War I prompted them to reflect on the fragmentation of Western civilization and question both the Newtonian model of irreversible linear time and Enlightenment's teleological idea of progress.[83] Drawn to unrelenting pessimism, many of this generation's key intellectual figures looked for a new paradigm of thought and action that would inspire change and perhaps countermand the adverse effects of these phenomena. They found it in the concept of messianism, as it was articulated within Kabbalist tradition—the very tradition they and their parents had to eradicate, or at least subsume under a more vital commitment to humanity, for the purpose of Emancipation and acculturation. Much of Jewish continental philosophy of the first half of the twentieth century was thus preoccupied with resurrecting the messianic and adapting it to the circumstances of modern Europe.[84] These efforts, as previously suggested, find their most emblematic expression in the works of Benjamin and Levinas.

"Reflection on the nature of history," according to Stéphan Mosès, "seems to have been a constant element in Benjamin's thought," leading him to consistently grapple with such questions as "how can we talk about history?" and "how can a chaos of events be made intelligible?"[85] These queries, however, were not addressed in an effort to legitimize the prevalent methods of conceptualizing history. Rather, Benjamin recognized that such methods forced time into a debilitating Newtonian model "that claims to reconstitute the past by accumulating 'facts' and to predict the future by ignoring the role of radical novelty, that is, utopia, which constitutes its essence."[86] A more honest historical consideration, for him, would bracket out this model, and all its attendant assumptions, from consideration. What arrives as a result of this bracketing, Peter Fenves explains, is an idea of time that does not function as irreversible progression along a straight line but rather as "a curve that is everywhere continuous yet nowhere differentiable: it is so sharply turned at every point that it proceeds without direction, neither progress nor regress, and every one of its stretches is not only like every other but also like the course of time as a whole." Since this time "runs counter to history," the task of a proper historical method is to look in the moment for that which "recapitulates—without ever exactly repeating—the whole of time."[87] It does not wish, in Mosès's words, "to follow the evolution of historical processes but to immobilize them, that is, to describe their privileged connections (in synchrony and not it diachrony), to identify the utopian elements in these connections and to evoke them in the form of images, to decipher that utopian moment precisely in everything that challenged the established order in the past, and finally to read the figure of utopia in the double *theological* and *political* model of messianism and Revolution."[88]

Benjamin's "*theological paradigm* of history"[89] dates back as far as his early essays on language. In these texts, the German philosopher contextualizes messianism through a discussion of the three stages of language's genesis: in the first stage, language is that of the divine word, where there is perfect coincidence between the word and what it describes; in the second stage, where Adam names the animals, a breach in the identity between language and reality takes place, but there still remains a certain harmony between them; and in the third stage, the magical power of naming is no longer available to language, and it is reduced to a simple means of communication.[90] The Fall from originary speech is most felt in modern times, which represent the height of the third stage. It is therefore important for Benjamin to highlight the possibility of moving language away from its communicable functions and advancing it—through insightful translation—toward the revelation of primordial truths. Here, according to Mosès, one finds the philosopher most indebted to Kabbalah: Thus,

> the process, which Benjamin defines as "messianic," and whose end simultaneously means a return to the origin, evokes the conception of history specific to Jewish mysticism, which has always conceived of the messianic end of history as the realization of the ideal plan implied in the Creation. In this sense, it means less a simple restoration of the origin than the realization, through the changes of human time, of all utopian potentials coded, so to speak, in the original program of the human adventure. This is a view of history that, although it is certainly not linear, is not cyclical either, since its end does not coincide purely and simply with its origin. . . . The restoration of the paradisiacal language goes through the movement of verbal invention itself, so that the return to the original is in fact produced through the creation of the new.[91]

As may be gleaned from this passage, Benjamin's theological paradigm does not see each moment as similar to the next in a mutual embeddedness with history's telos, but rather defines them as qualitatively different. The moment, for him, carries the traces of a bygone communion with God, from which humanity has been exiled. And since these traces only offer a partial and particular view of that immemorial past, it also holds within it its own particular future—or, more correctly, an array of potential future trajectories. This is why Benjamin asserted the importance of remembrance in Jewish thought. Remembering is the activity of locating and actualizing/animating the past inside the present so as to realize an inherent horizon; in the spirit of Lurianic mysticism, it is a way of proving human agency in the face of history's unstoppable thrust and of realizing the messianic within worldly reality rather than having it be the result of a metaphysical force. Yet for remembrance to be so revolutionary and messianic, it must take on the form of engagement that does not succumb to history but looks for meaning in fissures in its seeming continuity. Only through such a mystical perspective—or "auratic," to use a well-known Benjaminian term—can a moment be revealed as a monad of time as a whole, manifesting past and present simultaneously.

Toward the end of Benjamin's life, these theological ideas, which were present throughout his work, undergo a clear political turn. Such is the case of the formative essay "Theses on the Philosophy of History" (1940), written during the philosopher's Marxist phase and under the shadow of World War II. Benjamin's principal claim here is that history has always been constructed by the victors, the ruling elites, to reflect their own story and values, and that in the process of this construction, the heritage of the vanquished was repressed and hidden behind the (oppressive) idea of historical progress. This message is crystallized in the essay's most enduring metaphor—the "Angel of History." Addressing Paul Klee's *Angelus Novus* (1920), Benjamin imagines the Angel, an ideal present-day perspective on the past, as being forced by progress to assume a position where it is unable to salvage moments of this "unwanted" history—hidden pockets of resistance—from behind the facade of historical continuity. The task of the historian, Benjamin states, is to succeed where the Angel has failed, which is to say: succeed in capturing a moment *into a dialectical image* that renders visible a trace of repressed history and, in the light of a present-day political context, projects toward a utopian future. This "image" unveils history as "the subject of a structure whose site is not homogenous, empty time, but time filled by the presence of the now [*Jetztzeit*],"[92] and subsequently allows the present to be seen, in Mosès's words, as "both political—since it is in the name of today's struggle that it takes up the heritage of the losers of history—and theological insofar as those sparks of hope hidden deep in the past are also 'bursts of the messianic age.'"[93] To the extent that this theological-political "now-time" is, according to Hannah Arendt at least, "an equivalent to . . . the mystical *nunc stans* [Eternal Now],"[94] the historian is able play the role of the mystic, who experiences and mediates a revelation to his people. Like in Lurianic mysticism, this act does not make the historian-mystic a Messiah but rather an enabler of messianic redemption in the here and now of human reality. Yet unlike Lurianic mysticism, and in reflection of the traumatic historical background of the essay's writing, the redemptive process is seen as founded on upheaval that can break open the historical continuum. Only on the debris of such an explosion, Benjamin seems to say, can the oppressed transcend the conflicts of history and shift the trajectory of the future, potentially obtaining the ultimate unity and reparation that were heralded in mystical-messianic literature.

Like in Benjamin's case, the philosophy of Levinas, to quote Matthew Del Nevo, is first and foremost "cosmological, and as such, kabbalistic,"[95] in the sense of placing the individual in the ethical role of Messiah "aimed at *redeeming the times*."[96] Levinas's messianism, Michael Morgan explains, is not "apocalyptic and catastrophic" as Benjamin's, but it is "similarly redemptive and episodic or momentary."[97] Accordingly, for Levinas as for Benjamin, "time becomes unhinged,"[98] and it is this very unhinging that allows temporality to work ethically in favor of those most vulnerable to its hazards. In this capacity, the French philosopher pushed against two prevailing modes of temporal understanding: objective, where time is measured change, understood through reference to astronomical events or clocks, and subjective, the Bergsonian *durée*, where time is a stream of experiences understood from the perspective of the self. While recognizing the coincidence of both these temporal modalities in our everyday reality, Levinas nevertheless believed that they do not exhaust the story of time. Rather, for him, there exists a different temporal modality, a modality of revelation, which gives meaning to time as a whole, and to our reality in general. The temporality revealed is exactly that of the Infinite, which can also be understood as an "ab-solute past with respect to everything that is shown, signaled, symbolized, announced, remembered, and thereby 'contemporized' with him who understands."[99] It is also, in Levinas's eyes as in the eyes of mystics, the divine absolute, that which "preceded all presence and exceeded every contemporaneity in a time which is not of human duration, nor a falsified projection, nor an extrapolation of duration, is not a

disintegration and disappearance of finite beings, but the original ante-
cedence of God relative to a world which cannot accommodate him, the
immemorial past which has never presented itself, which cannot be said
with the categories of Being and structure, but is the One, which every
philosophy would like to express, beyond being."[100]

To the extent that this temporal order can be revealed, it is only
through an "irreducible disturbance": an interruption that, in Levinas's
words, "is not taken up by the context interrupted, to receive a meaning
from it, . . . because it was already ab-solute."[101] For such a disturbance to
occur, however, "a stranger is . . . needed, one who has come, to be sure,
but left *before* having come, ab-solute in his manifestation." This fundamental Other, the philosopher tells us, can force on us "*a divergency and
a past* which no memory could resurrect as a present,"[102] but only at the
cost of exposing its vulnerability in "the nakedness of a face that faces,
expressing itself."[103] The humbled face of another retains a disturbing
enigma, to which the proper reply is to assume moral responsibility for
the Other, which in the philosopher's perspective, means also to commit
oneself to that Other's preservation. For in the particular face one finds
the face of Absolute Enigma on the scale of infinity, which demands an
audaciously generous response of self-sacrifice. And by facing infinity
with such generosity, the individual "restores to each instant its full signification in that very instant: all the causes are ready to be heard."[104]

This charge of responsibility is not contingent on a particular
moment in time, a particular encounter; rather, we are always already
responsible.[105] In this respect, "an opening of the *time of suddenness*, which
is the beating of the Other in the Same,"[106] does not only reveal an immemorial past, even if this past determines its meaning; it also opens up
to an unending future. Such future-orientation should not be confused
with that which finds meaning in the face of death (as for Heidegger);
rather, Levinas believes that existential meaning extends well beyond
dying.[107] The future of which he speaks is therefore outside of profane
temporality—it is a future of unending obligation, the condition of a
(divine) commanding to which death is no limit. To Levinas, who had
lost much of his family in the Holocaust and was himself interned in
a Nazi prisoner camp, it was imperative to fix one's eyes on this future.
For only through its horizon can a sudden upheaval be justified, since it
allows us to discover the temporal structures of our existence, in which

the purpose of recollection and anticipation becomes clear.[108] In his mind, this is the way to redeem past trauma and reinterpret the deity that allowed its existence—a God now seen solely through a naked face. This theological-political concern for redemption, in turn, reveals Levinas's affinities to the posttraumatic mystical-messianism of Luria: in his demand for the restoration of an immemorial past that transcends our understanding of history but is not unconnected to our reality; in his belief that this restoration can be achieved democratically, through the face-to-face encounter of every subject with his or her Other; and most of all, in his insistence that such a meeting carries with it an ethical responsibility for the well-being of the Other, which one must undertake ad infinitum in order to substitute destructive apocalypse with utopian reparation.

The relevance of these mystical-messianic temporal constellations— Benjamin's "now time" and Levinas's "unhinged time"—to the study of *The Secrets* and *Bruriah* is not only justified by their ongoing use within cinema studies scholarship,[109] but also by their growing presence within Israeli public discourse, which reflects on similar—albeit arguably less sophisticated—messianic formations of New Age spirituality.[110] *The Secrets* unhinges temporality through a constant linkage between present action and a mythicized past—one that explicitly evokes the history of mystical-messianism. The film's plot is set in the ancient city of Safed, where Luria and his fellow Kabbalists developed their influential school of mystical thinking. In his study of the legends of Safed, Eli Yassif has argued that during the era of these mystics, this locale was considered a "mythical space" that serves as a threshold unto a transcendent sphere of divine presence and messianic temporality. Much like in the Benjaminian sense of "now time," the mystics' visions—their move from a "horizontal" to a "vertical" vector of existence—could be triggered at any given moment, through encounters with seemingly meaningless concrete sites and objects—a street, a house, a stone, a tree. These served as "runways" from which mystics disembark toward a different realm; and accordingly, to this day, the city—and in particular, the graves of medieval mystics within it—is considered as having the ability to engender ruptures in time and bring forth a measure of revelation. This sense of a mythical space appears in *The Secrets* through visual reference to sites of spiritual significance within Safed, including: "The Ari's Mikveh," where

Luria's body was purified following his death; the Ancient Cemetery, where major figures in Judaic history are buried; and the "Cave of Shem and Ever," the oldest study hall in Jewish history, whose supernatural powers have been proclaimed by many, including Luria himself. These sites' "magical" quality is enhanced cinematically by the choice to shoot them (or their stand-ins) at night while relying on candle- and torchlight as well as on ambient effects of fog and rain, so as to engender a dream-like mise-en-scéne. The delicate surrealism of such scenes, especially those that involve the reparation rituals performed for Anouk's benefit, appears to draw on the kabbalistic tradition of "midnight Tikkunim," which Luria rejuvenated as a ritualistic practice whereby the worshipper connects with the souls and cosmic knowledge of the righteous through prostrating at their tombs.[111] Accordingly, these scenes' stylization seems to rupture a concrete understanding of the historical moment and suggest the experience of a bridge between the present, the past of the Kabbalah mystics, and the immemorial given of messianic temporality. This sense of disjointed time is particularly evident in the aforementioned scene where Michelle and Noemi take Anouk to "The Ari's Mikveh." During their preparations, Noemi explains to Anouk that the ritual they are about to perform serves to bring about "a different state of consciousness." Later, during the ritual itself, it is Noemi who seems to undergo this shift in consciousness—she submerges in the water, and then after opening her eyes and seeing Anouk submerged as well, becomes overwrought and immediately resurfaces. This experience, the film leads us to believe, was one in which Noemi saw her mother's image present in the image of Anouk, thereby creating an evocative "dialectical image" in the Benjaminian sense. In this respect, Noemi engages the holy Mikveh as a "liminal zone between the real and the mythical"[112] and uses it, like Benjamin's historian, to reanimate a past in the here and now.

In *Bruriah*, a disjointed temporality that allows a past to intrude on the present is shown in a more literal fashion. From the outset of the film, we see the protagonist being plagued by incessant, fragmentary flashbacks to the occasion in which copies of her father's book were burned in the outskirts of Jerusalem. These flashbacks apparently serve as a catalyst for Bruriah's search for the lost book, and for her decision to ask Yosef for help in this quest. This prompting, in turn, leads Yosef to track down photographs that were shot thirty years before, during the

FIGURE 14. Noemi (Ania Bukstein) experiences a vision in the waters of the Mikveh. From *The Secrets* (Avi Nesher, 2007).

actual burning. The arrival of these images creates a sense of rupture, not only because they bring a past scene into the present, but also because they are visually aligned with Bruriah's flashbacks; additionally, the fact that the images are procured from real-life photographer Alex Libek, who is "interviewed" on-screen by Yosef, also adds to this sense of heterogeneity, by which a documentary quality intrudes into the fictional plot. This double intrusion sets up the most substantial temporal rupture, when Yosef presents the pictures to Bruriah. At this moment, the film's heroine sees herself as a young girl, and the resulting "dialectical image" then triggers a new and more complete flashback of the book-burning scene. In confronting such multilayered temporality, Bruriah seems to go through a process of Benjaminian remembering, which does not preserve memories of the past but reactualizes them for the present. Like with Noemi, the state of revelation is so overwhelming that it reduces her to tears. These anguished reactions seem to carry the traces of traumatic events (death, ostracizing); accordingly, they give credence to Benjamin's point that an awareness of now-time is always connected to an upheaval and colored by shades of the apocalyptic.

Significantly in terms of the films' feminist charge, the unhinging of temporality in and through them allows for an epiphany that orients the subject toward taking responsibility for vulnerable *female* others. In

The Secrets, the responsibility of being an ethical agent falls on Noemi. Though this shift is anticipated by her decision to attend the Midrasha, she truly begins to take responsibility for the Other through her interaction with Anouk—and specifically, at the moment of temporal rupture when she recognizes the dead mother of her past in the present *face* of the living Anouk. At this moment, she sees through Anouk's eyes the other Others: her mother, Michelle, and the rest of Judaism's disenfranchised women. This recognition foreshadows the wedding scene at the end of the film. In this scene, emphasis is placed on an exchange of glances between Noemi and Michelle, a muted dialogue between vulnerable faces that takes place separately from the procedure of the matrimonial service itself. The exchange sets up Noemi's resignation, the forfeiture of her rights to Michelle's love, as if demanded by Michelle's tearful eyes. Yet this charge actually helps Noemi perfect her ethical positioning, since in Levinasian terms, an ethical relationship can only exist in a state of asymmetry between self and other, where the other is completely vulnerable to the self. For Levinas, love, which is symmetrical in its requirement that emotions be reciprocal, can never be truly ethical. By accepting the charge of letting go, Noemi reintroduces a measure of asymmetry into her loving relationship with Michelle, and as a result, becomes responsible for her.

Bruriah also establishes the possibility of an ethical relationship between women, the likes of which is suggested in the tale of Ruth. The unhinging of time confronts Bruriah with an image of her younger self as Other; and it is this encounter with the repressed younger self, and specifically with her *face* in both photograph and flashback, that empowers the protagonist to assume responsibility for fellow women. This is manifested symbolically in the attempt to recover Talmudic Bruriah's true story through the search for the book as well as more literally in the attempt to help a friend get divorced in the rabbinical courts. Such efforts may be overshadowed by Bruriah's ultimate return to the fold of the family and her assumption of the role of wife and lover; indeed, it may be argued that the central ethical shift in the film is Yaakov's, whose encounter with the image of the younger Bruriah catapults him into a quest for subjectivity, which culminates in the reunion with his wife. Such a resolution may be deemed a failure for Levinas because he sees Eros as an impediment to ethics. Yet this sexual encounter can also be seen exemplifying what Sam Girgus, following Luce Irigary's critique of and elaborations on Levinas's philosophy, would define as a "reconciling [of] the ethical challenge of transcendence with the immanence of the demands of [a woman's] own sexualized body."[113] By bringing ethics into Eros by way of an embrace, this film may thus suggest "the possibility of achieving transcendence in immanence rather than accepting experience as confined by the visible horizon."[114]

According to the Talmud, "three things come unawares: the Messiah, a found article, and a scorpion."[115] These are also the three main coordinates of mystical-messianic temporality, through its medieval Kabbalistic and modern philosophical renderings. Mystical messianism is always about the restoration of an article once lost and now found: an immemorial past before creation as in Luria, which in Benjamin and Levinas is also doubled as the repressed past of the oppressed. This past is evoked within the present to countermand a prevailing temporal order that is ethically flawed. Consequently, the act of restoration is forever marked by the impending threat of a scorpion lying in wait—by the sense of apocalypse that Luria and Levinas preserve as a shadow while Benjamin brings to the fore. Yet it is through this threat that the possibility of a better future—the future of the Messiah—can arguably

FIGURE 15. Bruriah (Hadar Galron) looks at a picture of her younger self. From *Bruriah* (Avraham Kushnir, 2008).

be realized. The responsibility of facilitating this messianic redemption, however, falls not on a superhuman but on human beings; there may be those who are more skilled in obtaining the necessary revelation—a mystic, a historian—but the capability is there for all to exercise, in an act as easy and as revolutionary as a face-to-face encounter. The protagonists of *Bruriah* and *The Secrets* play their part in this messianic ideal—as historian-mystics, who draw out a past through disturbances in the flow of linear time, and use it to transcend the crippling ambivalences of linearity, toward a different future where Judaic women will not be oppressed. Such a future does not fully materialize in the confines of the films' narratives, which ultimately capitulate to a powerful patriarchal mechanism. Rather, it reveals itself as a possibility through the fissures of this mechanism—in the instances of disjointed temporality that "flash up at a moment of danger" and leave an afterglow of utopia in their wake. These are ephemeral trance visions more than concrete actualizations, meant to cajole an audience into pushing beyond the limits of the filmic text and imagining/experiencing a different sort of gendered relationship within Judaism.

Looking beyond (Im)Modesty

During a period of heated debate on gender-based segregation in Israel's public buses, eminent law professor Zvi Triger provided two main reasons for why this expression of Judaic "modesty" policies should be considered problematic: first, that it presents a clear case of "sexual harassment," since "the relegation of women to the back of the bus is clearly 'an insulting or debasing reference' to them in connection with their gender or sexuality";[116] and second, that beyond being illegal and morally flawed, it is also self-defeating, because in their desire "to 'clean' the public sphere from any manifestation, real or perceived, of female sexuality," religious Israelis "in fact put [this] sexuality at the center of attention."[117] Though warranted, this argument appears overly focused on Israel's religious constituency as the origin of modesty policy making, thereby sidelining the secular community's contribution to the sexualized imagination and libidinal economy surrounding the topic of gender-based segregation. Without disputing the legitimacy of secular Israelis' hope that women be released from Judaic segregation, the extreme fervor that typifies their contemporaneous critical discourse seems to indicate a more convoluted emotional motivation than mere indignation. In this respect, it may be argued that encounters with modesty-based segregation in the public sphere have served the Israeli secular community (or at the very least, large parts of its male contingent) to perform a dual movement: on the one hand, to flirt with its wish of exposing the "hidden" religious woman and making her a sexual object; and on the other hand, to disavow its own androcentrism by foregrounding the androcentric tendencies of a religious Other. As such, the forced hiddenness of the devout woman becomes the condition through which the secular mind can naturalize an impulse to see her immodest.

Female-centered Judaic-themed Israeli films tend to mirror this complex dynamic. Their focus is on religious women who challenge the constraints of Judaic patriarchy, and to this extent, their agenda embodies progressive feminist values. At the same time, however, these texts almost always reduce their protagonists' challenge to issues of sexual modesty while marginalizing or disavowing other sites of resistance. This focus inevitably plays into the craving to exoticize the religious woman, and ultimately, to unveil her mysteries. Such desire, in turn, is augmented by the fact that these films rarely expose the female body to full view. As Mary Ann Doane argues in the context of Rita Hayworth's iconic strip-tease act in *Gilda* (Charles Vidor, 1946), the basic impulse is not to show full nudity, since that will expose "the female body as the site of negativity, of lack and hence, of the possibility of castration." Rather, it is the "very process of peeling away accretions of layers" that will never arrive at its expected climax, the "continual flirtation with perception" that avoids the "full look," which ultimately sustains interest here, since it does not entirely undercut a woman's assigned role as fetish.[118] In a similar manner, it could be argued that the religious woman, possibly the last magical fetish in a society in which female bodies are increasingly exposed and demystified, stands at the center of these Israeli films' attempt to enact a "logic of striptease." Accordingly, such texts provide their predominantly secular audience with the "pleasures" of exposing their religious protagonists while simultaneously "saving" them from the bounds of modesty.

While partaking in this double bind of (im)modesty, certain Judaic-themed films like *The Secrets* and *Bruriah* nevertheless work to oppose it through an appeal to the anarchic experience of disjointed mystical-messianic time. The feminist nature of this appeal responds to a contemporary cultural milieu that is already accustomed, in the spirit of the New Age, to retool Kabbalah for the purposes of feminism. Kabbalistic literature offsets commonplace understanding of God as male by showing its being and influence to be the product of a complex relationship between male *and* female qualities.[119] The female qualities, placed under the general heading of Shekhinah, have inspired Jewish feminists to situate them as a means of empowerment vis-à-vis Judaic androcentrism. This made it essential, in the words of Luke Devine, "to remove *Shekhinah* from the original context," which in Kabbalah tied it to certain patriarchal tenets and perspectives. In so doing, Shekhinah emerges as "an amalgam of traditional and personal images; a fluid reflection of the individual feminist and their immediate spiritual context which is often 'private' and non-denominational."[120] What sustains this fluidity is the New Age emphasis on revelatory visions, where the bounds of human temporality are supposedly transcended. These revelations arguably appear to hold within them the promise of a new and more egalitarian existential order—one that may exist beside our normal order, like the cinematic screen exists beside our familiar reality. It therefore stands to reason that films like *The Secrets* and *Bruriah* would use cinema's "magic" to bring such visions of "messianic redemption" to life and entrance us into seeing that, to quote Scholem, "the power of evil has been broken, [and] all those differentiations also disappear which had been derived from it."[121] In this filmic revelation, feminism's values may suddenly (re)emerge from within Judaic tradition and work against Judaism's double bind of (im)modesty, thereby placing on viewers the supreme ethical obligation reserved (by Benjamin) to the historian-mystic: "to stay, awaken the dead, and make whole what has been smashed."[122]

3

RITUAL IN FILM, FILM AS RITUAL

The Vicissitudes of Prayer

In true prayer belief and cult are united and purified to enter into the living relation. The fact that true prayer lives in the religions witnesses to their true life: they live so long as it lives in them. Degeneration of the religions means degeneration of prayer in them.

—Martin Buber[1]

During the winter months of 2020, Israel faced the effects of a global COVID-19 epidemic through quarantines that kept the nation's citizens enclosed in the solitude of their homes. In a bizarre coincidence, Jerusalem's Israel Museum prepared to mount an exhibition around that time whose theme chimed with the zeitgeist of forced isolation: *Seated in Seclusion*, an exploration of Bratslav Hasidism's practice of secluded praying in nature (*Hitbodedut*), through photographic documentation of the chairs left behind in the wake of prayer. In their curatorial statement, Eran Lederman and Sharon Weiser-Ferguson chose to downplay the ritual's place within a theocentric cosmology in favor of its relevance to secular "consumer culture"—and specifically, to this culture's New Age pursuit after rites of "spiritual repair, a concept aligned with contemporary views on sustainability."[2] By an (un)happy accident, this relevance was thrown into sharp relief through the exhibition's conjunction with a worldwide pandemic, with Hitbodedut unexpectedly offering the museum's mostly secular audiences a way of approaching their forced isolation in positive terms—that is, as a means of spiritual restoration. Thus, it came to be that *Seated in Seclusion* not only reported on but also furthered the process of religious rituals being assimilated into Israel's secular ethos. And in so doing, the exhibition also left room to wonder: Should this process be seen as secularizing the once holy, or rather as sanctifying that which is ostensibly secular? And how may an exhibition—as a medium of secular ritualism—be best situated in relation to these two possibilities?

If *Seated in Seclusion* makes evident the ability of religious rites to be both inside and outside secularity in the post-Enlightenment era, this slipperiness is grounded in the definitional nature of ritual itself. As Timothy Nelson explains, ritual "is one of those slippery words . . . which is so useful, but which, when you try to define precisely what it refers to, seems to deconstruct right before your eyes."[3] What overdetermines this fluidity is the dynamic relationship between two dimensions that arguably set ritual apart from other social activities: "formality," which, in Nelson's words, relates to the "repetitive nature of ritual, or to its temporally regular performance and the style of the act itself, often characterized as rigid, standardized, or invariant;"[4] and "expressivity," which refers to, in Catherine Bell's phrasing, the "forms of mental content or conceptual blueprints [that] ritual, like action, will act out."[5]

As a recurring formalized event expressive of abstract beliefs and values, the ritual finds its natural home in the religious world. Yet the inclusive nature of formality and expressivity has allowed scholars and laypersons alike to extend the reach of ritualism beyond the confines of religion into a variety of "secular" activities. Such measures effectively revealed the existence of a ritualistic dimension within general human behavior and helped challenge the definition of religion as a sui generis phenomenon. At the same time, they also made it difficult to distinguish between ritualistic and nonritualistic activities, diminishing the precision and usefulness of "ritual" as an operative term. Instead of rendering ritual an unusable category, however, Nelson suggests that we relate it primarily to those activities perceived as separate from everyday reality by their practitioners—a separation that demands the employment of an overtly differentiated, symbolic frame of interpretation. These activities therefore become ritualistic by virtue of being "defined . . . in terms of *privileged* behavior . . . by the actors themselves."⁶

Within the academic area of religion and film, several scholars have argued that the filmic experience constitutes a mode of "privileged behavior" and thus should be spoken of in terms of ritual. In an introductory gloss of the field, S. Brent Plate states this claim in no uncertain terms: "Cameras and rituals," he writes, "*frame* the world, *selecting* particular elements of time and space to be displayed. These framed selections are then projected onto a broad field in ways that invite viewers/adherents to become participants, to share in the experience of the re-created world."⁷ In Plate's framework, the bracketing of filmgoing through various devices (a special venue, particular screening times, darkness, previews), combined with the filmic text's overt positioning as a mythical representation of "another world," draws the viewer to employ a ritualistic frame of reference and interpret his or her experience as "symbolically dominant." As a result, the film theater is imagined as an alternative place of worship, one that historically came into its own just as organized religion began its fall from (popular) grace. This, in turn, leads to the supposition that, as Edgar Morin once argued, "no one who frequents [cinema's] dark auditoriums is really an atheist."⁸

The present chapter addresses the topic of ritual as it intersects with the filmic medium, both in terms of ritual on film and of film as ritual. Per the example of *Seated in Seclusion*, this intersection is fleshed out, on the levels of culture and medium, in relation to a specific rite—that of Jewish prayer, which has often been described as the essence of Judaic ritualism, if not of Judaism in toto.⁹ Accordingly, two connected lines of inquiry are undertaken. The first involves a close reading of the representation of prayer in Judaic-themed Israeli cinema. Thus, if prayers are seen as privileged platforms for engaging in divine communication and expressing the social ethos for a collective of faith, then this analysis of their filmic rendering would seek to uncover Israeli cinema's perspective on the value of these objectives—a perspective that is tinged by profound ambivalence, for it seeks to locate the place of religious tradition within a social reality of an avowed secular character. The second line of inquiry explores these cinematic works as drawing attention to the ritualistic nature of film spectatorship, and specifically to spectatorship's analogical relationship with the praxis of Jewish prayer. This exploration is used to qualify the dominant theoretical paradigm in the religion and film field, which analogizes filmgoing with participation in typical religious rituals, for example that of Holy Mass. At the same time, building on the philosophy of Martin Buber and cine-phenomenology of Vivian Sobchack, it offers a more nuanced view on this analogy, which takes into account the function of ekstasis in both praying and film spectatorship (as they are commonly practiced). Ultimately, whether discussing prayer on the screen or in front of it, analysis herein does not encompass all facets of this ritual, a phenomenon whose full complexity could hardly be accounted for in such a limited frame. Rather, the discussion centers mainly on a single, albeit significant, characteristic: the relationship between personal and communal worship.

Jewish Prayer: Personal and Communal

Insofar as one looks at it as a ritualistic system, "the religious phenomenon," according to Ron Margolin, appears to operate "on two planes: the external-communal plane, which is in plain sight, and the internal-personal, which is focused on the individual's inner world."[10] With the external-communal plane, religion works to provide a cohesive social identity to its adherents, one based on a cosmic sense of order and meaning, and from which a set of rules, values, and conceptual norms is derived. In contrast, the internal-personal plane would highlight the "mental and therefore more subjective elements of religious life; that is, the conscious and direct contents of the individual's subjective life as they are shaped under the influence of religion, whether it be done through the social functioning of religion or whether it be done through personal choice independent of religious-social conditionings."[11] There is no straightforward distinction between these "subjective" elements and the collective frameworks established in religion's external-communal dimension. Indeed, internal and external often work hand in hand, as when the interpellation of communal frameworks allows the individual to identify with a social role, itself prescribed on the grounds of some cosmic truth. Yet as Margolin insists, there are also "many instances where it is possible to note a gap between the external aspect of religious behavior and the internal aspect attributed to those behaviors."[12] Thus for him, though the distinction between external-communal and internal-personal may at times appear more artificial than organic, the existence of such gaps makes its employment both justifiable and necessary.[13]

Emerging from the edicts of ancient Jewish sages, mainline Judaic tradition has aligned its image of Judaism with the biblical congregation's communal character. This entailed, in Margolin's words, that "the heart of Judaism" would exist "in a person's fulfillment of God's external decrees within a Jewish social structure that is regulated by the Halakha. From this point of view, Judaism is a Halakhic ritualistic external system, which is known and evaluated by the Halakhic way of life that is shared by its members."[14] A Judaic emphasis on the communal, while certainly sidelining considerations of the personal, did not eradicate them completely. Rather, as Margolin also notes, "it is possible to distinguish the parallel existence of both planes, the internal and the external, throughout Jewish history."[15] By and large, the recognition of the personal within mainline rabbinical Judaism was meant to facilitate its support of the communal emphasis, or at least the curbing of its potentially disruptive effects on this emphasis.

The evolution of Judaic prayer bears witness to this dynamic. Thus, in the period of the First and Second Temples, the main form of worship was animal sacrifice, performed in Jerusalem by the priestly elite and witnessed by the multitude of laypeople. Prayer was not an integral part of this service and occupied a marginal role in Judaic ritualism in general. The destruction of the Second Temple, however, led to a major shift in its status. The absence of the Temple denied the Jewish people the possibility of worship through sacrifice; accordingly, the Jewish leadership (*Sanhedrin*) offered prayer as its substitute. The rise in the stature of prayer also required the fixing of its form once and for all. As such, in ensuing centuries the staples of Jewish prayer became common law: the times of services (for example, the daily prayers of Shachrit, Minchah, and Arvit), the content of prayer (for example, the Eighteen Benedictions of the Amidah prayer), prayer behavior, prayer accessories, synagogue rules and regulations, and so on. Though it was never fully finalized—which may be evidenced from the existence of various versions of the Jewish prayer book (Siddur)—as Jewish ritual practice became increasingly unspontaneous, according to Stefan Reif, it relied less "on the individual's concentration during prayer time and more on the general standards of religious behavior, of which fixed prayer became an integral part."[16] This accompanied a deliberate move to foreground fixed prayer as a congregational practice, founded on the ten-person quorum (*Minyan*) that only in its presence can major sections of prayers be recited, and on the synagogue as a gathering space from which prayers are best dispatched. In this "emphasis of the 'we' over against the 'I,'"[17] the religious leaders were hoping to give a sense of national cohesion to a Jewry fragmented by the Temple destruction and resulting exile.

In light of this historical trajectory, it becomes clear that Jewish prayer is, to quote Adin Steinsaltz, "essentially the prayer of the community and of the people as a whole. In principle, its structure, contents, and wording are geared to the needs, hopes, and sense of gratitude of the community, so that even the individual praying does so as part of the whole community."[18] This is undoubtedly true for congregational services, which combine the communal fixed form of the ritual with the physical presence of a community; there, the external-communal aspect of Jewish prayer receives its most powerful expression, which is arguably why these rites are foregrounded in Judaic tradition, even more decisively than in other monotheistic religions. Yet the same collectivizing impulse also operates, albeit to a lesser degree perhaps, within individual prayers that take place outside of the congregational service and under its shadow. Thus, as Steinsaltz comments, "even though a person praying alone is not present at that particular moment within a congregation, in a certain sense he [*sic*] nevertheless functions not as an individual, but part of an absent, invisible congregation." This communal aspect receives concrete manifestation through "physical orientation during prayer services: while worshipping, all Jews face, not in a particular direction, but toward one specific point—the Temple site in Jerusalem";[19] even more fundamentally, however, it is activated through the use of holy language in a fixed form that asserts the collective affiliation of even the most secluded and individualized of prayers.

This is not to say, again, that Judaic lawmakers have not been aware of the existing tension between the dominant external-communal aspect of prayer and an individual's inner religious life, especially within a congregational setting. According to Steinsaltz,

This tension is created by three factors involved in the communal prayer. First the worshipper himself [sic], when truly praying and not merely reading or mouthing the words, feels and thinks his own emotion and thoughts; even when he does not bring to his prayers all those personal concerns that have occupied him throughout the day, there are certain matters that he wishes to express and reflect upon in prayer. On the other hand, fixed prayer provides a train of thoughts, themes, and concepts imposed upon the individual from without, from the prayer to the worshipper. Yet a third component is the praying congregation itself, which, both as a whole and as a collection of individuals, affects each particular worshipper.[20]

In light of this tension, mainline Judaism attempted to incorporate the personal into the communal dimension, making the two work together synergistically while upholding the dominance of communalism. The attempt is most evident in the significance given to "intentionality" (*Kavvanah*) within the fixed prayer. At the most basic level, to pray with intent is to acknowledge that one is standing in the presence of God and is aware of the true meaning behind the words uttered.[21] As such, it is also meant to recreate the traits of an individual's spontaneous prayer, performed ad hoc, as a counterforce to the depersonalizing effects of rote participation in a rigid communal form of worship.

While representing the major thrust of Jewish thinking on prayer, this collective-centered model was not without its challengers. A subtle opposition came in strains within Judaism that, while still adhering to Judaism's communal dimension, stressed the importance of inner religious life.[22] Such is the case in formulations of mystical prayer as a means of direct communication with God, particularly evident in the Hasidic vein of Jewish mysticism, where according to Margolin, "inner religious life and patterns of inwardness of Jewish religious life had reached their apex."[23] By and large, Hasidism's interest in inner religious life was motivated by its principal project of achieving a close encounter with divinity. This dialogue was perceived as dependent on the sacred workings of personal devotion—workings that were potentially threatened by the incessant stream of communal demands and their binding of the subject to a (collective) structure of social needs and requirements. Accordingly, for Hasidim, it became important to champion "the redemption of the individual," and specifically his or her internal capacity to work within a communal practice in a manner that "may elevate the soul, until reaching a *true clinging* to the divine being."[24] "Clinging" (or "cleaving," *Devekut*), as an intensified form of Kavvanah, assumes that God exists everywhere in the immanent world and therefore tasks the Hasid with engaging this world, including through religious practices, in intimate fashion so as to dissolve its materiality (*Bitul Ha-Yesh*). During those ephemeral instances when such dissolution is made possible, Hasidim are supposedly able to overcome the barriers that separate them from divine essence, discovering inside their particular being the traces of a godly unity that embraces all levels of existence. In this respect, as Scholem explains, their Devekut does not serve "as an active realization of the concrete, but as a contemplative realization of the immanence of God in the concrete."[25]

While personal Devekut may take place at any moment of a Hasid's life, its privileged realization was in prayer. On this, Louis Jacobs remarked that "the Hasidic elevation of prayer over other religious duties, even over that of study of the Torah, is not in keeping with the Jewish tradition."[26] Rather, prayer became for Hasidim the preeminent exercise in transcendence, a ritual that should be pursued through deep reflection (*Hitbonenut*), one imbued by the proper Kavvanah that connects the individual's innermost soul to the content of the prayer.[27] This procedure, which Jacobs describes as to be "completely absorbed in prayer, to lose the self and 'strip off one's corporeal nature' (*Hitpashtut Ha-Gishmiyut*), to burn in longing for the divine,"[28] could and was performed in communal settings. Yet such occasions made it difficult for the Hasid to maintain the level of complete concentration required in contemplation, forcing on him a measure of compromise.[29] Accordingly, in the spirit of legitimizing internal religious life, several Hasidic *Tsadikim*, like R. Nachman of Bratslav, stressed the practice of Hitbodedut, during which the Hasid sequesters himself in a remote (often bucolic) location to enter into a private meditation. In this quietude, Tomer Persico elucidates, the worshipper is supposedly able to transcend the separation between consciousness's subjective content and the objective data received by the senses, thereby enacting a vision of "existence as one perceptual whole, read as the experience of an individual's unification with the surrounding world, which in turn can be perceived as the one true divine reality."[30] In turn, such intimacy, for R. Nachman at least, serves as grounds for a highly personalized form of mystical praying, where the Hasid would pour his heart out to God, using familiar language in direct address.[31]

Thus envisioned, the challenge of Hasidic prayer was directed against the ritual's communal emphasis, which was believed to proportionally reduce the individual's spectrum of religious involvement and minimize the possibility of divine encounters. Hasidism's goal, however, was not to abolish communalism so much as to create a stronger balance between it and prayer's mystical-personal impulse. This delicate balance, in turn, was unsettled through the subsequent evolution of neo-Hasidism, amid the consistent proclamations about the "death of God." Fueled by certain strands of philosophical writing (for example, the oeuvre of Friedrich Nietzsche), as well as catastrophic historical events (most notably, the Holocaust), this supposed "death" disconnected the communal-external systems of Judaism from their source of cosmic legitimization and consequently destabilized their standing as the premier meaning-making structure of Jewish consciousness and identity. In this context, then, for many Jews it became meaningless to pray, since the divine addressee was allegedly "gone," and consequently the human subject became the center of the universe. Yet with the lingering presence of God still remaining palpable in the collective memory of much of modern Jewry, this "death" was insufficient to eradicate the desire to pray altogether. What could be done, then, with the ambivalence of these "prayer wounded"[32] Jews, who wish to pray but cannot? Neo-Hasidism's answer, which is particularly relevant to the present discussion, attempted to overcome this "crisis in prayer" by recovering God as an addressee, though in a manner respective of the contemporaneous de-legitimization of Judaism's communal form. Its solution was one that, in Margolin's words, stressed the "subjective emotional contents of the religious individual as a way to allow the modern subject to come in personal contact with religious life while ignoring [its] institutional and social aspects."[33] Such valuation of personal over communal, in turn, was imagined as permitting the individual to search and potentially "re-discover" a god that is not wholly bound by the standard collective structure in which He has been located and from which He has "disappeared"—a god with which only a mystical-personal dialogue can be engaged.

Expressed by many Jewish thinkers, this view received its clearest and arguably most influential articulation in the philosophical writings of Martin Buber. In terms of contribution to western philosophy, Buber is perhaps most known for his theory on dialogue as the basis of human relationality. According to Buber, humans function in relation to external entities: other humans, the world, and God. This relationship can take two forms. In the first form, the "I-It," one would meet another entity but fail to establish dialogue; there is no recognition of the Other as equal. In contradistinction, the second form, the "I-Thou," does offer such recognition of equality, and therefore allows the subject to overcome biases, engage in true rapport with all that is encountered, and become more whole in the process. These forms do not exist in an either-or scheme but slip into and emerge out of each other. Yet of the two, it is the "I-Thou" relationship that is most fleeting and rare. Its elevated status leads Buber to argue that when addressing an Other as Thou, one encounters the perceptible presence of the "eternal Thou"—the unfathomable God, the infinite or Ein-Sof of mystical experience. Thus, for Buber, "every time we allow I-Thou relations to arise, . . . we cease to be alone because we allow the 'spark' of the Eternal that resides in us to connect with the 'spark' of the Eternal that is in the other." By placing the eternal Thou in a dialogical relationship with "Man," Buber mitigates divinity's alleged radical transcendence, and hence, in the words of Alexandre Guilherme, renders "the re-connection with God [as] something that can be achieved despite the divisions and compartmentalizations of modern life."[34]

Even with such a cursory summary of Buber's philosophy, it may be possible to discern the immense influence Hasidic thought held over his work. Buber had a lifelong affair with Hasidism, which resulted in his edited anthologies of Hasidic lore and volumes of commentary on Hasidic life. More profoundly, however, his notion of dialogism was inspired by the Hasid's encounter with a hidden God on the plane of immanence, and thus may be deemed neo-Hasidic. As Israel Koren argues, Buber equated the I-Thou relationship with the Hasidic notion of Devekut, as a form by which the subject emerges out of itself to connect to a Wholly Other. He also drew on the Hasidic recognition that Devekut cannot be pursued indefinitely in order to assert his understanding of I-Thou as a fleeting phenomenon, emerging out of the I-It only to return to it shortly after.[35] Furthermore, he took from Hasidism the notion that the genuine dialogue, which is Devekut-based, must be performed through the world of things, through the "somethingness" that allows glimpses into a divine void. Accordingly, he foregrounded the Hasidic-infused belief that God may be encountered anywhere, and that in effect, there is always a dialogue with Him. In this framework, prayer also becomes for Buber dialogical in nature. Following the Judaic logic that favors praise over petition in prayer,[36] he did not regard this dialogue so much as a conversation in the literal sense, where the subject asks for something and God answers. Rather, the dialogue of prayer is first and foremost, in Buber's mind as in much of Hasidism,[37] a human response to a standing invitation by God to become intimate with His presence and see the world through His eyes.

While Guilherme argues that "this understanding applies to 'prayer' as public worship or private devotion,"[38] it seems that the thrust of Buber's philosophy focuses on private devotion as expressing, in his words, "the living prayer, the immediate saying of the Thou, and in linking it with the life of the senses."[39] As such, Buber's neo-Hasidic perspective tends to radicalize Hasidism's stance on prayer by taking its *emphasis* on a personalized engagement, mainly in Kavvanah but also occasionally in secluded performance, and making it the sole model for religious prayer. This radicalization, for Persico, comes "at the cost of canceling the significance of the external, . . . in direct breach of the framework offered by Hasidism's leadership."[40] Accordingly, to the extent that Buber affirms community, it is only as a collection of individuals bound to each other through the "common quality of relation with the Center"—their shared intentionality toward the eternal Thou through its specific reverberation, the Thou. Per this view, in not submitting to the demands of communal liturgy through its appeal to mystical experience, the individual's personalized prayer paradoxically ensures the community's "authentic existence."[41]

Buber's foregrounding of the personal fits well within twentieth- to twenty-first-century New Age mentality, which sees the individual as the origin and center of spiritual meaning. It is no wonder then that his philosophy has resurfaced as an important intermediary between the Hasidic challenge to Judaic orthodoxy during the eighteenth to nineteenth centuries and contemporary Jew Age culture, a major part of which can be defined as neo-Hasidic.[42] As such, Buber can also be seen as a catalyst and shaper of the contemporary "thirst" within Jewish culture "for internal religious activity, i.e., a connection with divinity whose focal point is in the individual's innermost soul."[43] This thirst has expanded the Buberian solution to the modern "death of God" crisis, contributing to what Smadar Cherlow has dubbed as "the resurgence of prayer." Focusing on Israel, Cherlow claims that not only has prayer become more prevalent within the postmodern–New Age cultural landscape, it has also turned more diverse, offsetting the centrality of mainline Judaic custom by incorporating esoteric norms from the margins.[44] This process often takes form through Buber's dual emphasis: on the one hand, the suspicion toward the institutionalized communal dimension of prayer, and on the other hand, the affirmation of a personal mode of piety as a way of reaching out to a (mystical) god that is not wholly reducible to religious dogma. Such mystification and privatization of praying activity thus appear as the necessary conditions by which, in Cherlow's phrasing, "prayer is transformed from ritualistic routine or Halakhic duty into a living rite."[45]

Ritual on Film: Cinematic Prayers

The struggle to turn ritualistic routine into a living rite reverberates through the representation of prayer in Judaic-themed Israeli films. As such, Buber's philosophy—which has held considerable influence over contemporary negotiations of Israeli identity[46]—gives us important cues to understanding how this struggle, and its attendant ambivalence, are negotiated on screen. As will be shown, the Buberian emphasis on the "I," echoed through the New Age focus on personal experience and privatizing of religion, comes to the fore in these films' affirmation of individual intentionality in the context of prayer. This affirmation does not necessarily lead to the delegitimization of communal prayer, though that occasionally takes place. Nevertheless, even when this form is left unquestioned, personal prayer overshadows it as the most viable mode for divine communion. Thus envisaged, cinematic prayers on the Israeli screen flesh out the possibility of, but also the difficulty in achieving a mode of "self-transcendence,"[47] to use Sagi's term—a state of ekstasis that counters the prevalent "death of God" discourse, not through recommitting to age-old rituals but via an open and direct dialogue, which joins one's innermost soul to a divinity unbound by the coordinates of religious dogma.

A text that exemplifies this dynamic is the made-for-TV film *Shofar* (2001), directed by secular filmmaker Daniel Sirkin and scripted by the ex-Haredi writer Dov Elbaum. The film's Haredi protagonist Amram Zakuta, a scribe (*Sofer Stam*) earning his meager income by copying *Mezuzah* scrolls, finds it difficult to connect with his mentally disabled son, Yitzhak Shlomo. One day, while staying with a neighboring woman, Yitzhak Shlomo blows the ceremonial ram's horn (*Shofar*) and immediately after, the neighbor's pregnant daughter reports that her water broke. This chain of events leads the neighbor to hail the child as a having "special" powers. As news breaks of this supposed wonder, people line up outside of the Zakutas' apartment, asking for a prayer blessing from the father and a Shofar blowing from his offspring. While the wife Yaffa attempts to shield her child from exploitation, Amram becomes enamored with the new popularity into which Yitzhak Shlomo has catapulted him. Spurred on by Elharar, a local wheeler and dealer, he then abandons his scribing duties and takes on the role of a "miracle working rabbi." His dreams of glory are ultimately shattered, however, when during a synagogue meeting for the benefit of one of Elharar's shady enterprises, Yitzhak Shlomo refuses to blow the Shofar and is subsequently taken away by an angry Yaffa. Understanding that fame had corrupted him, "Reb Amram" leaves the synagogue to rejoin his family. There, in a moment of intimacy, he hears his son utter the word "Mezuzot" for the first time. So enthralled by this gesture, which seems to have bridged the distance between their two worlds, Amram takes the Mezuzah parchment and draws on it a caricatured face of a young religious boy, provoking a rare smile to extend across his son's face.

The world of *Shofar* is one where the words of prayer have lost their sacredness. The main representatives of this world of religious language, Amram and Elharar, embody different facets of this decline. As a scribe, Amram is surrounded by words, yet his relationship to them is not one of true comprehension but of thoughtless copying. Becoming a rabbi by popular demand, he understands his authority as stemming from the power of his words. Yet the absence of a close bond to language, a particular Devekut that connects personal devotion to communal expression, seems to render his prayer powerless. While Amram fails to truly connect with language, Elharar, on the other hand, completely distorts its explicit devotional use. This is not only manifested in private quarters, when he uses language of religious discourse to fraud the people arriving at Zakuta's doorstep; even publicly he seems to treat words like a smoke screen, as when he uses the time of congregational gathering in the synagogue to discuss business with an associate. These differences notwithstanding, for both characters the communal dimension of language, whether uttered in private or in public, has more to do with communal needs than with communal devotion. God has disappeared from the words of their prayers, arguably through a long tradition of collective use that is more about establishing social controls than channeling the believers' personal piety toward divine ears.

In contrast to profane prayer, Yitzhak Shlomo's Shofar blowing seems to operate more spiritually. Zakuta's son does not belong to the world of language and is unencumbered by its use—or rather misuse—in the furthering of human interest. Accordingly, his "prayers" originate from a prelinguistic sphere, through the sonic workings of music. Since blowing the horn does not involve the mediation of words, one can assume a stronger connection existing between Yitzhak Shlomo and the Shofar's sounds than is often found between a praying subject and the language of prayer. Thus envisioned, the Shofar emerges on-screen as a communal vessel of worship that is devoid of profane-social appropriations and hence can facilitate an enhanced state of devotion, in which emanated sound seemingly transports the individual out of quotidian reality and onto a transcendent plane. This perspective, in turn, resonates with the Kabbalistic view that God may be most effectively approached through blowing the horn, for this is an act of embodying the divine voice.[48] As such, Yitzhak Shlomo's use of the horn emerges as an attempt to recuperate what Theodore Reik called "the totemistic god" of old,[49] extracting it from a communal language that has been, so the film seems to argue, corrupted through its reduction to social uses. It is no wonder then that the first recipient of the Shofar sound, the pregnant neighbor's daughter, reacts in horror. For as Reik explains, the desired objective of Shofar blowing in contemporary Judaism is to shock listeners with memories of a time when objects such as a horn echoed the incarnate, audible presence of God on earth.

FIGURE 16. Yitzhak (Daniel Peri Nadav) blows the shofar. From *Shofar* (Daniel Syrkin, 2001).

With this in mind, the film's resolution may be understood as allowing room for a change in the status of prayer language. If at the beginning of *Shofar*, Yitzhak Shlomo destroyed the blessings of his father's Mezuzah by blackening them out with ink, at the end he finds himself being part of the practice of uttering sacred language. The pronouncement of "Mezuzot" nevertheless does not mark entry into the order of Halakhic language and Law of the Father, so much as the release of language from Halakhic constraints, drawing it near to the unmediated voice of divinity. This move, in turn, spurs a complementary gesture from the father: he draws an image, which like the sound of the Shofar, is a nonverbal form that may avoid the trappings of communal words and manifest more authentically the presence of God. That this "coming together" between father and son occurs away from a group setting seems to underscore the film's main point: a revolution in worship can only be realized in relation to individual effort—that is, in the context of personal Devekut.

Similar negotiations appear in Religious Zionist filmmaker Shalom Hagar's made-for-TV drama *Shrouds* (2010). At the outset of the film, protagonist Nachum finds new employment in the religious organization responsible for burial in Israel, Chevra Kadisha. He is taken on as a trainee and is taught the ins and outs of Judaic burial rites. As the plot unfolds, it becomes clear that Nachum's choice in seeking this position, which places him on the margins of religious society, involved a particular familial tragedy: some time before, his baby girl died of SIDS; now, as his wife is pregnant again and on bed rest, he feels the need to resolve this previous loss and find room for the new life that is about to enter the household. This negotiation of death on a daily basis takes an emotional toll on Nachum, especially when he has to take care of a couple whose infant had just died. Yet through the work, and his meaningful encounters with colleagues, the protagonist ultimately attains peace of mind, and after his child is born, also a renewed comfort in parenthood.

At the center of *Shrouds*, so it seems, is an attempt to unveil the hidden practices of burial preparation, which have rarely been shown on screen within a Judaic-themed film. In revealing these practices, the film also foregrounds their inherent ambiguities, which derive from the complex standing of the dead body within Judaism. The corpse is considered in Judaic thought to be the most profane form of human corporeality. Accordingly, the avowed function of Judaism's burial ritual is to resanctify the body before laying it to rest, while contextualizing the death to the deceased's loved ones through a meaningful framework of actions and symbols. Yet more than acts that attempt to facilitate a transition between existential states, these rituals function most in the form of containment. In the various scenes of bathing and cleansing the corpse, one can infer a desire to block away the spread of its contamination into the social body; the same desire operates in the Judaic custom of hiding the dead body for most parts of the burial procedure, including its interment covered in shrouds from head to toe, which seems to support a regime of visibility that denies the existence of profane death. For practitioners of the preparation services, as the film clearly shows, the rote performance of ritualistic acts allows for a certain distance from the corpse's "taintedness." For the mourners, the ritual's assigning of symbolic meaning to various parts of its process serves to sublimate raw emotion into thoughtful comprehension. Yet as Nachum's case proves, the ritual, as a practice of bracketing, is insufficient in containing emotion to and intimacy with the deceased; rather, the act of containment delivers a promise of tranquility that is not realized, thereby creating the lingering sense of loss. Consequently, the protagonist's journey seeks to connect personal and communal religious life—to find the place of corporeal intimacy and unbridled emotion in ritualistic acts whose purpose is the regulation and even exclusion of such elements.

The film's emphasis on the minutia of burial preparation, which turn it into a "burial procedural," exposes the challenges that this search is bound to encounter. For the mourners, their exclusion from intimate contact with the deceased allows the ritual to perform its ordering tasks, setting up boundaries between the living and the dead in an effort to maintain communal decorum. These boundaries are breached only when grief demands a place within the ritual, as when in one scene, a woman and her son go into the preparation room, and at a moment of spontaneous emotion, the son breaks out of his ritualistic positioning and throws himself onto the corpse of his father. If the ritual is able to minimize such points of interpenetration between live subjects and dead bodies, it is mainly for the benefit of mourners and not for those in charge of burial. The undertakers are bound by a state of constant proximity to the deceased due to their intense handling of the body through rites of cleansing. While the preoccupation with procedural detail creates an invisible barrier between mortician and corpse, such separation is not complete, for as one of Nachum's coworkers explains, some things, like the stench of death, cannot be washed away from one's skin. Nachum's challenge within this ritual is to negotiate the intimacy of a bond with the dead: to find a corporeal and emotional connection to the corpse, which is not blocked off through the concentration on ritualistic detail, but that also does not overshadow and disrupt meaningful connections with the living. It is a way of opening up a formalized communal ritual, with its inscribed social hierarchies, to the fluidity of individual sentiment—or rather, recognizing that such sentiment has existed in the ritual all along.

The tension between the formal distance that ritual creates and the place of intimacy that may be occasioned are also evident in the film's stylistic treatment of the burial preparation. Great effort is undertaken to foreground the beauty of ritualistic preparation, using various aesthetic means. Thus, for example, the high contrast–low key lighting provides the corpse with an ethereal look, which is augmented by the flickering of light through the drops of purifying water that are frequently applied to the dead body; the proliferation of close-ups of isolated body parts accentuate the delicate and fragile nature of their anatomy; and the austere decor separates the corpse from the background in such a way as to add a sense of purity and symmetry to the ritual setting while suspending it from the time and place of everyday practices. These stylistic measures seemingly turn the body into a work of art that demands spectatorial distance. In this respect, they correspond to the dead bodies in the opening of Ingmar Bergman's *Persona* (1966), which are represented in fragmentation, placed against a neutral and blank background. The difference between the two texts, however, is that the bodies in the Bergman film are shown to be static, removed from the setting of ritual preparation, as *tableaux non-vivant*. The dead bodies in *Shrouds*, however, are presented amid the process of their preparation, and accordingly, the abstracting qualities aestheticization bestows on them are placed in constant friction with the movement of the undertaker's hands over limbs, which brings concrete reality to bear. These movements, accentuated by accompanying camera motion, "dirty" the cleanliness of the hyperaestheticized body of a Bergman corpse, and insert intimacy where once there was only alienation.

While the burial preparation scenes push these meanings aggressively to the fore, it is in the scenes of prayer that one finds their most nuanced and elegant treatment. Three of these scenes take on a crucial importance in this context. In the first, occurring at the beginning of the film, a Chevra Kadisha employee is shown teaching Nachum how to recite the *Merciful God* funeral dirge (*El Malei Rachamim*). The way by which this prayer is explained places an emphasis on its communal service to the mourners. Though God is the subject of the prayer, He is absent from the undertaker's consideration; rather, what is stressed is the performative elements of the recitation and how they may respond to and affect particular emotional responses in the listening audience, bringing it together. Thus, at a certain moment in recitation, the coworker explains, an undertaker must pause in order to "let the family feel like [he] is totally with them"; and, when a time comes to include the deceased's name in the prayer, the recitation must be in a low voice to indicate both respect and emphasis. The undertaker, by this account, is not emotionally invested in the prayer but rather performs investment for the benefit of his audience; and then, as the coworker states, "after 15–20 minutes it's over and done with, and you can be at home drinking coffee." The communal language of prayer, in this context, is therefore meant to create the image of a bereaved collective rather than an appeal to God. But it is a hollow language, absent of a personal dimension.

The second significant scene involving prayer takes place later in the film. Here Nachum is faced with a couple who, as previously mentioned, has just lost their infant child. The experience of preparing the baby for burial proves unbearable for the protagonist, considering his own tragic personal history. Consequently, he chooses to accompany the bereaving couple in prayer. The prayer, *Baruch Dayan Emet*, seeks to explain away the death as the result of God's true judgment, and thus contain the disruption of its effects on the regime of belief and the routine of observance. By asking the parents to repeat the words of the blessing, Nachum essentially forces on them a framework of containment that denies their grief, deemed excessive and unruly by Judaic doxa. The parents, in turn, find it difficult to locate a place within this communal prayer for their emotion and intimacy with the dead; the language, which seeks to restore order to a collective-in-crisis, cannot account for their loss or their rage. It is thus in the gaps of the prayer, at the moments when the speaker needs to pause between the utterances of verses to recover composure, that spontaneous, personalized sentiment and even Devekut claim a presence in the ritual. It is also where physical intimacy is achieved, over and against the distantiating procedures of burial, as is seen in Nachum's attempt to reach out to the mourning father by placing his hand on the man's arm.

FIGURE 17. Nachum (Kais Nashif) in solitary prayer. From *Shrouds* (Shalom Hagar, 2010).

The entrance of emotion and intimacy into ritual reaches its apex in the third prayer scene, which takes place at the film's denouement. The meeting with the infant's bereaved parents had unsettled Nachum, and in returning home, he sits with his wife, and the two begin to weep together. This cathartic moment is then quickly followed by an extended presentation of Nachum's prayer the morning after. The prayer is for the most part shown in a long (90-second) static shot, from a relatively wide angle. The extended duration of the shot draws the spectator's attention to the changing rhythms of Nachum's movement in prayer. While the gestures presented are not separated from the norms of prayer, their intensity, heightened through a burst of music, underlies the presence of Nachum's emotional life in the ritual. This is not a case of performance without intimacy, as in the first scene, nor does it entail the breaking of ritual for the purpose of allowing emotion to surface, as in the second scene. Rather, what is presented is a seamless integration of emotion and intimacy into the ritual itself—the same holistic relationship between rite as a communal ordering mechanism and the personal as a vibrant, unruly force, which Nachum attempted to locate within burial practices. Importantly, for the first time in the film, the protagonist does not perform a ritual in relation to another dead or living being. This prayer is performed in seclusion from wife, mourners, or coworkers, and its words are recited silently, as if to further emphasize the absence of the community that is mirrored through them. It is a singular moment when Nachum attempts to enter into a personal relation with his God—a divine being that is not bound by the social barriers that Judaism continuously tries to uphold through its communal rituals. In this respect, to use Abraham J. Heschel's formulation, the film touches on "our great problem" with Jewish prayer: namely, "how not to let the principle of Kevaa [fixity] impair the power of Kavvanah."[50] Its answer to this issue seems to be that only through actively securing a place for the individual in a fixed collective ritual can one potentially activate intentionality and learn, via divine dialogue, "the art of awareness of God, the art of sensing His presence in our daily lives."[51]

If *Shrouds* and *Shofar* express deep suspicion of institutionalized, communal prayer practices and language, it is never to the extent of their outright dismissal. Other texts, however, are far more dismissive. One such film is *To Take a Wife* (2004), written and directed by the brother-sister team of Shlomi and the late Ronit Elkabetz. Inspired by the filmmakers' childhood experiences, the plot follows a Masorti family during a particularly challenging weekend. The mother, Viviane, and the father, Eliyahu, are at odds with each other. She feels stifled by his over-bearing behavior; he feels threatened by her constant pleas, complaints, and threats. Their apartment becomes a veritable war zone, with their children getting caught in the crossfire. The sudden appearance of an old flame leads Viviane to imagine an alternate existence, beyond the constraints of her marriage. Yet she ultimately declines his advances, recognizing that an escape would compromise her standing with her off-spring. She thus stays put, and when Shabbat comes around, the marital feud erupts again, in earnest. This time no resolution is met, with each side breaking away to its neutral corner, Viviane to her living room sofa, and Eliyahu to his seat at the synagogue.

As with the Elkabetz siblings' subsequent collaborations (*7 Days* [2008], *Gett: The Trial of Viviane Amsallem* [2014]), *To Take a Wife* high-lights the tension between a rigid communal ritual and the demands of personal desire and interpersonal dynamics. Within its diegesis, rite is used internally to maintain peace, order, and harmony inside the home (*Shlom Beit*) as well as externally to keep up appearances and sustain a legitimate standing within the community. It thus appears to have less to do with divine dialogue and more with meeting the mundane needs of seeming respectful and demanding respect on a familial and greater social level. This operation of respectability, in turn, is bound by a gender asymmetry—of charting out not only the outer borders of the commu-nity but also the inner boundaries that separate male dominance and female subservience. The weight of tradition, and the overarching pres-ence of a masculine God, make it possible for the male characters of this and other Elkabetz films to foreclose on the liberties of the women in their lives, forcing them into disenfranchisement.

The sense of enclosure is foregrounded by the choice to shoot most of the film in the confines of the family's apartment, and largely using tight close frames. The constrained physical space that emerges as a result of this visual strategy seems to press Viviane into action. She is aware of her compromised role within her family; she understands that the religious authority and the collective image that it sustains give her little room to maneuver in achieving a greater measure of freedom. Yet with her back to the wall, she has no choice but to resist. This resistance comes, among other things, in the form of subverting rituals, and most visibly, those of the Shabbat. For Eliyahu, religious observance is key to setting himself apart from his wife and other people who are less devout; it is the hierarchal position from which to assert strength. Therefore, when he demands that his wife keep the Shabbat and forces the same observance on his children, it is with the intent of maintaining his stature as a respected ruler of the home. Viviane's subsequent nonconformity to the letter of Shabbat rites thus acts as a rebuttal to the state of marginality imposed on her by religious patriarchy and its communal ritualism; she places herself outside of patriarchal reach, in an unregulated and personalized realm of operation.

This very challenge so frustrates Eliyahu that he must retreat from his home to the synagogue—a space where an all-male congregation can still claim its collective identity through ingathering and a common language of prayer. Fittingly, the synagogue scene is shot in an uncharacteristic wide angle, which shows the congregation that is solidified through the communal act of praying. Within this shot, Eliyahu is positioned in the middle, on an elevated podium; he reads the Torah scroll as part of the prayer rite and thus situates himself as the voice of the collective. Yet the burden of carrying this voice seems too great, so he breaks down during the service and begins to cry. The recited words from the Book of Hosea, describing the way in which the prophet abused his "whore" wife amid fears that she would leave him for a former lover, seem to demand his endorsement of an androcentric collective vision as a condition for his achievement of popular respect. Eliyahu, however, is visibly distressed by this demand, for reasons that remain unclear. Perhaps it is frustration at his inability to rise to the standards of masculine behavior, as prescribed by his people. Such may be too harsh a criticism toward a man who, after all, is affectionate enough toward his wife to not believe in the legitimacy of Hosea's unbearably harsh punitive measures. It thus appears as if Eliyahu's silence comes as an almost reluctant subversion of the constraints of collectivity, tantamount to Viviane's own dismissal of Shabbat as a ritual that places her at a disadvantage. He is absent of words that would express his subjectivity and hence is only able to operate through silence—through nonlanguage. As such, Eliyahu severs, if only momentarily, all connection to the congregation, and the god to which it prays—a god whose good graces have now seemingly disappeared. And while his taciturnity carries the traces of trauma at God's disappearance, in Buberian terms it also permits a different kind of dialogue with a divinity unbound by mortal definitions: for "only silence before the *Thou*—silence of *all* tongues, silent patience in the undivided word that precedes the formed and vocal response—leaves the *Thou* free, and permits man [*sic*] to take his stand with it in the reserve where the spirit is not manifest, but *is*."[52]

If the "death of God" remains an implicit theme within *To Take a Wife*, in Raphaël Nadjari's *Tehilim* (2007) it becomes a central preoccupation. At the outset of the narrative, an observant family undergoes an upheaval: while driving his two children—the eldest Menachem and the youngest David—the father Eli drives the car off the road; after Menachem goes out to find help, he returns to the car to discover that his father has vanished. This disappearance throws everyone into disarray. Eli's father and brother demand that the family home be proclaimed "a place of prayer" where people could come and recite chapters from the Book of Psalms so as to hasten Eli's return. On the other hand, Eli's wife Alma, who is less observant, tries to close ranks with her offspring and reclaim the familial space for her own. Caught in the middle, Menachem first supports his grandfather's enterprise of prayer, which by now

Figure 18. Eliyahu (Simon Abkarian) breaks down during communal services. From *To Take a Wife* (Ronit and Shlomi Elkabetz, 2004).

has evolved into the publication of prayer books under Eli's name. In an effort to widen the circle of praying, he convinces David to distribute the books together to passersby on the street, along with some money stolen from his mother, meant to be given to charity (*Tzdaka*). When the grandfather and uncle hear of this, they become infuriated with Menachem, claiming that the prayer books were meant only for Eli's community members and not for random people. Upset by their reaction, which he seems to interpret as a betrayal, Menachem returns home and asks for his mother's forgiveness. In the end, Alma, Menachem, and David are shown to receive a certification of Eli's missing person status, thereby suggesting their resignation to the fact of the father's disappearance.

As a text about modern devotional existence, *Tehilim* deals directly with a crisis in prayer. This understanding is made explicit in the opening sequence that shows a religious study session, in which Eli and Menachem participate. At the heart of the discussion is the question of how to pray when one does not know the direction of Jerusalem. The rabbi proposes that God, and not His residence at the Temple, is of import in the act of prayer. Accordingly, praying is a matter of directing one's heart not to a physical site but to a metaphysical center that defines the Jews as a community of belief; or in the words of the rabbi: "if one is standing in the East, he should turn towards the West; if one is in the West, he should turn towards the East; if in the South, he should turn towards the North; and if in the North, he should turn towards the South; and so, all of Israel shall turn their hearts to one place." This community, in turn, is defined differently than the collective known as the "Jewish People"; it is not bound by the collectivizing impulses whose symbol is the historical-religious capital of Jerusalem, but rather by a mystical unity that connects—in Buber's sense—the *personal* experiences of God.

Quickly after, however, the film challenges the resilience of this unity through Eli's disappearance, which symbolizes the potential disappearance of God as the community's focal point. The grandfather and uncle respond to this disappearance through disavowal: they assert God's continued presence at the heart of the Jewish people by clinging to Judaism's collective rites, and they use this assertion, ipso facto, as a supposed guarantee for Eli's future reappearance at the heart of the family. Alma, on the other hand, was bound to a sense of greater unity only through her husband, and with his absence, can no longer sustain much faith in the communal rite; theologically speaking, her trauma enacts the predicament of the prayer wounded, where neither the solace of belief nor the freedom of atheism are available, but only the constant negotiating of perspectives from the past when God was alive and from the present when He is long dead.[53] In the face of these two avenues, the film's protagonist, Menachem, is asked to make a choice, and this choice is appropriately manifested through a gradual shift in his view on praying.

While prayer in the film is mainly discussed by characters as a petitionary form meant to influence God's favor, its main function seems to be to create a sense of collectivity, a "strength in numbers" to overcome the fear that the disappearance will be permanent. Or at least this is the initial function of praying for Menachem, who, when Alma asks his grandfather and uncle to take their prayers outside of the family home, shouts that they must stay and pray because he needs "a family." This need for an expanded family is also what motivates him to distribute the prayer books to people on the street, and thereby create a wider web of support. Yet in performing this act, he discovers the limits of Jewish prayer as a communal form. If, as the rabbi in the opening sequence claims, prayer allows "all of Israel to turn their hearts to one place," then for Menachem's grandfather and uncle, there is a need to delimit this fluid mystical communion to those who are found to be occupying the proper "devotion." In this context, the grandfather is especially discriminatory, not only against people outside of Eli's congregation but also against Alma, whose religious education—and by implication, her moral fiber—he finds lacking. Though it takes him time to internalize this, Menachem subsequently comes to the conclusion that for his grandfather, his "spiritual guide," a community of prayer is more about exclusion than inclusion, about collecting rather than communing.

In giving up on this vision, Menachem aligns himself with his mother and her pragmatic approach to life in the shadow of absence. This shadow has an atomizing effect on those who are unwilling to ignore it and pursue a sense of collectivity through a communal language of ritual. If God is dead, then humanity becomes the world's center; to accept that, the film seems to say, is to accept a redefinition of communalism as one founded on the individual, or at the utmost, on his or her immediate family. Such is the message rendered visible by the final sequence, which ends on Alma, Menachem, and David sitting in silence at a Jerusalem bus stop after a visit to police headquarters. The immediate family becomes the universe, joined not by a shared tradition but by a shared trauma, a painful absence that must be worked through but cannot be denied. Their bond at this moment is forged without words, perhaps because language, as displayed in prayer, has failed them. In a reality where God's disappearance is proclaimed, prayer as petition is meaningless. And in any case, it seems to have always been more focused on solidifying a collective's boundaries, and grounding them in discrimination, than in approaching God. But does this mean that prayer has no place in such a universe, shrunk to nuclear family size? As in *To Take a Wife*, the silence, accentuated through the use of a lengthy take, looks to delineate a new mode of worship, which draws from personal religious life and not the communal power of traditional rite in order to achieve the goal of self-transcendence. In its sphere of nonlanguage, this quietude suggests that it is possible to isolate the Halakhic God, the one defined by language, as the deity that has disappeared, and consequently to reclaim the palpable presence of an unfathomable God as the center of a different kind of communion—one absent of the collectivizing impulses signified by the Jerusalem Temple as preeminent symbol of the "Jewish People." The extent to which this proposition is legitimized remains unclear, for the abrupt cut ending the final shot-sequence leaves little room for a comforting resolution to the pain of God's supposed death.

While such films as *Tehilim* and *To Take a Wife* point to the disappearance of God and the resulting crisis of prayer, others seem to counter such troublesome possibilities with affirmations of both God and prayer, as praying appears to elicit miraculous responses from a divine source. Since these cinematic texts stand at the center of the next chapter, they are not discussed in detail here; rather, a representative work—*God's Neighbors* (2012), directed by Masorti-born filmmaker Meni Yaish, who had "undergone some process of repentance [*Teshuva*]"[54]—can be used to show how the patterns of prayer representation operate in such films. The film's protagonist Avi, a born-again Bratslav Hasid with an avid interest in electronic music, lives in an urban working-class neighborhood. Together with his two repentant friends Kobi and Yaniv, he enforces religious observance on residents and neighbors, oftentimes through violent means. During their various run-ins with Halakha violators, Avi

FIGURE 19. Alma (Limor Goldstein, *right*), Menachem (Michael Moshonov, *left*), and David (Yonathan Alster, *center*) sit in silence at a Jerusalem bus stop. From *Tehilim* (Raphaël Nadjari, 2007).

and his friends meet Miri, who becomes a target for harassment as a result of her "immodest" attire. The young Hasid quickly discovers that he has feelings for Miri and begins courting her, to the great chagrin of his vigilante squad mates. The budding romance causes a rift between the friends. Consequently, Avi is not present when Kobi is stabbed by two Palestinians amid a turf war altercation. Struck by remorse, he agrees to join some local gangsters on a revenge spree into Jaffa. At the height of this rampage, however, he is faced with the choice of shooting an Arab resident of the city, and in spite of his friends' urging, decides not to. This decision, in turn, leads him at the film's conclusion to forgo the path of violence and build a loving relationship with Miri instead.

Through its narrative elaboration, *God's Neighbors* supports two concomitant Hasidic beliefs: "that God is invisible yet omnipresent in His created world, that the world is thus clothed in an endless variety of guises, all of them equally illusory, all of them in fact disguises, concealing the single, too awesome countenance";[55] and that there is "a human obligation to lay bare the divine element in all things and gain knowledge of the unity of existence despite the multiplicity that greets the eye and to nullify the distinct and separate existence of things in one's thought."[56] In this framework, the film positions Avi as carrying

out the "human obligation" of exposing God's "awesome countenance."
As a religious repentant, he stands at the crossroads of secular and religious social practices, and his lifestyle clearly shows a seamless oscillation between the two categories. Yet unlike his fellow repentants on
the modesty squad, Avi ultimately deserts an oppositional stance that
favors one social order at the expense of the other and instead posits
the possibility of a unified social whole—one indicating, and perhaps
even repairing, a state of cosmic unity. In accordance with this position,
the protagonist's musicality plays a vital role. Not only is Avi enacting a
meaningful cultural dialogue by combining religious language and secular style in his music, but he is also, by the very choice of music as a
means of expression, gesturing toward the medium's role in the Bratslav
perception of a unified universe. For R. Nachman, as Ora Wiskind-Elper
explains, musical expression was "a complex vehicle: most basically, it
is a precious component of human creative experience; yet it serves,
as well, as a metaphor to speak of the most esoteric truths."[57] These
two functions were inseparable in the rabbi's eyes. The metaphorical
power of music resided in its ability to effect unity in a manner that
is not easily amenable—and that could actually be seen as defiant to—
categorical conceptualization; consequently, it was helpful for R. Nachman
to speak of the sphere of divine oneness as a melody that orchestrates
the variety of songs existing in nature.

Whether this integrative capacity turns Avi into "an Israeli Every-
man"[58] (as Yaron Peleg argues) or into the emblem of "Mizrahi-Breslov
shared territory"[59] at Israel's periphery (as Merav Alush-Levron claims),
what remains vital to his message of communal unity is a reliance on collective religious forms. Such is particularly evident in the film's opening
and closing, which feature significant prayer-centered rites. In the first
scene, Avi performs the Kiddush prayer that ushers in the holy Sabbath,
and shortly after, spearheads a violent altercation with local youngsters
whose loud music disturbs his Saturday rest. Contrastingly, in the last
scene, the protagonist, his father, and Miri, partake in the Havdalah
prayer ceremony, which hails the end of Shabbat and the beginning of
the work week. Together, these sequences function as symbolic book-
ends to Avi's coming-of-age story: as Peleg explains, "the opening scene
'sanctifies' Avi and anoints him as a kind of local Jeanne d'Arc who goes
out to fight for God and country. The concluding scene shows that he

has matured and learned to differentiate—to literally make *Havdalah*, which means 'separation' in Hebrew. Both scenes take place around the Sabbath table. In the opening scene, Avi and his father dine alone. In the concluding scene Miri has joined them as Avi's bride-to-be. This neat and happy ending is a reward for Avi's good behavior and a fulfillment of his quest for meaning and purpose."[60] Not only, however, is this a confirmation of Avi's arrival at inner unity, but of the possibility of facilitating outer unity as well. Thus, for Alush Levron, "the last scene gives us a glimpse into the new and harmonious world that Avi has achieved. . . . The Havdalah rite and this harmonic familial scene signal Avi's release from the entanglement he felt during the Kiddush ritual that opened the film. At the end of the Havdalah, the film's concluding song, played on voice-over, expresses love for humankind and self-recognition: 'Love your neighbor as you love yourself, and know one's inner soul.'"[61]

Seen through these two prayer rituals, it appears that *God's Neighbors* calls for a return to the traditional collectivity of mainline Judaism—so much so that Peleg reads this message as "certainly ironic"[62] considering Israeli Zionism's former rejection of this collectivity as a legitimate social bond. The irony is nevertheless mitigated when considering that the most poignant moments of prayer in the film—those that "generate miracles and function as a mystic means for endowing meaning to various upcoming events"[63]—take place away from collective rituals, or as such rituals break down. Two such moments stand out. In the first, following a quarrel with Koby and Yaniv over his reluctance to participate in violent regulation, Avi goes to the seashore and performs prayer in the Bratslav fashion of Hitbodedut. He speaks to God mostly in the unstructured and informal form of everyday address, explaining that he loves His rules but also loves Miri who flaunts these rules, and asking for a sign from above as to whether she is the one for him. Later, during a casual conversation, Avi explains to Miri that when one randomly opens the Book of Psalms to read a verse, this verse will testify to the person's current existential state. When Miri follows this operation, the verse arbitrarily chosen is the foundational articulation of Judaism's position on proper womanhood—"In her chamber, the king's daughter is glorious." The sudden arrival of this well-known phrase, for Avi, comes as a divinely ordained sign that Miri is right for him—that she is a favored child of God, sent to aid in his devotion rather than lead him astray.

This "miracle" was already foreshadowed through the remarkable conclusion of the Hitbodedut prayer, where by Alush-Levron's account, Avi's immersion into the water at dawn is pictured vividly and beautifully as "the expression of the sublime and draws us closer . . . to the same profound inner spiritual dimension that Avi experiences in his unmediated meeting with God."

The second instance takes place later, as Avi drives with a few vigilantes to exact revenge on Arab residents of Jaffa for the hurt put on his friend. During the drive, the protagonist reaches for his Book of Psalms and starts reading from it. The verse read arrives from Psalms 144: "Praise be to the Lord my Rock, who trains my hands for war, my fingers for battle." Rather than accept this message literally, as he did earlier with Miri, Avi seems to invest himself in the quote's deeper purpose, a plea to God for salvation from one's enemies. Through an intimate rapport with divinity, he tacitly recognizes that inner hatred, rather than an outer threat, is his worst enemy, and as a result, decides not to fire on his intended Arab victim, whose pleading stare creates "a short moment of mutual human recognition." The significance of this miraculous transformation is further asserted through the subsequent scene, where in a congregational prayer at the synagogue, as his head is covered by his father's shawl during the "priest's blessing" (*Birkat Cohanim*), Avi begins to cry. While the scene begins with what, in Alush-Levron's mind, is "the sublime" manifesting through "a flash of a supreme light,"[64] its sublimity arrives at an apex in the extended moment of weeping. This moment may signify the collapse of collective ritual, but it also points to the significant role tears may play in the context of prayer, according to R. Nachman: namely, that of "completing the process of connection with God . . . an internal movement of bonding, the successful outcome of belabored spiritual work reaching its final destination."[65]

The potency of these private devotions does not invalidate the significance of collective rites that surround them throughout the film, including in its final moments. It does nevertheless define personal "mystical prayer" as the privileged mode of spiritual engagement, which legitimizes communal prayers as its faint shadows, meant less for approaching God as to creating a community of faith in His name. As such, *God's Neighbors* registers a need for reorienting traditional Judaism in the manner of Buber's neo-Hasidic project—to allow, through the individual's

FIGURE 20. Avi (Roy Assaf) crying, covered by his father's prayer shawl. From *God's Neighbors* (Meni Yaish, 2012).

idiosyncratic appeal, for a truer and more authentic relationship with God than is presumably offered by communal worship. Yet though Avi's actualization of true communion does manage to bleed into and revitalize communal practice, the process in itself seems particularly fragile, for it rests on the individual's power to resist the demands of a tradition he or she ultimately wishes to affirm. Consequently, even in a cinematic text that supports Judaic faith, an unresolved tension between the personal and the collective, the free-formed and the regimented, still exists. Through its existence we may therefore detect the difficulty of incorporating religious ritual into an Israeli social ethos so persistently overdetermined by the supposed "death of God."

Film as Ritual: Spectatorship and Prayer

Through their shared thematic focus, the representations already discussed foreground the significance of self-transcendence via ritual in Israeli-Judaic life. At the same time, and on an even more implicit level, these cinematic texts also point toward something else—the suggestive relationship between the self-transcendence of religious ritual and that of cinematic spectatorship. For as Vivian Sobchack makes clear, "films focused on 'spiritual' or 'religious' subject matter [tend] not only to represent but also *present* and *solicit* transcendent or 'spiritual' states of being from each viewer."[66] They perform this task by waking us through thematic focus to "a major conundrum of cinematic figuration and sensual intelligibility,"[67] whereby our experience of the screen has to do with being materially bound yet simultaneously sensing "a unique exteriority of being—an *ek-stasis*—that locates us 'elsewhere' and 'otherwise' [than] our lived body's 'here' and 'now.'" This state of "transcendence in immanence," Sobchack further notes, "occurs constantly in myriad circumstances both trivial and significant, quotidian and ritual—including those such as going to church or the movies, in which *ex-static* transcendence is not only purposefully solicited but also formally shaped and experientially heightened."[68]

What is suggested in Sobchack's argument—the analogy between filmgoing and partaking in liturgy within congregational spaces of worship (especially in the context of the rituals of Mass)—is in fact quite a common assertion within religion and film scholarship.[69] Representative of these positions, and influential in their articulation on the subfield as a whole, has been the work of religious scholar S. Brent Plate. In several studies, Plate countered religious tradition's longtime rejection of cinema as dangerously secular, arguing instead "that religion and film are *like* each other, and that their similarities exist on a formal level."[70] This formal similarity, according to him, is founded on the operation of both as "worldmaking": "a performative drama in which humans [like] costume designers and liturgists, scriptwriters and sermon givers, cinematographers and saints, projectionists and priests . . . attempt to make meaning of the spaces, times, and people that make up our life."[71] Plate's view sees the performative function of worldmaking as centered on re-creation, which is to say a process where reality is taken apart and then reassembled in a new way. Though this "new world" is distinct from the "real world," the two remain bound by each other. The existence of such a bond, in turn, "puts people in touch with the world again in new ways. In both [religion and film], one is connected with their world only by experiencing another world."[72]

On the basis of this understanding, Plate attempts to further strengthen the comparison between religion and cinema by arguing that myth and ritual, decisive terms in religious nomenclature, are also central to the operation of cinematic "re-creation." In cinema and in religion, according to him, the re-created world is mythical in the sense that it operates as a cosmogony, offering the individual meaningful ways to connect with a universal order. As such, myth is played out in both spheres as a way of warding off meaninglessness by providing answers to existential questions of origin, identity, and purpose. These answers, in turn, become available to society through the practice of ritual retelling and reenactment, which invites audience attention and participation. Accordingly, this argument stipulates that films function like rituals, taking mythical content as their "expressive" dimension and actualiz- ing it via concrete "formality." This formality operates on the level of the filmic text, as when Plate argues that "filmmakers work with and manipulate afilmic space, time, form, movement, color and sound in ways that look and feel similar to how rituals are experienced through the use of sensual things like flowers, music, candles, symbols, cosmic relations and images."[73] It also operates on the level of spectatorial con- text, separating film viewing from everyday experience and bestowing on it, as in "the Jewish tradition of the Sabbath," the ritualistic aura of "an active, vital time."[74] Together, these elements stand as the foundation of Plate's central analogy, where "the *altar* and the *screen* are . . . structured and function in comparable fashion,"[75] presumably inviting the subject to partake in a liturgy and assume the posture of prayer.

As far as the model presented by Plate relates cinema to a dynamic of religious ritual, and specifically a dynamic of prayer, it seems most vulnerable to criticism on the grounds that it equates cinema's ritual- istic expressivity with the category of myth. Plate's reliance on myth allows him to surface a historical continuation between the sphere of religious tradition and that of cinema, arguing that film art appropri- ates religion's myths across time ("transmediality") and updates them to the requirements of the here and now ("intermediality").[76] The benefits of such a conceptual move are arguably overshadowed by the disadvan- tage of constricting the world re-created on screen to the contours of a religious myth—contours that assume some cosmic structure, which is organized through a spiritual or godly being and foregrounds a vision of a better reality in light of it. An argument that films always point to an idealized existence sanctioned by a spiritual beyond seems incongruous with the cinematic landscape's actual diversity. Even those filmic texts that relate directly to a religious framework do not necessarily function in this way, as the aforementioned representations of Jewish prayer in Judaic-themed Israeli cinema clearly indicate. These seem less invested in allowing access to the world as it "ought to be" and more with manifesting the challenges of the world "as it is."

Should this mean, however, that the comparison between film and religious ritual is to be cast aside as ineffectual and even erroneous? Such an assertion would overly discount the lingering presence of a film-as-ritual relationship within popular discourse, as encapsulated in J. Hoberman and Jonathan Rosenbaum's statement that "purely as phenomenon, the cinema has provided the simulation of religious epiphany on an unprecedented, assembly-line scale."[77] If this presence is taken as testament to some bigger truth about film experience's cultural standing as "privileged behavior," then perhaps it would be better not to dismiss the film-as-ritual comparison but rather recover it in a different, more qualified way. Inspired by the lessons of the films already discussed, the following suggests one possible mode of recovery, which does not stress the specific contents of films/rituals and their relationship to myth but rather focuses on their standing "purely as phenomenon"—that is, on the experiential-phenomenological dimension, as it interlinks and defines their formality and expressivity. To render this comparison concrete and detailed, the category of religious ritual is discussed only in relation to Buber's Hasidic-inspired model of perception-based prayer, a decision that both recognizes the customary definition of prayer as epitomizing religious practice and the particular relevance of praying that is linked "with the life of the senses" to comparisons with cinema's specific sensorial operation. In terms of the category of film, the discussion makes use of Sobchack's influential model of cinematic spectatorship, primarily for its phenomenological emphasis. Before commencing on a comparative description of these models, it would be worthwhile to first articulate its desired outcome. Thus, through an analogy between film spectatorship (phenomenologically understood) and perception-based prayer, it becomes apparent that both forms involve seeing the physical world as an introspective image (an internal vision "from the inside out") of a transparent (if not outright disembodied) "body." In this perceptual act, the relationship of conjunction and dissonance between world (as a physical continuum) and worldview (as a parsing out of this continuum) is unveiled in its utmost intimacy and intensity. As a result of this impression, and under the aegis of formal means that separate the experience from "everyday life" and heighten its effects, the participating subject feels as if he or she has gained a privileged perspective on the intersubjective structures of being-in-the-world—a measure of ekstasis or transcendence of the self toward a broader perspective on the modus operandi of human existence.

A phenomenological understanding of film spectatorship is grounded in phenomenology's perspective on the dimensions of "being-in-the-world." At the risk of oversimplifying an already elusive philosophy, phenomenology aims to provide an account of our known reality through an intimate engagement with the world of experience—the "life-world" (*Lebenswelt*).[78] Our life-world is not reducible to an object (a planet, and such) but is the plane where things appear as themselves—where they meaningfully cohere. This space, for phenomenologists, possesses a unity that evades definition and may only be sensed through the primal and primary operations of the body and consciousness. By virtue of being part of the world, human agents possess a unity that corresponds with that of the reality that surrounds them. Yet this unity is not one that can be simplified to "mirroring," which in turn indicates a certain fundamental separation between the human body and what lies outside of it, allowing the body to occupy a transcendental perspective over its exterior. Rather, body and worldly objects are related through an intimate relationship that, while not abolishing difference, does collect them into an uninterrupted texture of existence. Within this bond, the human body, actualized first and foremost through perception, interacts with the world in a manner that speaks of a tacit reciprocity. Out of the multiple possible modes of being-in-the-world, which make up human unity, a person projects himself or herself into the world *intentionally*, as if realizing a particular project. This intentionality makes manifest a particular facet of the world, a particular context, which gains meaning through the interaction (what Husserl explicates as the action of *Noesis* on *Noema*). In this, it is not so much that the subject constitutes the world as responds to an invitation to deal with the world in a certain way—to follow a possible path that is always already part of the unified horizon of possible experiences. The experience that is acquired herein is not reflective but perceptive, serving as the foundation for all future thought that attempts to define and organize the world "objectively." It discloses, in the words of Merleau-Ponty, a "world which precedes knowledge" and "of which knowledge always speaks."[79]

Judging by the account just given, it may seem as if phenomenology sees experiential familiarity with the world as achieved solipsistically. Yet this is not the case, since phenomenologists, while situating the embodied subject as the locus of "presuppositionless" experience, have also recognized the important contribution of intersubjectivity to subjective "being-in-the-world." Robert Sokolowski sets up the terms of this relationship in lucid fashion:

> When I experience a bodily object, such as a cube, I recognize it as an identity in a manifold of sides, aspects, and profiles. The manifold is dynamic; whatever perspective I may have on the cube at any moment, I can move myself or the cube and generate a new flow of sides, aspects, and profiles. . . . My experience is a mixture of the actual and potential: whenever certain sides and aspects are given, I cointend those that are not but that could be given if I were to change my position, perspective, ability to perceive and the like.
>
> The mixture of actual and potential is heightened when other perceivers come into play. If others are present, then I realize that when I see the object from this side, the others do actually see it from some other angle, an angle that I would possess if I were to move to where they are. What is potential for me is actual for them. The object therefore takes on a greater transcendence to me: it is not only what I see and could see, but also what they see at this moment. Furthermore, I appreciate the object as so transcending my own viewpoint: I see it precisely as being seen by others and not just by me. That level of its identity is given to me. The object is or can be given intersubjectively, and it is presented to me as such.[80]

Though somewhat simplified for heuristic reasons, Sokolowski's description is useful in clarifying how subjective and intersubjective modalities are interweaved in our engagement with the world. On the basis of a definition of the life-world as this common manifold, a horizon of possible significances that all beings occupy, phenomenologists spoke of the self's recognition of the Other as "someone *like* me." We are all somewhat undifferentiated, to the extent that our intentional agency is bound by shared organizations of existence. This commonality breeds identification, or in the words of Merleau-Ponty: "if I am consciousness turned toward things, I can meet in things the actions of another and find in them a meaning, because they are themes of possible activity of my own body."[81] Fundamentally, such identification is not deduced; rather, I *experience* the Other through our sense of bodily and affective togetherness. And this experience allows me to perceive the Other's embodied activity as manifesting an intentional project that may be different from mine, but nevertheless is not outside the realm of my pre-reflective intelligibility, and hence may be incorporated in some form or another into my own vision of being.

In spite of its importance, intersubjective identification has proven to be the most difficult challenge to the phenomenological desire of "returning to the things themselves"—which is to say, to our pre-reflective perception of "things." Such a return is meant to divulge a realm of total sensory involvement that Merleau-Ponty termed "wild thought" and associated with a child's immersion in the world. This immersion is gradually forsaken under the pressures of an intersubjective communication through signs, which prompt the child to adopt a notion of selfhood and enter into the codes of culture. As a system of categorical distinction that displaces the unity of the life-world, culture abstracts and distorts the child's "embedded" experience. It does not, however, entirely sever ties between experience and the life-world, for this connection allows culture-based knowledge to appear natural and all-encompassing (as if belonging to the world) instead of constructed and limited (as the product of intersubjective attempts at conceptualizing the world).

Phenomenologically speaking, cinema is not removed from these structures of being-in-the-world. Rather, as Sobchack has cogently argued, "cinema uses modes of embodied existence (seeing, hearing, physical and reflective moment) as the vehicle, the 'stuff,' the substance of its language" and "the *structures of direct experience* (the 'centering' and bodily situating of existence in relation to the world of objects and others) as the basis for the structure of its language."[82] Thus, the level of wild thought or meaning—"the pervasive and as yet undifferentiated significance of existence as it is lived rather than reflected upon"[83]—is

what constitutes the foundation of film experience. The filmic text "perceives and expresses itself wildly and pervasively before it articulates its
meanings more particularly and systematically as this or that kind of
signification, that is, as a specific cinematic trope or figure, a specific
set of generic configurations, a specific syntactical convention."[84] It is
this level to which viewers respond most profoundly and that provides
the cinematic form with its ground of legibility. Thus envisioned, for
Sobchack at least, the cinematic medium presents a special case in
human communication.

In spite of this shared foundation of being, our experience of film
is not equivalent to an isolated and direct human experience of reality.
Rather, to the extent that film provides us with access to the life-world
we all inhabit, it does so *intersubjectively*. In terms of the dynamics of
seeing, Sobchack argues that as a carrier of vision, the film is perceived by
the viewers as having a "body" of its own—a body "like their own"—that
is made possible by, but is nevertheless irreducible to, cinema's technology and its human operator. This body, according to her, "need not be
visible in its vision—just as we are not visible in our vision as it accom-
plishes its visual grasp of things other than itself." Yet, it is "always implicated in its vision, just as our whole being as embodied informs what
we see and makes us present to the visible even as the visible appears as
present to us."[85] Thus foreseen, the cinematic experience functions as a
doubled vision: as "a dialogical and dialectical engagement of *two* viewing subjects who also exist as visible objects (if of different material and
in different ways)."[86] Within this dialogue, as we incorporate the film's
vision into our own, we recognize it as the experience of an Other, entailing a certain gap, a "third" space of shared vision. Accordingly, Sobchack
explains, "the spectator's significant relation with the viewed view on the
screen is *mediated by, inclusive of*, but *not dictated by*, the film's viewing-
view. The spectator's experience of the moving picture, then, entails the
potential for both *intentional agreement* and *intentional argument* with
the film's visual and visible experience."[87]

If our engagement of film appropriates the basic form of human
intersubjective being-in-the-world, it is only to a degree. For, as Sobchack
reminds us, intersubjectivity entails the recognition of a sentient Other
who is "like me." What is directly given to the viewing subject is only the
Other's visible body, which is acknowledged as the expression of a parallel

consciousness. That perspective of another on the life-world—its own internal "introceptive image"—is never experienced directly but instead is inferred from the Other's visible posture. Such is not the case of cinematic experience, however. There, my encounter "does not present me with the other's activity of seeing as it is inscribed through and translated into the activity of a visible 'visual body.' Rather the film's activity of seeing is immanent and visible—given to my own vision as my own vision is given to me. The film's vision does not visibly appear as the 'other' side of vision (the other's 'visual body') but as vision lived through intentionally, introceptively, visually as 'mine.'"[88] This is not a case of inferring an internal vision, then; in contradistinction to a "standard" intersubjective experience of manifesting a life-world, here an internal vision is made visible for consumption by those to which it is external.

In presenting an introceptive image "from the inside out," film allows us to occupy the impossible position of *literally* seeing through another's eyes: of *directly* experiencing, "not just the objective world but the very structure and process of subjective, embodied vision."[89] As a result of this situation, we not only *perceive* but also *perceive perception*, arriving in turn at an awareness of the intersubjective manner by which we both experience and, even more importantly, establish knowledge of reality. Thus imagined, this awareness understands the visible in film experience not as world but rather as worldview that arrives from and is given through the material of the world, a representation that emerges from but is still separate from the "thing itself." This, in turn, allows us to produce, by Sobchack's account, "a *radical reflection* on the act of viewing and its relation to our being-in-the-world."[90] It may be argued that such a reflection is not always salient: the binding of self to screen through a shared ground of embodied existence can give the spectators the impression that they're viewing the world "as it is," laid out as *their particular viewed* rather than as a distinct introceptive image of another. For Sobchack at least, it is only at points of rupture in film experience, where the distance between "perceive perception" and "perception" becomes noticeable, that we begin to consciously see our perception as founded on a dialogue with other internal perceptions, which though emerging from the stuff of the life-world, nevertheless present a limited vision of it. At the same time, Sobchack's definition of this reflection as radical—which assumes critical distance as its only possible framework—may render it too narrow for engaging cinematic spectatorship as a whole. In contrast, a case can also be made that the immersive attention typifying "normative" spectatorship is always accompanied by the tacit acknowledgment that somehow, what I see is not entirely "mine" even as it appears as such and consequently always provides me with a subtle reflection, an undercurrent of a "phenomenology of vision." This undercurrent is buttressed through the formal separations of the conventional cinematic setting, which we *never lose sight of.* These arguably give—or at least contribute to—the impression that film viewing itself is "privileged" and hence "ritualistic"—which is to say, an event that, through the materials of everyday experience, detaches itself from this experience to offer a broader perspective on how it is (intersubjectively) constructed.

Prayer, at least according to Martin Buber's religious-existentialist account of the ritual, lends itself to a similar phenomenological description. In Buber's terminology, the world is marked by "an expansion into its own being and reversal to connection."[91] These movements, which serve as the foundation for worldly relationality, are embodied in the two basic existential attitudes occupied by human beings toward what is external to them: "separation" and "meeting." The first attitude does not involve a *true* engagement with reality; rather, it is performed internally, between the subject and an image of reality that must be dissected, analyzed, and possessed. In this mode, the subject "declares itself to be the bearer, and the world round about to be the object, of the perceptions," erecting a barrier between subject and object as a result.[92] If partition denies the essence and particularity of the object by turning it into a "thing" that I "experience" (that is, arrange) and "know" (that is, appropriate), then these qualities are redeemed through a corollary gesture, that of a connection that takes the subject out of the boundaries of the self (without its dissolution) and toward a meeting in the world. This meeting does not entail a conceptualization of that which faces the subject; rather, it is a measure of openness that is predicated on the gesture of addressing the Other. The relationship is direct in the sense of being absent of controlling ideas and fundamental biases. It is also dialogical in that it is always founded on a reciprocal invitation to connect—or rather to actualize the movement of connection that always already undergirds the life of the universe.

To be sure, for Buber both partition and meeting are necessary attitudes within life. This necessity, however, does not entail their equal valuation. For even if partition, by Buber's own admission, is not inherently negative,[93] it still can be made negative through overreliance, which serves an impulse "to manipulate nature, e.g. seek resources to fulfil our needs, and sometimes use people as means to an end."[94] In contrast, a dialogical meeting is the sole form of "real living" and hence cannot but exist in "grace."[95] Buber recognizes such inspired existence in the early stages of infancy, where before the formulation of self, the child perceives a reality absent of barriers. There, infant and world are bound by a togetherness that makes them respond to each other in a meaningful way, without placing this engagement under conceptual constraints. During this engagement, "in the instinct to make contact (first by touch and then by visual 'touch' of another being) the inborn *Thou* is very soon brought to its full powers, so that the instinct ever more clearly turns out to mean mutual relation, 'tenderness.' But the instinct to 'creation,' which is established later (that is, the instinct to set up things in a synthetic, or, if that is impossible, an analytic way—through pulling to pieces or tearing up) is also determined by this inborn *Thou*, so that a 'personification' of what is made, and a 'conversation,' take place." Thus, out of the tenderness of mutual relation with the objects of the world comes an engagement that pulls things apart and tears them up—a conversation that is executed, first and foremost, on the level of society and its web of intersubjective relations (and codifications). In Buber's view, the effects of this synthetic practice are unavoidable but may be mitigated if its nonsynthetic grounding is "kept in mind."[96]

The act of "keeping in mind," for Buber, is bound by a certain verbal order—by the articulation of the word "Thou," which speaks to a basic sense of connection over and against our tendency for separateness, verbally manifested through the word "It." Buber chose Thou as the word of relation because of its spiritual connotations, realized most commonly within the context of prayer. Such connotations are important for him since, per his theological perspective, every approach to the Thou is also, by extension, a gesture toward the eternal Thou.[97] This divine encounter, in turn, does not take the subject beyond the world, since Buber believed that a person "is only an individual living really with the world . . . in real contact, in real reciprocity of the world in all the points in which the world can meet man."[98] In light of the importance placed on this connection, it is understandable why he would also underscore the need to connect prayer, in true Hasidic fashion, to the "life of the senses." Within the context of prayer, perception becomes the means to invite in those worldly things with which the praying subject must come into "real contact."

Perception-based prayer—in the sense of worship with one's eyes wide open—may not always succeed in achieving this contact. Language is form, and as such stands in contradiction to the formless nature of lived experience; consequently, to engage lived experience through words stands the risk of reducing this reality to the realm of It and denying access to its formlessness. Yet even if such a level of immediate experience is not achieved, what is nonetheless made more commonly available by this prayer is an awareness of the basic intersubjective mechanism of our being in the world. At the moment of transposing the word "Thou" on a viewed reality, this reality ceases to be only my view, but also simultaneously an introceptive image of it, attributable to a body whose physical posture is invisible to me. In sensing this simultaneity—of perceiving and "perceiving perception"—we come to intimately realize the ways by which the basic principle of "tenderness" in the world drives us to experience reality through the eyes of another subject. It also highlights how the introceptive image appropriated from others is essentially a frame of understanding, a "worldview" that emerges from the materials of the "world" but must be transposed on them in order to render this world conceptually meaningful for human subjects. These dynamics of awareness, in turn, seem to prompt Guilherme's assertion that prayers in a Buberian sense are not "attempts to bring about a change of outcome or of influencing the outcome of events," but are means of providing us "with the 'space' to reflect upon ourselves and issues, to reflect upon our attitudes towards others and other's attitudes towards us, as well as upon events taking place in our lives." Such a definition, however, fails to recognize that before all else, prayer provides a privileged platform from which to reflect on the structures of our intersubjective existence. It is this reflection—often more subtle than "radical," and activated in part by the separation of prayer time from "profane time"—that serves as the foundation for Guilherme's more "refined" social and ethical reflection.

It is also what relates perception-based prayer with the experience of film spectatorship.

As far as comparisons go, the one presented here between film spectatorship and perception-based prayer is vulnerable to questioning on the grounds of obvious differences in kind. One major dissimilarity is located on the level of phenomenological engagement between watching a film and reciting the words of a prayer. Such differentiation does not only signify possible distinctions regarding agency, but even more importantly, with reference to the phenomenological definition of the world as the self's interlocutor—as possessing another "body" that interacts with the subject dialogically. Thus, in film spectatorship, spectators *directly* perceive a vision that is not their own; in a Buberian model of prayer, on the other hand, the praying subjects directly perceive a vision that is their own, yet one that, especially when the fixed prayer text is involved, has a "foreign" verbalized perspective superimposed onto it. Such differences are significant and should not be disregarded. Their effect, however, can be allayed by highlighting the features common to both modes of engagement. Accordingly, it is worth noting again the primacy of perception, not only in film spectatorship but also in Buber's model of prayer. For Buber, the ground of meaning-making is perception: this is where the I-Thou exists most purely, and from which the first acts of forming, of turning Thou into It, come to be. As a result, though placing emphasis on the "word," he sees perception as the major axis around which both It and Thou revolve. This, in turn, leads to another basic similarity: namely, that the formlessness of perception in both film spectatorship and Buberian praying is placed in a dynamic relationship with a form that is ascribed to an Other. Both the film and the prayer have built-in views on the world. The conjunction—and disjunction—of these perspectives with the basic sense of being-in-the-world as activated via perception is what allows the two media, regardless of their medium-specific dissimilarities, to be uniquely capable of bringing awareness to our fundamental modes of human experience.

The second major difference between praying and film watching, already established but requiring a second mention, is that often the former is bound by an avowed recognition of a divine sphere, a god, while the latter rarely operates along these terms. This dissimilarity, again, is substantial, and may not be fully dissolved even through

Buber's binding of the eternal and localized Thou into a metaphysics of the concrete. Nevertheless, its effects can also be lessened by reorienting our engagement with spectatorship and prayer so that the focus will fall more strenuously on the nature of experiential action than on the question of addressee.[99] Such an emphasis allows us, according to Sagi, to define prayer as a response to a fundamental desire to transcend the exigencies of experience and obtain "a moment of reflexivity, wherein a human's being is exposed in its totality."[100] An equivalent movement of self-transcendence, as noted by Sobchack, exists also in film, permitting the subject to similarly acquire (or at least feel as if acquiring) a more comprehensive perspective on his or her state of being. By looking at this shared ekstasis, it is possible to then offer a different reading of both film and prayer's ritualism, one that distances its expressivity from reference to cosmological myths but does not make it lose its standing as "privileged behavior" in the process. This definition is not meant to dismiss differences between the media's conceptual frameworks for situating self-transcendence but arguably lets us to still keep sight of their common ground, and by implication—to still legitimize a comparison between filmgoing and religious ritual that has held considerable purchase on modern culture.

Significantly, the comparison as outlined here diverges on two counts from Plate's analogical model of cinema-as-ritual. The first site of divergence centers on the question of personal versus communal, which has been the major theme for much of the discussion in this chapter. In making a claim that "religion and film are *like* each other," Plate is not invested in the media's personal dimension but rather foregrounds "the role of cinema in establishing communal life, often usurping the role that religious traditions have had in previous times."[101] While not dismissive of the collective functions of cinema and religion, which bind the subject to communal law, the comparative model proposed herein foregrounds the personal dimension in religious/cinematic experience. Buber's reflection on prayer affords us such an emphasis, for as previously explained, he regards its experience as highly individualized. This perspective, in turn, permits him to chart out enough distance between the religious community and its "cultic" operations to provide a different image of the collective—not as a hardened collection of individuals but as a *shared* experience that links separate engagements with a *common* metaphysical center. A similar dynamic is surfaced in the phenomeno-logical account of theatrical filmgoing. By this account, spectators do not necessarily participate in a collectivizing ceremony when congregating in the film theater; rather, under the cloak of darkness, they often exer-cise the freedom to experience their own distinct inner lives, and achieve personal agency, while communing in front of a single screen. The act of locating a personal cinematic experience, in turn, also expands con-sideration of cinema beyond the theatrical exhibition setting, which was underscored by Plate and other scholars, mainly because of their desire to strengthen the conceptual bond between filmgoing and churchgo-ing. This extension seems necessary in light of the shift in film experi-ence toward increasingly individualized screening contexts. These bear more resemblance to personal prayers than to participation in Mass and constitute a community that is reminiscent more of a fluid and ephemeral Buberian communion than of the rigid collectivizing of reli-gion's "cult."

A second point of divergence has to do with the central question of why we partake in film and prayer. For Plate, cinema and religion's pre-occupation with worldmaking is meant to help its participants in *making sense* of the world by becoming aware of the conditions of being-in-the-world. This basic understanding, in turn, leads him to claim that in both film spectatorship and religious ritual, making sense takes on the form of adhering to a cosmological, utopian, and moralizing order, as when he argues that "we go to the cinema and to the temple for recreation, to escape, but we also crave the re-creative aspects, maintaining the canopy of meaning over our individual and social lives as we imagine how the world could be."[102] The model suggested here is aligned with Plate's insofar as it presumes the act of *making sense*—of organizing the world's multiplicity into terms (and more elaborately, worldviews) made coherent in light of language and culture—as the main goal for praying and spectating. At the same time, it diverges from Plate's argument by stipulating that, in the space of these experiences, "making sense" func-tions first and foremost as a reflection on the aforementioned order—not as a confirmation of it. Additionally, and perhaps more importantly for this volume's overall argument, the present model also does not pre-suppose that "making sense"—as worldmaking—is the *sole* service these experiences provide their purveyors. Instead, it accepts the possibility that praying and film viewing can also be about world-unmaking—that is, not necessarily being invested in rendering a world *sensible* through the known terms of coherence, as in mystically unraveling these terms to expose their adherents to the ineffable mystery of reality. Buber is not opposed to making sense through I-It and its sphere of world-views yet wishes this operation to be in the main a steppingstone for a deeper form of experience—an extreme ekstasis that removes the subject entirely from the realm of I-It. The concept—the word—of "Thou" encapsulates this process. "Thou" may capture intricate and profound conceptual understandings of its referent; yet these understandings, even when not "harden[ed] into an object,"[103] do not evoke the referent itself. In Buber's mind, such evocation is made possible only when one summons the whole of one's being to the recitation of the word in prayer. At that moment the word-as-form—together with the terms and worldviews encapsulated in it—completely unravel, supposedly allowing the subject to access a fleeting vision of a mysterious totality. This experience, in turn, is also accessible to film spectators under certain conditions. At moments when the terms of coherence break down, as has been suggested in previous chapters, an opportunity arguably arises to sense "something else." Sobchack provides one possible account of what this "something else" might be when she writes that "the camera seeks [an] *ekstasis* in the 'flesh' of the world: it offers up a profane illumination of objective matter that, in its unrelenting 'hereness' and 'nowness' opens into an apprehension of something ultimately unfathomable, uncontained and uncontainable—not only in the thing on which we gaze but also in ourselves."[104] Moments like these—when ekstasis becomes so extreme that it no longer provides a wider perspective on how we come to know the world but completely disconnects the viewer from sensible terms or worldviews and produces a certain "unknowing"—may be said to actualize an aspect of film experience that bears some resemblance to the mystical facet of ritual, which focuses on facilitating privileged interactions with a persistent enigma.

Such a project of unraveling film's expressive dimension and engaging a mysterious totality of the life-world is difficult to realize—so much so that most films avoid it altogether. But even when left unpursued, the wish for unraveling may still be there, lurking in the shadows of our sense-making endeavors, compelling us to look at the screen. Indeed, the presence of this impulse, this hope, may be said to also sustain the power of film-as-religion in the discursive zeitgeist of a "death of God." For, as Buber reminds us in this chapter's epigraph, religions degenerate when true prayer no longer lives within them: when one cannot summon the entirety of being so as to overcome—or bracket out—worldviews and enter into an unmediated rapport with a greater mystery. And if religions have arguably failed in their task of providing such communion, could not cinema be uniquely positioned to take their place? In order to entertain this view, we must move away from perspectives on spectatorship that stress its affinity to categorical thinking and look elsewhere for a paradigm that traces attempts at undermining these categories via an extreme ekstasis. It is in this paradigm that the term "faith" would become useful—not in the object-related sense of "belief" (*Emuna*), but in the phenomenological-existential gesture of "trust" (*Emun*), an openness to suspend categories and remain, uneasy and unfixed, in the unifying experience that supposedly ensues.

4

HASIDIC TALES ON FILM AND THE QUESTION OF CREDULITY

Beyond the private tunes of any system of knowledge is the melody of faith—this song invests the light of *Ein sof* itself.
                                                    —R. Nachman of Bratslav[1]

The ascent of Hasidism in the late eighteenth century has been widely recognized as a significant transformation within Jewish history. Its beginnings were humble—small groups of devout believers that gradually coalesced around the larger-than-life figure of Baal Shem Tov (Besht), a mystic and healer. The generations after the Besht's demise (1760), however, saw the steady expansion of Hasidism as a religious movement, its rise in popularity among the masses, and its formulation of defining institutions (most importantly, that of the righteous leader [*Tsadik*] and his court [*Hatzer*], as well as the dynastic structure that ensured the survival of the community). This evolution occurred, in no small part, due to a general dissatisfaction with the traditional mode of religious practice and a concurrent destabilization of the social orders that organized (European) Jewish life. Hardly heretical as their opposition within mainline Rabbinical Judaism made them out to be, Hasidim did not wish to abolish the Halakha and its edicts but rather to revise and revive them in a manner that would make the experience of a presumed God, and emphatic devotion, more accessible. Hasidism's reliance on Kabbalah mysticism, with its promise of divine encounters, as well as its greater emphasis on the spheres of world and self as important ingredients of this encounter,[2] served as the cornerstones of this agenda. To a certain extent, these foundations allowed the Hasidic movement to unsettle the hegemony of erudition by legitimizing states of knowledge that transcend (in the case of the Tsadik) or are ignorant of (in the case of the common Jew) the heuristic forms of Talmudic study. Such possibilities were explored more fully in the Hasidim's appeal to the general population, arguably in an attempt to provide it with a greater sense of agency within the spiritual world. Quite appropriately, then, they appear less in the movement's Midrash literature, which aimed to provide a complex and specialized theological framework for the Hasidic vision, and more in its folkloristic works, which held no such aspirations.

Of the variety of folklore creations within this cultural landscape, none was as prominent or influential as the Hasidic tale. More than any Judaic sect before it, Hasidism valued stories. Their narratives of righteous and laypersons undergoing trials of devotion were used as ways of attracting members to the movement from walks of life that were rarely serviced with such passion by the mainline rabbinical institution. Yet the story's function was not only one of expanding the Hasidic grassroots base of support. Rather, as Tsippi Kauffman explains, Hasidim regarded storytelling, first and foremost, as "a holy activity,"[3] which revealed certain foundational and hidden truths about reality. As such, to make these stories available for the masses became less a matter of choice than of obligation—an unrelenting impulse that led to the formation of one of the richest repertoires of Judaic storytelling, both in sheer volume and in creative ingenuity.[4] And accordingly, for the Jewish world outside of Hasidism's courts, the story became the principal way through which one could gain insight into the Hasidic imaginary as it developed over time.

It was not a matter of chance, then, that the Hasidic tale stood at the focus of the Jewish Enlightenment's virulent attacks against Hasidism. As a movement, the Haskalah emerged in the aftermath of European Enlightenment's eighteenth-century heyday, with the goal of reconstructing traditional Jewish society in light of modern values and providing more opportunities for Jews to assimilate into their host cultures. Haskalah adherents saw Hasidim as the main obstacle in realizing this objective, figuring Hasidic devotion as a bastion of superstition unfit for a modern world of reason and scientific "wisdoms" (*Chochmot*).[5] This image was fueled to no small measure by the Hasidic folktales, since these feature experiences that blatantly defy rational reasoning, and to which no alternative contextualization outside of the theological is offered in any methodical way. Consequently, to battle their influence, Haskalah writers tended to create parodies of Hasidic tales, using the genre to lampoon Hasidim as bumbling fools, if not outright charla-tans.[6] At their hands, the supposed ineffable truth that Hasidic tales were meant to expose became the epitome of credulity.

Nevertheless, the entrance of Hasidic tales into Haskalah literature, albeit in parodic form, also signaled their subsequent acceptance by the precincts of "enlightened" Jewish secularity.[7] Indeed, by the late nine-teenth century, Hasidism became a source of inspiration for many young Jewish intellectuals who grew disillusioned with the promise of progress and the edification of rationality inherent to Haskalah's Enlightenment project. While the Hasidic movement itself became more and more iso-lated, neo-Hasidism foregrounded and reworked some of its ideas, mak-ing them accessible to a wider (secular) audience. Again, a principal site where this transformation took place was in Hasidic folktales, which many neo-Hasidic luminaries collected (in adapted form), studied, and/ or wrote variations in the their styles and themes. But where in previous years the folktale was used in parodic fashion to mock the Hasid while elevating the learned Maskil, here it was the other way around.[8] The potency of this refashioned image allowed the Hasidic tale to become a legitimate part of the general Jewish literary canon and ensured that it would serve as the foundation for subsequent cultural creations—literary or otherwise—throughout the twentieth and twenty-first centuries, even when their audiences were not necessarily observant or even Jewish.

The prevalence of neo-Hasidism within Israel's contemporary Jew Age cultural landscape has led to a robust interest in Hasidic tales, on platforms both academic and popular.[9] A clear testament to this interest has been the adaptation of tales to the screen by several Judaic-themed Israeli films. While not meriting it worthy of methodical interroga-tion, scholarship nevertheless acknowledged this appropriation of folktale elements on more than one occasion. Such acknowledgments often reiterated Haskalah's dismissive position on Hasidic story-telling's supposed antimodern credulity, regarding the genre's filmic rendition as geared toward "feel-good" naive escapism.[10] The following discussion occupies a different stance, which stresses the tale's tendency to be—and to foreground its own being as—historically situated. This situatedness, it is argued, attuned Hasidic storytelling to the subtleties of Jewish reality as well as to the competing ways—traditional-religious and modern-secular—in which these subtleties were read. By virtue of its attunement, the genre was consequently able to cultivate a middle ground of religiosity, where a religious-traditionalist outlook could be adjusted to the standards of secular modernity.[11] It is this capacity for adjustment that has arguably appealed to Judaic-themed films: the tale as a form, not of credulous escapism, but of an incredulous grasp of reality's complexities, which may offer new avenues for negotiating the ambivalences of Israel's secular-religious landscape. By affirming the Hasidic tale's "realism," even at "fantastic" moments, these cinematic texts may thus be said to challenge an "enlightened" position that stresses "credulity" to make short shrift of religiosity's usefulness in Israeli culture. Yet as the chapter's final section indicates, the implications of this challenge extend well beyond the Israeli context, allowing us to also contest the terms of credulity as they have been traditionally applied to film viewing in toto.

Hasidic Tales and Religiosity

Like many folktale traditions, the original context of Hasidic storytelling was not that of written transmission. As Joseph Dan established, written literature during Hasidism's early stages was of the Midrash variety—didactic-sermonic explications of key theological and ritualistic ideas. This conservative and reputable literary form, Dan argues, was well-suited to be the public face of a movement in the process of establishing its legitimacy.[12] Nevertheless, under the Besht's guidance and influence, a practice of oral storytelling also simultaneously developed during this formative period. Hasidic stories originated from Tsadikim such as the Besht and R. Nachman of Bratslav, who often recounted them in casual settings, and were later distributed by professional storytellers throughout the burgeoning Hasidic world, achieving great popularity.[13] In the early nineteenth century, the growth of the story's appeal—combined with the movement's expansion and a diminished need to rely solely on Midrash literature—eventually provoked a desire to move from oral to print tale-telling. The publication of the first Hasidic tale collections—*Praises for the Besht* (*Shivhei Ha-Ba'al Shem Tov*) in 1815 and R. Nachman of Bratslav's *Book of Tales* (*Sefer Sipurei Ma'asyiot*) in 1816—was perceived as a necessary and crucial step for the movement's expansion.[14] So monumental was the importance placed on the arrival of these volumes that they soon became central works in Hasidic lore, overshadowing in their impact the Midrash literature that preceded them. Yet paradoxically, the significance and success of the two collections also stunted the growth of printed storytelling, in part for fear of adding to the Besht's and R. Nachman's authoritative voices, and for opening the movement up to parody by Haskalah intellectuals.[15] Therefore, it took time for new tale collections to emerge on the scene, and when they finally did in the 1860s, their dissemination grew exponentially, making printed materials the preeminent platform for Hasidic stories.[16]

The enthusiasm by which Hasidim took to this enterprise of publication testifies to the viewpoint that, though previous Judaic traditions used stories for their various social and theological ends, only Hasidism provided the tale with a predominant position in its landscape of cultural creation.[17] This emphasis can be explained by Hasidism's desire to achieve wider popularity, especially among sectors of the Jewish people previously unattended to by the rabbinical establishment and various mystical schools.[18] As opposed to Midrash literature, with its demand for a high level of Judaic literacy, the traditional Hasidic tale did not provide a complicated account of theology, at least not on an explicit level, and consequently made Hasidism's spiritual message available for a larger audience.[19] In addition, the clothing of this message in story form allowed Hasidic writers to elevate known Tsadikim to demigod stature and perpetuate their reputations, while at the same time acting therapeutically on listeners/readers by "sweetening" the painful truths of religious observance.[20] Such pedagogical and propagandist objectives, however, do not fully explain the centrality of the tale within Hasidism, as they fail to account for its distinguishing attribute within the history of Jewish storytelling—its sanctity. Thus, drawing on the teachings of Medieval Kabbalah, Hasidism emphasized the immanent presence of God within physical reality, and the need to cling to and expose this presence through material activities (*Avodah Bagishmiut*). Reading and telling stories were imagined as such activities, and accordingly, were imbued with distinct theurgic capabilities.[21]

The dynamic of clinging and exposing is not only limited to the mechanics of Hasidic storytelling but is often mirrored within the narratives themselves. The Hasidic tale's narrative attributes are notoriously difficult to pin down and have resulted in a diversity of scholarly interpretations.[22] Scholars such as Dan, for example, concentrate on the primacy of the Tsadik as a key defining feature of the Hasidic narrative, which effectively functions as hagiography.[23] Other writers such as Yoav Elstein counter the Tsadik-centered evaluation of Hasidic tales by highlighting stories in which ordinary Hasidim take on crucial roles. These stories emphasize that neither erudition nor wealth are necessary or even desired conditions for achieving privileged access to God, and that sanctity can also exist—and perhaps chiefly exists—in people and activities that at face value epitomize the profane. The Tsadik's role here is limited to the recognition of sacredness in the ordinary subject, which in turn serves to solidify the authority of the sage as he who "possesses superior knowledge and can penetrate the external layers of reality in order to assess the true nature of an individual."[24]

The definitional challenges with respect to the protagonists of the Hasidic narrative extend also to their plotlines, which are too diverse in kind to allow for a simple categorization. Generally speaking, it may be argued that the Hasidic story, following the basic patterns of the folktale, often foregrounds a state of existential exile. This exile and resultant yearning frequently necessitate a journey of some sort[25]—whether that be an actual journey from a faraway land toward home,[26] or through more minor movements between the community's interior spaces (familial or religious-institutional) and exterior ones (of labor, leisure, and such).[27] This physical journey often involves trials and tribulations, culminating in human acts that disclose divine presence. Yet these stories are not only about godly revelations in physical reality but also about the reception of such phenomena—about the internal process of characters achieving and manifesting devotion.

The emphasis on *personal* devotion and epiphany within the Hasidic tale, according to Elstein, points to a "society-breaking" tendency, because it affirms a mindset that bypasses normative social understandings and codes.[28] This tendency, Kauffman argues, is inherent in the medium of storytelling itself. In her mind, the story intrinsically includes a variety of voices and viewpoints because it "centers on the specific person, the existential condition, relationships, and emotions, rather than on the norm, the law, the always-true abstract maxim."[29] An intrinsic dwelling in the contingency of a particular here and now, in turn, invites a form of "contextual thinking," whereby the audience member can "participate in developing [the story's] spiritual message in a way that suits his [sic] personality and existential state."[30] The unprecedented foregrounding of the tale form within Hasidic culture, in Kauffman's mind, signals the movement's desire to make room for relative flexibility in message and experience—to create "another polyphonic religious focus, equal in value to the Hasidic *derashot* [Midrash literature], on the one hand, and the halakha, on the other, both of which represent the normative and general perspective."[31] Though polyphony exists in the Hasidic tale even when there is a strong authorial voice—one that naturally represents the edicts of Hasidic Judaism—it is heightened within narratives that undermine this voice by foregrounding the spontaneous religious acts of individuals; their experience of ecstasy stands in contrast to rote participation in ritual, and therefore may be considered "subversive, if not necessarily transgressive."[32] These narratives in particular testify to the tale's flexibility in bypassing some of the thornier divides between Judaic and secular perceptions of reality at the historical moment of its making. In so doing, they also point to the genre's explicit intent of charting out a common ground of individualized—and spiritualized—religiosity where such oppositional worldviews can coexist.

This flexibility is mirrored through the tale's formulation of what the modern mindset would define as "reality" and "fantasy." The conventional definition of Hasidic storytelling as escaping reality—as nonrealistic in the sense of producing a diegesis incongruent with modernity's commonsensical understandings of the real—can be countered by evidence that many traditional tales structured their diegesis "on a distinctly realistic ground; the stories depict the unmistakable characteristics of Eastern European Jewish life, including recognizable names, occupations, toponyms, person-home and person-livestock dynamics, landscapes, living arrangements, rituals and holidays."[33] Within an attempt to "apologetically"[34] legitimize Hasidism, narratives used this ground to fashion a multivalent and nuanced portrait of reality, highlighting the intricacies of conflict between Hasidim and their opponents from both the Jewish and the non-Jewish communities. Hagiographic tales often focused on episodes in a Tsadik's life during which he was viciously persecuted (as in the canonical hagiographies "The Miracle of the Nineteenth of Kislev" and "Rabbi Nachman's Journey to Palestine," chronicling the travails of Chabad founder R. Shneur Zalman of Liadi and R. Nachman of Bratslav, respectively). Other stories that are less Tsadik-centered focus more on generic social conflicts: for example, around the exploitation of poor Jews by rich Jews, or the abuse of Jews by gentiles (and especially gentile nobility). In these cases, according to Yassif, the Tsadik functions as an "intermediary figure," to the extent that he elevates the poor and topples the rich Jews, challenges the gentile elite and rescues the Jewish community from harm.[35]

What the traditional tale's "realism" had to contend with is a Hasidic perspective that defies Enlightenment's instrumental reason, with its tendency to split the world to discrete units, and offers instead a cosmic vision where categorical separations are dissolved into an overarching divine unity.[36] This questioning of a real made legible through rationality is apparent, for example, in R. Nachman's famous proclamation "I don't know," which recognizes that the "human intellect" can never "capture the infinite light" but only reveal, at best, "the edge of its ability, its inability to attain."[37] Similarly, Chabad lore spoke of "the bounds of knowledge" and their fundamental incapacity to deliver "the unknowable, inconceivable realm"[38] that permeates all things. In both cases the championed solution for rationality's faults is one of radical ekstasis—of a "faith that transcends intellect and comprehension," which leads to "the nonrational peak of the *unio mystica*."[39]

In facing the call for self-transcendence, the enlightened mind is met with a fundamental dilemma: "Is this departure from the standards of rationality essentially an unknown yet true aspect of reality? Or is it only an illusion, the result of faulty perception, with no connection to outside reality at all?" Rather than foreclose on discussion by siding with one option over the other, the Hasidic tale preserves a measure of "uncertainty,"[40] which consequently opens up a space for agreement across contrasting views. For this purpose, those aspects of storytelling that favor the irrational are adjusted in such a way so as not to automatically incur their dismissal as "fantastic" by modern standards of credulity.

On the most basic level, adjustment meant that mystical unity is often contextualized and couched in emotional terms, at times at the expense of reliance on the unreality of mythopoetic tropes (as those of Kabbalah mythology).[41] Love in particular has played a central role in Hasidic theosophy, and by extension, Hasidic storytelling.[42] Thus, focusing on social integration made possible through the connecting emotional thread of love serves to testify, within the tale, of a greater cosmic unity. Concurrently, in creating a tale of emotionally based social integration, audience members are prompted more easily to integrate themselves within the story. As a result, a strong union of theurgic significance is engendered between storyteller and recipients, whereby the former is able to provoke revelatory experiences in the latter.[43]

Within this moment of unity, revelation in the eyes of the recipient is cued by the appearance of diegetic miracles. While the miraculous places the greatest strain on instrumental reason, its presentation within the tale allows for this challenge to be mitigated. Thus, as Dan details, Hasidic stories display various forms of miracle that correspond to different modern understandings of what constitutes as "fantasy." The least fantastic miracle, in that it can be explained as a purely subjective phenomenon, is what Dan calls "wondrous experience"— namely, an experience of revelation that the Tsadik undergoes and then recounts, but to which there is no proof outside of, perhaps, its toll on the Tsadik's physical state. More fantastic is the "wondrous knowledge," where revelation is manifested through the clairvoyance of the Tsadik, which allows him access to secrets from the past, people's innermost thoughts, things that are taking place in the cosmic sphere, or events that will occur in the future. Most fantastic, however, are "wondrous deeds," in which the Tsadik "operates in material reality and changes the laws of nature, performing veritable 'miraculous' acts."[44] Yet even here there is a hierarchy in the level of fantasy, with only some miracles being "exuberant," while others being "simple" and therefore more *believable*.[45]

This adaptation to modern notions of incredulity became even more extensive, as well as less defensive, within neo-Hasidism. As a cultural movement, neo-Hasidism responded to the bifocal challenge imposed by Haskalah on young European Jewry during the fin de siècle period—of the painful alienation from traditional Jewish identity and from God.[46] This response took the form of vindicating the Haskalah's principal object of ridicule—Hasidism, and its storytelling in particular.[47] As part of Hasidism's recovery, neo-Hasidism became highly invested in publishing collections of traditional Hasidic stories and in writing original stories within the parameters of the genre. The literary products that came out of this endeavor, however, took on a different shape than the Hasidic origin. Through reworked and original stories, neo-Hasidism popularized a highly selective image of Hasidic Judaism, one that disproportionately highlighted certain aspects of Hasidic thought and folklore.[48] These features were chosen on the basis of their capacity to inspire modern-liberal Jewish society. Such was the case, for example, of the neo-Hasidic emphasis on Hasidism's valuation of inner religious life, which served to affirm for modern Jews the possibility of a spiritual experience without having to commit to theological erudition and the observance of Halakhic laws; or its emphasis on Hasidism's appreciation of worship through physical acts, which gave modern Jewry the occasion to disassociate God from a position of absolute transcendence and make Him part of the everyday world; or its emphasis on Hasidic anthropocentrism and populism, which allowed the Jewish diaspora to imagine a religious stance that takes its lead from individual needs rather than institutional (rabbinical) demands. These and other traits were foregrounded at the expense of those that did not sit well with the outlook of modern Jews at that time, like Hasidism's adherence to a devout traditional lifestyle, its avowed elitism (in the form of Tsadik dynasties), its use of Kabbalistic theosophy and resulting systems of symbols and practices, as well as its quietist tendencies, which undermined personal identification with the immanent world. Ultimately, neo-Hasidic stories sought to strengthen a reliance on individuals' "inner worlds in order to make sense and verify the truth of their religious life,"[49] placing greater weight on ecstatic experience than on divine miracle. As a result, their depiction of the miraculous allowed for its appropriation—from a modern perspective—as an idiosyncratic "subjective" impression of something in "outside reality" that can also conceivably (and more persuasively) be explained in "objective" terms.

This dynamic is clearly evident in Martin Buber's seminal contribution to (neo-)Hasidic storytelling, which turned it into a familiar genre not only for modern Jewish culture but also for European culture at large.[50] Buber's first major publications were, in fact, collections of Hasidic stories: *The Stories of R. Nachman* (1906) and *The Legend of Baal Shem* (1908). In preparing the collections, Paul Mendes-Flohr explains, Buber did not wish "to translate these creations—these legends and symbolic fairytales related by the Hasidic masters—but to 'retell' them. Selecting various motifs from Hasidic stories, which in his judgment captured the distinctive message of Hasidism, Buber would 'relieve' these motifs and the message they conveyed, retelling them as he experienced them."[51] Through this process of "retelling" and "reliving" the "distinctive message of Hasidism," Buber was able to lay the foundation for his modern philosophy on Judaism and universal spirituality. Thus, in his stories, simple Jews are often elevated to the level of Tsadikim, and both are removed from the institutional contexts of rabbinical Judaism[52] in a manner that indicates Buber's own valuation of subjective religiosity over structured religion. Religiosity, in turn, is most visibly expressed within these stories through devotion via everyday activities, a rhetorical gesture that served to shift focus toward the human experience of sanctity, colored by modern notions of personal freedom and individual agency.[53] In his introduction to *The Stories of R. Nachman*, Buber places this experience under the heading of "mysticism," understood as "a temporary conscious reaction against the dominance of the rule of the intellect" that allows for a vision where "in the midst of an unspeakably circumscribed existence, indeed out of its very limitations, there suddenly br[eaks] forth the limitless."[54] By highlighting the populist nature of Hasidic mysticism, he expanded the purview of this mystical system—this extreme ecstasy that unravels the limits of coherence toward an image of the world's underlying unity—so as to include the commoner and not only the enlightened mystic. Concurrently, through this expansion, Buber was able to further his claim that although mysticism may be a universal quality, it is found most potently in Jews.

Buber's model of neo-Hasidic religiosity—which refers to a divine presence that is suitably nebulous and worldly so as to not incur intractable modern resistance—appealed to subsequent purveyors of neo-Hasidic tales during the twentieth century (such as Isaac Bashevis Singer and Elie Wiesel), and in turn fed into the current landscape of New Age Jewishness—which, as already suggested, is markedly neo-Hasidic and therefore intensively engaged with "retelling" Hasidic tales. The tales' contemporary retelling is found not only in written texts but also in audiovisual ones. Cinema in particular has offered fertile ground for this type of adaptation, often transposing the Hasidic tale from its original shtetel context into a modern setting.[55] By offering such an update, Judaic-themed films test the relevance of the genre's religiosity to Jew Age culture as "a model for a unique life, one situated in the here and now,"[56] which can accommodate religious understandings to modern sensibilities. As accommodation is a fraught process, it breeds ambivalences, which certain filmic texts push to the fore while others elide. Understanding a film's position in relation to (neo-)Hasidic religiosity thus requires delving into its negotiation of ambivalence, which affects its attitude toward a fractured society (the "real") and an all-encompassing divine unity (the "fantastic").

Hasidic Tales on Film: Between "Real" and "Fantastic"

Judaic-themed Israeli cinema has tended to follow the transnational pattern of Hasidic-tale film adaptation, situating the genre's narrative tropes to a contemporary background. By choosing a familiar setting, these films are able to highlight Hasidic storytelling's "realistic" tendencies in neo-Hasidic fashion. They avoid the criticism of "utter credulity" by sidestepping the mythopoetic—especially in terms of Kabbalistic symbolism, magic, and cosmology—and by stressing the immanent over the transcendent as their site of primary operation. At the same time, their depiction of this immanent reality shows awareness to the nuances of social conflict and avoids reducing them to the Manichaean schemes of myth (which occasionally dominate modern perspectives on social reality as well). From this awareness, these texts mobilize the details of a conflicted social landscape in order to put forward the side of Israeli-Judaic life that would be admissible (if not entirely acceptable) by Israeli-secular definitions of what life is and should be. Such measures seem to reveal an overarching desire to find room for religion within a modern understanding of (probable and proper) reality rather than to claim that no such room exists through an escape from this understanding. These films' message is therefore one of religiosity, as flexible as it is ambivalent, which emerges from the stuff of Israeli social existence to capture a possible common ground for integration across traditional/religious–modern/secular perspectival divides.

Unsurprisingly, this integrative religiosity, itself a derivative of Hasidic tales' fluid understanding of reality, is often articulated through, grounded in, and enhanced by the actions of religious repentant characters. Mainstream ultra-Orthodoxy, and mainline Israeli Hasidism in particular, follow the prevalent notion of secularity and religion as "a cultural binary," a zero-sum game in which the religious subject must "choose a side: that of spirituality or of materiality; of Haredism or of secularity; of the 'great sages' or of the 'celebrities.'"[57] In contrast, the position of the "born-again" Israeli Haredi, as exemplified in the practices of the major Hasidic repentance movements Chabad and Bratslav, is far more intricate. Rather than be fully absorbed in their host communities, these Hasidim operate as "liminal personae," straddling both the religious and the secular worlds and embodying the resultant ambivalences.[58] This straddling, in turn, creates a de facto proximity to modern-liberal sensibilities that "softens" the repentants' commitment to ultra-Orthodoxy's "strict religion."[59] Consequently, by bringing the life of Hasidic repentants to the screen, Judaic-themed films render palpable and confront us with ambivalences on the fault line between Israeli religion and secularity; in so doing, however, they also point to possible sites where such ambivalences may be mitigated, with the help of a (neo-)Hasidic religiosity that is cognizant of modern definitions of reality and attempts to integrate itself into them.

Importantly, within the Hasidic and especially neo-Hasidic vein, the films' protagonists are not religious sages but simple and flawed individuals, "hidden Tsadikkim" more than established mystics. Their religiosity, in turn, is formed through an uneducated, almost intuitive mode of faith, rather than through religious erudition. Indeed, too much religious education seems to hinder the characters' ability to access what is figured as the true ground of mystical communion—"pure feeling, i.e., as liberated from the bonds of ideational or halakhic dogma and centered on an internal emotional connection to the soul."[60] Stressing the affective in neo-Hasidic fashion,[61] these films foreground a very personalized piety—one that does not necessarily negate the congregational settings of Judaism, yet is most effective when removed from them. It is there that the protagonist can mine his/her emotional depths; it is there, as well, that he or she finds the emotion most vital for the task of facilitating social and cosmic unity—love as the integrative feeling par excellence. Though at times drawn to negative emotionality, which divides instead of repairs, these characters' capacity for love allows them to build bridges over seemingly unbridgeable gaps—within their communities, but also from without. And since love is shown as a power for social cohesion, the film's diegetic logic—following that of (neo-)Hasidic stories—suggests that this emotion can also expose divine presence as intimately implicated in these characters' lives.

Revelation comes at miraculous occasions connected to the protagonists and at times is prompted by their own actions (as in acts of prayer). Within the (neo-)Hasidic tale, miracles point to the existence of a divine world, and in being so cosmological—full of apparitions that "neither the reader nor the character (who shares the same ontological assumptions) can explain by the logic of [a rationally understood] world"[62]—they court dismissal as "fantastical" by the "enlightened" mind. Accordingly, through the inclusion of the miraculous in their plots, the cinematic offshoots of (neo-)Hasidic storytelling run the risk of undermining their attempt to legitimize cosmic unity for modern sensibilities by figuring it in emotional rather than cosmological terms. In order to mitigate this risk, these films open the revelatory moment to other plausible explanations than the miraculous. They do so by steering clear of "exuberant" revelations, focusing instead on the simpler manifestations present in the tale genre, which appear more "out of the ordinary" than decidedly theophanic. Such supposed miracles are bound by everyday reality, to which the tale and its cinematic renderings are committed, and they keep God as a nebulous presence, distinct from the imposing dogmas of religion and in line with the tenets of New Age spirituality. Consequently, these Judaic-themed filmic works are able to maintain revelation's evidentiary claims to some degree by providing it with an air of plausible deniability—that is to say, by making it less offensive to a modern worldview.

Gidi Dar and Shuli Rand's *Ushpizin* (2004) is a particularly celebrated example of this intricate and elusive representational pattern. The film follows a born-again Bratslav Hasid couple—Moshe and Mali (played by then married couple Shuli and Michal Rand, also born-again Hasidim)—as they make preparations to celebrate the holiday of Sukkot.

Moshe and Mali are experiencing financial difficulties, which adds strain to a relationship already burdened by the couple's inability to conceive a child. As Sukkot approaches, however, their fates suddenly appear to improve—they receive a sizeable sum of money by way of donation, and a friend even locates a seemingly abandoned ceremonial hut (*Sukkah*) for them to use during the holiday. Most auspicious in this happy turn of events is the arrival of two unexpected visitors—Eliyahu, Moshe's friend from the pre-repentance days, and his partner in crime Yosef—who have escaped prison just in time to help Moshe and Mali perform the required task of hosting guests (*Ushpizin*) in their Sukkah. What seems fortunate at the outset, however, quickly turns out to be disastrous—the Sukkah, which was thought to have been abandoned, is shown to be someone's actual property; and the Ushpizin, who were so happily welcomed into Moshe and Mali's home, abuse their hospitality by creating problems for their hosts, pitting the whole apartment building against them. Tensions rise until Eliyahu and Yosef cause a disturbance in the building's atrium, which prompts residents to call the police, and Mali to depart to her parents. In an attempt to appease his longtime friend, Eliyahu makes his "famous" vegetable salad and unknowingly destroys in the process an expensive Sukkot citron (*Etrog*) that Moshe bought with the donation money. This enrages Moshe, and he is able to contain his anger only through practicing secluded prayer in the woods. Hitting rock bottom, his spirits are nevertheless finally elevated when, while dismantling his Sukkah, Mali arrives to let him know that she is carrying his child. The film ends in the celebration of the child's *Bris*, which Eliyahu and Yosef also attend, bearing gifts.

Ushpizin's various dramatic twists and turns take place in Mea Shearim, a Haredi neighborhood in Jerusalem, which in this context becomes a metaphor for Israel's ultra-Orthodox society. On-screen the religious enclave is figured as an intricate web of alleyways, whose enclosedness contributes to the creation of a tight-knit community. This sense of "living in close quarters" is most visibly manifested in the architecture of Moshe and Mali's apartment building, a two-story structure with a large inner square. Inside this building, the lives of inhabitants interpenetrate each other, particularly in the shared courtyard that seems to inevitably force human interaction. Friction may ensue, but the film seems to show that constant contact causes, at worst, an opportunity for forgiveness, and, at best, a chance for helpful cooperation. In this sense, the atrium, and the neighborhood and world that surround it, do not function negatively along the lines of a Foucauldian panopticon, but rather positively, as a Hasidic court that affords its members protection and sustenance.

The landscape-as-court of *Ushpizin* creates an impression of religious insularity, which is emphasized by the strategy of rarely presenting geographical spaces that are associated with Israeli secularity. It is for this reason, perhaps, that Peleg argues for a definition of the film as essentially "a story about an 'eternal' community, one that exists in a timeless zone of religious rituals and practices, disconnected from historical time in any meaningful way."[63] But while this argument may have merit in relation to the film's spatial organization, its explanatory power is limited when it comes to discussing narrative action. Thus, rather than detach itself from the contemporary realities of religious life into "a timeless zone," this film appears cognizant of the timely challenges of maintaining insularity within a largely modern-secular national setting, and wishes to dramatize and potentially resolve them through the intrusion of Eliyahu and Yosef into Moshe and Mali's courtyard. In this sense, though *Ushpizin* does aim to "to paint a more positive picture of [the ultra-Orthodox] community for a generally hostile secular Israeli public," this effort does not come necessarily at the price of pure escapism. Rather, as much as the Hasidic tale is not as socially "naive" as Peleg would have us believe,[64] so is this narrative not as "neat and attractive"[65] as his argument makes it out to be, exploring real-life social conflicts with great nuance rather than suppressing them entirely.

At face value, the film seems to present social tensions between secularism and Judaism in the Manichaean dialectic of evil versus good that undergirds mainline ultra-Orthodox ideology, yet closer inspection shows a much more complex and equivocal understanding of these tensions' underlying conditions. The representation of physical space, for one, includes only two distinctly secular sites—Eliyahu and Yosef's prison and a Jerusalem restaurant where they dine. This choice, in turn, seems to reduce the secular landscape to the categories of criminality and leisure that are vulnerable to moralistic dismissal. The fact is, however, that these sites are not necessarily presented in a negative light. Thus, we are never given glimpses of the prison from within and are therefore relieved from experiencing the often-brutal conditions of imprisonment; instead, what we do experience is the attractive desert landscape that surrounds the prison, and which lends beauty and even sanctity to this secular site. Concurrently, the restaurant is not a place of corruption or even wastefulness, but rather is a modest establishment whose sole purpose is to answer basic nutritional needs. As such, it is "kosher" enough to allow a Bratslav Hasid to enter and ask Eliyahu for a donation to religious charities.

Similarly, the characterization of main secular figures also features equivocation and nuance, even as these are couched within an explicit binary structure of reference. Thus, at the outset these characters are clearly shown to be a disruptive force within the peaceful ultra-Orthodox neighborhood—a disturbance that is associated with their social standing as criminals. True to his family name, Eliyahu Scorpio can be as venomous as a scorpion, and in contrast to prophet Elijah, to whom his given name obliquely refers, is anything but the proverbial guest whose visit bodes well for the household. Though not always as belligerent, Eliyahu's partner-in-crime Yosef is an unsavory character as well, supporting Scorpio's machinations and causing harm as a result.[66] These negative traits, however, are counterbalanced by positive and redeemable features. In the case of Eliyahu, his antics are ultimately motivated by a mistrust of Moshe's intentions, and when Moshe becomes hurt by his actions, he attempts to offer reconciliatory gestures. As for Yosef, in his childlike demeanor he often exhibits an openness to Moshe and Mali's lifestyle that Eliyahu lacks, and at times mitigates his friend's hostility out of respect for their hosts. Accordingly, these characters, like the spaces most related to them, seem to render the film's position on Israeli secularity and its attendant modern worldview as multivalent rather than as monolithically damning.

Nor is the religious community presented in one-dimensional terms. Spatially, *Ushpizin* does present us with a human landscape that is colorful and vibrant, filled with alluring images that render it appealing to the eye. At the same time, the film also exposes us to images of abject poverty that collapse the spiritual to base needs while highlighting the ways in which capitalist mentality and practices pervade the lived realities of religious characters (for example, in the business of selling high-priced citrons, the constant panhandling for charity money [*Tzdaka*], and the obsession with private property and ownership of Sukkahs).[67] Indeed, of the various observant characters, only one—Moshe's rabbi—seems a righteous and holy sage. The others are flawed: like the Hasid Ben Baruch, who despite his good nature and loving personality, is guilty of neglect in not discovering the true proprietary condition of the Sukkah he takes for Moshe; or the Hasid Gabai, owner of the Sukkah, who does forgive Ben Baruch and Moshe for their "crime," but with a grudge that seems excessive in light of the fact that he has an additional newer Sukkah of his own. And finally, the residents of Moshe and Mali's building are often characterized as cantankerous in a manner that is not entirely justified by the intrusion of secular Jews into their insular community. It therefore stands to reason that at the aforementioned climactic moment of his existential crisis, when Moshe cries to God for help, this act is performed outside of the neighborhood's limits, in a bucolic setting that connotes purity over and against the impurity of the community's ghettoized existence.

Indeed, it is this fiction on the necessity and merits of complete communal insularity that the film subtly attempts to critique. The entrance of secular Jews into the religious community exposes the desire of Hasidim to use insularity to buttress a position of moral superiority over modern secularism. Accordingly, at the instances when Eliyahu and Yosef collide with the residents of Moshe and Mali's building, their similarities become even more noticeable than their differences. For example, close to the end of the film the two escaped prisoners decide to have a party in the middle of the courtyard. They fire up the grill, put their music on full blast, and start drinking and dancing. The residents shout at them to stop, and one Bratslav Hasid in particular gets so riled up that he calls out "animals" to their faces. Another resident intervenes and asks the Hasid to temper his anger, offering to speak with Yosef and Eliyahu more politely in order to appease them, but the two jailbirds at that point are far too intoxicated and energized to respond to such subtle pleas. Mali descends down the stairs and attempts to negotiate between the factions, but she quickly finds herself shouting both at the two "guests" and at the indigent neighbors. As spirits gradually run higher, Yosef draws out a meat skewer, and Mali, in retaliation, grabs one too, forcing him and Eliyahu to cease their disturbance. Though halting before any violence was perpetrated, the altercation lasts long enough to undermine unequivocal claims to Hasidic moral superiority. It may be true to say that the Hasidim's indignation was provoked, and that some of them even wanted to resolve the clash peacefully. But at the moment of altercation, when push quite literally comes to shove, it is difficult to distinguish between the behavior of religious and secular Jews. As one of the residents tells another, after the latter blames Yosef and Eliyahu for being blasphemous—"actually, it is you who are committing blasphemy."

In this sense, *Ushpizin*—as a Hasidic tale about "guests"—does not wish to escape the conflict between secularity and religion; rather, this conflict is seen as not only unavoidable but also necessary for the process of Judaic introspection. Such self-inquiry is made possible due to an inversion in the usual power relations of the secular-religious conflict—that is, in this film, we are not given the traditional image of a religious minority that intrudes on a secular majority, but rather the opposite vision wherein a secular minority intrudes on a religious majority. This position of strength defuses the sense of persecution that fuels ultra-Orthodoxy's binary mindset, forcing a more elaborate contemplation of the relationship between Haredi and non-Haredi Israelis while containing it within the protective limits of an internal religious drama. The film's spatial organization supports such an understanding. In one scene, for example, Yosef, Eliyahu, and Moshe are seen celebrating inside the Sukkah. They drink too much, and Eliyahu provokes Moshe's ire; the two exchange words, but the fight culminates in a warm embrace and subsequent singing and merriment. The scene then ends with the building's residents looking at the Sukkah from the outside with a puzzled gaze. The positioning of religious Jews outside the ceremonial hut marks its walls as a physical barrier between the Judaic and secular worlds. But separation is not clear-cut, for if the apartment building acts as a microcosm of religious life, then like the Sukkah that is found within the atrium, so is the presence of secularity understood as being *within* religion, as an integral part of Judaic existence rather than a foreign intrusion. The bewilderment of the religious Jews around the Sukkah seems to therefore indicate a frightening realization—that these secular brethren are perhaps "like us" and even "part of us."

It is in this particular drama of recognition, where religious Israelis acknowledge a shared ground of human complexity with secular Israelis, that religious repentants like Moshe and Mali play a decisive role. As

"liminal personae" who have made the transition from the secular to the
religious world, their existence is marked by a constant battle with social
ambivalence. *Ushpizin* seems to say that the self-consciousness emerging
out of such struggles—that which yields an understanding of religion
and secularity as kindred, or even as being implicated in each other—is
crucial for Israeli Judaism's coming to terms with the modern ethos of
Israeli society. Moshe and Mali, who carry secularity into their religious
existence, and who as a result epitomize the complexity that is shared
by both religious and secular Israelis, are thus the only ones who can
offer keys for the film's religious community to overcome its puzzlement.
Predictably, they are also the principal characters shown to be moving
between the Sukkah and the surrounding atrium and building. In this
spatial sense, they become mediators, offering their flexible religiosity as
possible proof that certain social chasms may not be as deep as to prevent
their bridging.

In contrast to the hardened fundamentalism of mainline ultra-
Orthodoxy, Moshe and Mali's religiosity allows for fluidity because, in
Shai Ginsburg's words, its law is "not the 'learned' legal one, but the
Law of Love."[68] Though their relationship is far from perfect, the two
characters love each other dearly, and this love is depicted as the bond
that helps them overcome the adversities of poverty and childlessness.
Additionally, this capacity for love is what undergirds their hospitality
toward Eliyahu and Yosef, which is put to the test on numerous occasions, and what draws out a similar capacity in these guests, permitting
them to integrate into the religious community, as symbolized in their
arrival at the Bris ceremony. So potent is Moshe and Mali's loving message that, along with the secular guests, the secular audience members
are also won over. Indeed, according to Peleg, *Ushpizin* performs a feat
of "innovation" by integrating "the modern comedic-romantic sensibility [with] the Hasidic one," prompting secular viewers familiar with the
former to accept the latter through it. Yet if the film does manage to
mobilize romance, so that "even the most hardened of secular hearts
cannot but rejoice with the destitute couple,"[69] it seems less a matter
of unholy union between secular and religious generic forms and more
about a particular evolution of the (neo-)Hasidic tale's emphasis on love.

In the best tradition of Hasidic storytelling, *Ushpizin*'s emphasis
on emotionality serves a greater goal than representing and facilitating

social integration on- and off-screen: that of revealing the greater cosmic unity of which social integration is but a part. Thus, the diegetic world the devout characters inhabit is filled with a diffused sense of providence, which manifests in the most mundane contexts and benefits all in equal measure. This is not an existence where God has retreated into a transcendent sphere; rather, He is, on some level, essentially approachable, and available for an intimate, loving rapport. Such is why Moshe and Mali speak to Him directly using the common appellation "Father"; for as Avi Sagi explains, "the god, to whom the believer relates as 'father' or 'tateh' in Yiddish, is one with which a person can be in immediate relation and without recoil, as facing a close friend, as me facing you."[70]

Through the love between individual and God, *Ushpizin* professes, the believer can affect divine movement, and ipso facto prove the existence of a greater cosmic unity. This is most evident in the establishment of a causal relationship between praying and miracles, which serves to illustrate Moshe's claim that "in a place where something is missing, it is either because it wasn't prayed for, or because it wasn't prayed for hard enough." Two events in the film establish this relationship. In the first, Moshe and Mali pray for God's help to overcome their financial woes in anticipation of the Sukkot holiday. Their prayers are then followed by the fortuitous happenstance of a nameless benefactor having $1,000 to spare, and choosing Moshe out of a list of many names to benefit from this sum. Here causality is established through rapid crosscutting between praying shots and shots of the benefactor picking Moshe's name. And if such filmic rendering is not sufficient affirmation of divine intervention, both Mali and Moshe later verbally recognize this handsome donation as a "miracle." The second event, taking place at the end of the film, sees Moshe, enraged by his guests' spiteful behavior, running to a remote forest on the outskirts of Jerusalem and begging God for an explanation of his trials and for His unending mercy. This prayer—performed in the Bratslav practice of Hitbodedut—subsequently leads to another "miracle," where Mali finds herself pregnant after many years of bareness.

While these sequences certainly assert the existence of bona fide miracles in our world, the assertion in itself is shaped in such a way that it cannot be dismissed as "a wonderfully naïve picture"[71] by modern standards of incredulity. Hence the revelations here do not fall in the category of "wondrous act," nor do they rely on some spectacular

FIGURE 21. Moshe (Shuli Rand) pleading for divine intervention. From *Ushpizin* (Shuli Rand and Gidi Dar, 2004).

imagery that is conventionally associated with theophany. They are also dissociated from the realm of mystical operation of the Tsadik rabbi, who is present in the film as a benevolent character but is not shown to have any direct link to the alleged miracles. Within this state of affairs, God emerges as a diffused entity—an "endless light" in Moshe's words—and consequently the emphasis moves from Him toward the *experience of Him* as an overarching unity in the hearts and minds of the main characters. Thus envisioned, even as the film attempts to establish a causal paradigm of "prayers being answered," it also affords the possibility for a modern-secular audience to "accept" revelations as "objective" events that can and should be interpreted through rational categories (for example, as coincidences) or at the very least diverts this audience's attention from revelations through focusing on their subjective/biased acceptance by the protagonist. This adaptation to the modern boundaries of plausibility is perhaps what caused one secular Israeli film critic to laud *Ushpizin* for "treating each of its 'miracles' with a slight irony—as a humorous chain of misunderstandings and happenstances—and as such, avoiding a didactic or evangelical presentation."[72]

Haredi filmmaker Rama Burshtein's second feature, *The Wedding Plan* (2016), follows *Ushpizin*'s path of affirming devotion through the

Hasidic tale structure yet does so with greater equivocation. The film centers on Michal, a born-again Bratslav Hasid, who following more than a decade of dates, is desperate to finally get married. After her fiancé breaks off the engagement during a food tasting, she remains committed to the nuptials, regardless. Placing faith in God to deliver a groom by the predetermined event date, the hopeful protagonist goes through potential candidates offered up by her matchmaker. While those fall through, a surprise prospect comes in the form of Yos, a popular secular singer, whom she accidently meets during a visit to R. Nachman's gravesite in Uman (Ukraine). The two hit it off, which later prompts Yos to visit Michal at her Jerusalem home and ask for her hand. In light of her own romantic tribulations—as well as those of her (secular) sister, who obsesses about a man who won't have her, and a roommate who decided to wed Michal's ex-fiancé behind her back—the protagonist is understandably overwhelmed by this impromptu proposal and rejects the suitor. Yet this leaves her without any alternatives, and she ultimately has to attend her own wedding ceremony sans a betrothed. Then, when everything seems lost, Shimi—the congenial owner of the matrimonial hall, who believed in her all along—steps up and proposes. As fate would have it, he had just recently become divorced, and Michal's audacious wedding plan convinced him that he should offer himself as a potential husband if no one else would wish the role. Baffled at first, it nevertheless dawns on the heroine that Shimi may be the one for her, and she accepts the proposal. This appears to have been the right decision, for in a brief epilogue, we see Michal, already married, looking at her husband with adoring eyes, as they sit around the Sabbath table, and he chants the famous lines from Proverbs: "Who can find a virtuous woman? for her price is far above rubies."

By and large, Hasidic tales are centered on male figures—most notably, the Tsadik—and carry the androcentric focus of Judaic tradition. Female characters therefore are generally marginalized and tend to receive less than favorable treatment within the narrative.[73] Nevertheless, it is still worth noting that, as Tsippy Kaufmann explains, "Hasidic women listened to Hasidic stories and also recounted them. Women are sometimes the heroines of these stories, and, as narrators, women become partners in molding the literary work."[74] Michal is a descendent of these women, who worked within but also resisted

Hasidic storytelling's patriarchal alignments. In terms of working within, this heroine is seen acquiring agency through the devout and fervent abidance of Hasidic dictates. Those include, first and foremost, spiritual acts allotted to women, from kneading and separating challah to becoming a dutiful wife, Michal's greatest ambition. Yet they also refer to duties placed on all members of the Hasidic congregation—men and women alike. For example, through performing the "inner work" of self-betterment and strengthening of devotion, Michal follows the path of "great women who viewed themselves as *Hasidot* and embraced [this] central aspect of daily Hasidic religious service that was personal and did not belong to the movement's public, institutionalized dimension."[75]

While Hasidism's institutional dimension encourages this kind of personal labor from the protagonist, other aspects of her deportment act in defiance of the community's patriarchal logic. Most defiant in this respect is her decision to go ahead with the wedding in order to directly influence God to supply her with a groom. Not only does a rabbi, brought in by Michal's mother, question this choice but also her female dressmaker, who internalized the patriarchal view that stipulates that such direct appeal is not the share of women. Michal responds to this view by saying that "the world was made for her," and that therefore she knows in her heart that God would provide. Such claims situate her, not on the level of a female Hasid (*Hasida*), but of a female Tsadik (*Tsadika*), with theurgic powers. This marks an aberration of the Hasidic norm, equating Michal with her biblical namesake—the daughter of Saul, who possessed not only "feminine" but also "masculine" traits, having been known to place *Tefillin* like a man. The Bible admonished Michal for her transgression, as several Hasidic tales did with likeminded women of the congregation.[76] *The Wedding Plan*, on the other hand, valorizes Michal's challenging behavior as worthwhile on a spiritual level. Accordingly, through neo-Hasidism's nonhierarchical emphasis on the individual, the film appears to locate in its protagonist a reflection of, if not outright connection to, the mystical unification of masculine and feminine in divinity, with which Kabbalah tradition has long been preoccupied.[77]

As a reconciliatory figure, Michal flushes out those parts of both religious and secular society invested in boundaries rather than bridges. In its commitment to the Hasidic tale's realist confrontation with social woes, the film certainly shows both communities to be rife with narrow-mindedness. In the religious sector, not only the dressmaker exhibits prejudicial attitudes but also other characters: for example, a client of Michal's business—a "mobile petting zoo"—makes derogatory comments about how a devout woman wishing to be wed should not be handling foul animals (in resonance with a tradition of Hasidic storytelling where the term *Hasida*—as in the feminine form of Hasid—is used negatively through association with its other meaning in Hebrew—the stork, an impure bird by biblical laws);[78] or a potential Hasid suitor who, as part of his general abstention from female impurity, refuses to look at Michal before she agrees to marry him and then proceeds to chastise her after she promises marriage on the stipulation that he looks at her first. On the side of Israeli secularity, the representative of narrowmindedness is Michal's mother. Although well-meaning—trying at one point to bring a rabbi to reason with her daughter—the mother is clearly opposed to the wedding scheme, out of anxiety about Michal's mental health and about society's judgment of her actions. More profoundly, however, it appears that the matriarch's reticence comes out of a deep-seated suspicion toward Michal's religious repentance, and religion in general, as manifesting irrationality and even mental imbalance.

In contrast to these, the film also shows several characters who are attracted to Michal's message of reconciliation—most notably her two romantic interests, Yos and Shimi. One would expect Yos, a popular entertainer, to epitomize the values of secular hedonism; yet the film's first real encounter with him takes place at R. Nachman's tomb in Uman, a site of pilgrimage for many religiously minded Israeli Jews. Though going there on a whim, his auspicious arrival at this holy site marks Yos as spiritually sensitive, and his conversation with Michal shows this sensitivity as forming a lingua franca of faith over secular-religious divides. While this bridge of religiosity binds the two characters together, it gradually becomes clear that Yos's openness is not sufficiently couched in religious terms to accurately meet Michal's needs. More appropriate in this respect is Shimi, who is anchored in the religious world, but nevertheless is encouraging of Michal's movement "out of its natural order." Thus the film's epilogue, as that of *Ushpizin*, manifests a reclaiming of Judaism's parameters and roles as the preferred framework for existence; the path leading to it, however, indicates that such parameters and roles may be made flexible enough to bring secularity closer to the religious fold, creating a firm ground of integration.

Though these relationships foreground love as the adhesive for social integration, they also position it as the basis for mystical revelation. A trace of R. Nachman's teachings is evident here, mainly in his figuration of love and longing as a spiritual force found "in the quest of the *Hasid* to approach his rebbe, in every Jew's desire to draw closer to God, even in the romance pulling the solid letters of the Hebrew alphabet to union with their soul, their vocal points."[79] Informed by these ideas, Michal's path seeks to integrate her not only with a suitable partner but with the Almighty. In order to achieve this dual goal, the protagonist is primarily tasked with locating the proper form of love that binds lower and upper worlds. The search for proper love moves her from actively looking for a groom in the name of God to fully submitting to God's will on her nuptials (or "go with the flow," as one woman advises her during a prayer session at Uman). Through her ultimate acquiescence, the protagonist is therefore positioned to actualize "a concept that is integral to the world of Hasidic values: the 'sweetening of judgment' [which] pertains to the ability of every individual to recognize the Divine 'judgments' that manifest in a certain situation, to accept the situation as given, and to act, from within this acceptance, to identify the mode of action that will elevate these judgments to their Source and thereby balance the relationship between divine judgment and mercy."[80]

By assuming the proper attitude toward love—accepting it as a cosmic rule, not enacting it as a human endeavor—the film's protagonist manages to get her miracle in the end: by sheer providence, Shimi finalized his divorce the week prior, and on her wedding day, with not another groom in sight, steps up to reveal his love for the wayward protagonist. That this moment is taking place on the religious holiday of Hannukah relates the film's apotheosis to the sphere of divine intervention. At the same time, it also associates Michal's miracle with that of "the cruse of oil," whereupon during the Maccabean revolt a small oil canister was found, whose contents were magically replenished so it could light the Temple Menorah for eight days. This association, however, belies a major difference between the two miraculous events: while the original "Hannukah miracle" is clearly fantastic by modern terms, Michal's rendition is more mundane and can feasibly be explained away as coincidence by

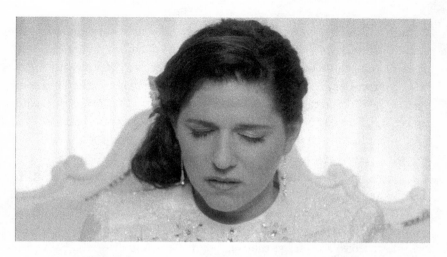

FIGURE 22. Michal (Noa Koler) about to realize her dream of matrimony. From *The Wedding Plan* (Rama Burshtein, 2016).

those same standards. Furthermore, the filmic miracle's couching in the emotional coordinates of interpersonal love aligns its aberration with that of secularity's principal romantic myth—of finding "the one" who is "made for me."[81] Together, these factors, in the fashion of (neo-)Hasidic storytelling, undercut the supposed "naivete" of *The Wedding Plan*, inviting secular viewers as much as observant ones to enter its mystical vision.

Erez Tadmor and Guy Nattiv's *Magic Men* (2014) pursues a similar interest in the role of the repentant within the religious-secular tension, yet unlike *Ushpizin* and *The Wedding Plan*, its protagonist is not a born-again Hasid but a secular Israeli. Avraham, who escaped Greece during World War II and settled in Israel, has just lost his wife. Following the funeral, he consents to travel to the Greek town of Arta and represent his municipality in a "twin cities" celebration ceremony. Upon arriving there, he discovers to his great chagrin that his estranged offspring Yehuda, a Chabad Hasid with whom he had no relations since the son's repentance process, was asked by the mayor to accompany him on the visit. Rather than follow the prescribed itinerary, Avraham evades Yehuda and attempts to locate an old magician friend who saved his life during the war. On his search, he meets the prostitute Maria, who offers her help. The demands of the visit get in the way, however, and Avraham is forced to suspend his quest and go with Yehuda and their chauffer to

Arta. En route, he quarrels with the driver, who leaves his two passengers on the side of the road. Maria comes to their aid, but ultimately departs, partly due to Yehuda's objection to her association with Avraham. Maria's departure strains the relationship between father and son, yet the two ultimately reconcile and agree to find the long-lost friend together. Upon discovering that he is now a nonresponsive resident of a retirement home, Avraham and Yehuda decide to deliver the friend to his son with a sum of money that would take care of his well-being. While at the son's home, however, they come to realize that this old man is not, in fact, Avraham's friend. Leaving him with his family, Avraham and Yehuda then embark on the journey back to Thessaloniki. As it gets dark, they park on the wayside and engage in a candid conversation, during which Yehuda receives a message that his pregnant wife delivered a baby girl. Avraham announces that he will visit the infant and the rest of Yehuda's children, and the two go to sleep. The following morning, Yehuda wakes up to discover that his father has passed away. He then accompanies Avraham's body to Israel and recites the Kaddish prayer over his grave.

Through its detailed depiction of the conflict between Avraham and Yehuda, *Magic Men* traces the effects of religious repentance on a secular family more closely than the other films discussed herein. Because integration into the Haredi world demands that they forsake all traces of secularity, repentants' relationship with their parents tends to be fraught with tension; here it is often the secular father who maintains contact with the repentant child, while the mother abstains out of resentment.[82] In *Magic Men*, however, the father is the one who actually severs relations with his son, even as the mother continues to visit him monthly. The apparent reason for the break is Yehuda's choice to inform on his father, who opened his butcher shop for business on the Sabbath even while carrying a "kosher certificate." Yet it is Avraham's disdain for religion that seems to be the decisive catalyst for the long-standing feud. This resentment surfaces, for example, when he denies his son the right to recite Kaddish over his mother's gravesite at the beginning of the film. It also emerges when, on the drive to Arta, Yehuda makes the chauffeur stop to rest until the passing of the Sabbath—a request that incurs Avraham's verbal protest, as well as his subsequent decision to eat nonkosher food during the Friday meal, in front of his son. So ferocious is Avraham's contempt that it seems to be motivated not only by an act of filial betrayal but especially by the way in which this act was undertaken—the very choice of abandoning the world of secularity for that of religion.

The film's inner-familial religious-secular conflict is played out largely away from the main characters' home—the geographical landscape of Israel. In this, *Magic Men* follows the Hasidic tale's use of a physical journey to a distant land as a way of facilitating change in the protagonists' lives and perceptions. The trip to Greece serves to isolate Avraham and Yehuda from the cultural context that places further pressure on their conflicting positions and circumscribes any effort of reconciliation. It also provides challenges and obstacles through which the characters are given an opportunity to reappraise their relationship. Yet unlike many Hasidic tales, where the "faraway land" is foreign enough to mark the return to the land of origin as "a coming home," here the journey takes the protagonists to a more familiar location. Greece, in this respect, is not an unknown territory, but one that is closely connected to the characters' past—to the wartime experiences of Avraham, which he attempts to retrace, and to the traditions and stories that were shared with the infant Yehuda. By having the two characters voyage there, *Magic Men* seems to mark history—far removed history, so removed that it seems virtually foreign—as a site that needs to be recuperated in order that father and son, secularism and religion, may be able to find common ground.

Importantly, this history is shaped by considerable trauma, with specific ramifications on the question of religious identity. Between the two main characters, the primal scene of interpersonal trauma may have been that of Yehuda's informing on Avraham's "nonkosher" business practices. Yet such treason is but a reverberation of an earlier traumatic betrayal: Avraham's wartime travails and subsequent displacement, which caused him to neither visit Greece nor speak Greek for decades after. If Avraham is fundamentally antireligious, it is perhaps because this watershed trauma in Jewish history—World War II and the Holocaust—made him question the need and legitimacy of Judaism. In this respect, his attitude is related to a broader Jewish disillusion of religion in the aftermath of World War II, which was channeled into mainstream Israeli secular-Zionism's not-so-tacit resentment of religious Jews during the nation's founding stages. Thus envisioned, *Magic Men* appears to suggest that for this resentment to be appeased, father and son must recover a past that preceded their traumas, and is linked with Greece: to relive their respective childhoods, when Yehuda bonded with Avraham over Greek stories, and when Avraham was at peace with his native land, prior to the monumental catastrophe that beset European Jewry.

This recuperation, it should be noted, does not necessitate an agreement on matters of devotion but rather a recognition of the common ground of emotionality that undergirds different belief systems. Out of the two characters, Yehuda plays the decisive role in surfacing this shared emotional base. Thus, he is not on a proselytizing mission to "convert" Avraham to ultra-Orthodoxy. Instead, what motivates him is a far less doctrinal and more human-relational principle—that of exhibiting a "respect for the father" (*Kvod Av*). By sidestepping evangelism, Yehuda is then able to reconceptualize the familial rift as bridgeable rather than not and pave the way for a recovery of past bonds. This ability, the film further suggests, stems from the flexible religiosity of a born-again Chabad Hasid who maintains secular ties and is reflected in his musical creation, which interweaves religious messages and a secular rap style. The musical emphasis, in turn, also ties Yehuda's religiosity with the Hasidic tale's fashioning of music as a form of "worldly" devotion, integrating inner life and everyday reality to foster interpersonal bonds as "a potent weapon against the social and economic hardships that weighed on [the] community."[83] Accordingly, through chiming in with this narrative trope, Yehuda's authority as a social mediator is given the weight of tradition.

Though anger as a force of divisiveness is part of the emotional ground both secular and devout share, *Magic Men*—like the (neo-)Hasidic tale—places greater emphasis on the integrative function of love. It could be said that at the film's outset, Avraham's main predicament is his absence of loving feelings. The encounter with Maria, however, opens up a new avenue for love—one that seems more humanistic than romantic, founded as it is on a proximity of national culture (Greek) and secular outlook. On the basis of this love, Avraham is mobilized into responding to Yehuda's advances and traversing the distance once created by religious observance and lack thereof. At certain moments even the association of Yehuda and Maria, the characters most socially distinct from each other, arrives at the heights, if not of love, then at least of affection. In this, the film rounds off its portrait of integration by not only linking

secular and religious Jews but also Jews and Christians—a reconciliatory gesture that is symbolically marked through the characters' names,
with Avraham referring to the father of Judaism, Maria to the mother
of Christianity, and Yehuda to the common Jewish (*Yehudi*) ancestry of
both religions.

Interdenominational bonds project onto the possibility of cosmic unity under one God, which in turn, following the (neo-)Hasidic
narrative pattern, receives palpable form in miraculous revelation. In
comparison to *Ushpizin* and *The Wedding Plan*, where the focalization is
through devout protagonists, *Magic Men* works primarily in relation to
secular Avraham's "modern" perspective and as such appears even more
sensitive to potential reproaches over naivete. This sensitivity translates
into a narrative evolution wherein both the secular protagonist and his
secular audience "learn" to distinguish between pseudo-revelations and
potentially real miracles. The first scene on this path takes place early
in the film. Avraham is at a local Thessaloniki bar when a television
show about searching for missing relatives appears on a nearby screen.
While watching, the anchorwoman suddenly addresses Avraham and
announces that his old friend has been looking for him for quite a while.
Avraham responds, and the two have a conversation, until the bartender
interrupts, and the scene returns to "normalcy." Here, the television
show's title—*The Light in the Darkness*—clearly evokes the language of
mystical revelation, yet the scene seems to indicate that the unexplain-
able is not so much supernatural as the product of individual halluci-
nation. This dismissal is followed up by the foregrounding of magic as
a rival discourse to that of revelation—one in which an abnormal event
is defined as "trick" rather than as proof of divine existence. The "trick"
aspect is highlighted in an early montage scene that shows Avraham and
Maria performing various "feats of magic": for example, when he stands
to the side of a parked bus and brings his hands together as the auto-
matic doors close; or when they perform swiping motions, seemingly
forcing the movement of a nearby revolving door. Such feats clearly constitute trickery—Avraham and Maria's actions do not cause the mecha-
nized effects to occur, and even as objective occurrences, effects of this
nature are hardly out of the ordinary. Accordingly, through these tricks,
the possible existence of a Transcendent that defies modern views of the
world is discredited.

As the plot progresses, however, the film alters its attitude toward this possibility—a change registered in the way that magic is depicted. The next central scene featuring magic has Avraham and Yehuda putting on a street show for passersby in order to earn some spending money. Their magical feats are different from those Avraham performed with Maria. These are no longer obvious tricks, their internal mechanism displayed in full view. Rather, they are operations whose outcome appears out of the ordinary (especially as they are shot in slow motion) and whose cause is not entirely laid bare. In making it more mysterious, magic stops being a barrier and starts acting as a bridge for Avraham and Yehuda to come together—as potentiality indicated in having them both wear clown make-up in order to blur their visible differences. Yet the placement of these feats in the context of a street show still lends them an air of deceit and as a result prevents the occasion from becoming a truly sound base for mystical unity.

It is only at the film's conclusion that magic ceases to be explicable (and dismissible) in terms of rational thinking. In the penultimate sequence, Avraham and Yehuda are in a parked car and have a candid talk for the first time in years. As the conversation winds down, Avraham asks Yehuda to pick a card from his deck. Yehuda picks the queen of hearts and places it back in the deck. Avraham then looks through the deck but does not extract the right card. Yehuda asks him where he placed the queen of hearts—is it under his pillow, as it was when they were younger? Avraham simply responds that the magic "didn't work,"

FIGURE 23. Avraham (Makram Khoury, *left*) and Yehuda (Zohar Strauss, *right*) performing magic. From *Magic Men* (Erez Tadmor and Guy Nattiv, 2014).

revealing it as a bad trick. Yet after he dies, in the final moments of the film, the card reappears in the most unlikely of places—in Maria's cigarette box, which she opens while on a date with a client, and between the pages of Yehuda's prayer book, as he reads the Kaddish over his father's grave. The sheer implausibility of these "magical" manifestations makes it difficult to write them off as tricks and turns them into something that is truly mysterious. Considering the exact character of the card—the queen of hearts—and the fact that it also appears with Maria, a female figure who helps Avraham and Yehuda rediscover their mutual love, *Magic Men* seems to indicate that such mystery can only be accessed through an emotional openness, a capacity for love; it is this common denominator that serves as the condition for both Yehuda and Avraham to transcend the bounds of categorical thinking. Yet the mysterious vision that was enabled through this emotional openness cannot be reduced to emotional terms; it exists as an "objective fact" belonging to the "outside world," independent of character mediation and interpretation.

If understood in mystical terms, this "fact" could be said to qualify as an example of "equalization" (*Hashvaah*), which Chabad Hasidism uses to describe "the equality of the divinity [through] the equalization of opposites and the finding of a median between entities contrary to each other in their external manifestation."[84] In this sense, by bringing together symbols of secularity (the card, the cigarette box) and religion (the prayer book), *Magic Men* equalizes them into a *coincidentia oppositorum* to manifest an underlining unity that binds them together. Nevertheless, such a reading of mystery, which figures it as miraculous, is not forced on the viewer; as a "wonderous act," this revelation is still modest enough to, in neo-Hasidic fashion, "deemphasize the significance of the 'truth value' of religious claims on a theoretical level."[85] Consequently, what remains present at the film's ending is a persistent enigma that can neither be rationally explained nor theologically contextualized and therefore is flexible enough to unite both secular and religious individuals in its midst.

Thus described, *Ushpizin, The Wedding Plan*, and *Magic Men* all follow in the tradition of Hasidic and especially neo-Hasidic tales, whose religiosity makes miraculous revelation palatable for modern audiences through the lessening of its "fantastic" valences. As such, if one were to accuse these films of "credulity," the designation would only be applicable

FIGURE 24. A card in the prayer book. From *Magic Men* (Erez Tadmor and Guy Nattiv, 2014).

in the self-conscious sense of "second naiveté": what Paul Mendes-Flohr, following Jewish-German philosopher Ernst Simon, defines as

> an approach that allows the children of Enlightenment to affirm religious belief while still respecting the doubts, hesitations, and skepticism that come with secular experience. What destroys belief is not the denial or rejection of the insights and sensibilities of modern, secular culture; if anything, these insights and sensibilities, and the knowledge-images they support, are given respect, transformed and incorporated into a new cognitive stance, which opens up to the transcendent truths that carry within them tradition's "old answers." Without giving up on the critical wakefulness of the secular order, "second naiveté" allows Man [*sic*] to experience God's presence, to open up to tradition's transcendental claims, and to bow down in humility and prayer.[86]

To the extent that "second naiveté" retains a desire to work within a theosophic understanding even while *incredulously* attempting to adjust to the modern mindset, it can never fully detach itself from modern definitions of the credulous. Such is clearly the case with the religion-affirming *Ushpizin* and *The Wedding Plan*, which support, to a greater or lesser degree, the ontological validity of "God's presence"—especially in their legitimization of the miraculous. These texts should therefore be considered "religious," even as they leave room for modern-secular audiences to accept their revelation through rational terms. Like these two films, *Magic Men* also foregrounds an overarching unifying presence that undergirds multiplicity, yet unlike them, it does not explain this unity away. Rather, it shows how traditional-religious and modern-secular readings of this multiplicity unravel and dissolve into mystery, epitomized by the climactic "miracle"—a true trance vision appearing on screen. In so doing, this film, more than the others, cajoles the viewers to self-transcend in radical ekstasis and inhabit the experiential indeterminacy typical of unio mystica. The resulting unitive state offers a response to the modern-secular mindset's quest to inhabit reality's hidden dimensions.[87] The question remains, however, to what degree such a remedy, removed not only from theological claims but also from those of instrumental reason, can find a footing within this mindset, without simply being dismissed as credulous.

Cinema, Credulity, and Faith

The cinematic adaptations of Hasidic storytelling discussed so far not only raise questions as to how miraculous revelation can be represented on screen but also as to how cinema can elicit *a revelatory experience*. In contrast to the spectatorial states outlined in the previous chapter's conclusion, which are more the norm of film viewing, this experiential position is much less prevalent and thus much more difficult to decipher. A fruitful starting point for this definitional task may be a statement made by Mexican filmmaker Carlos Reygadas on his reaction to the famous resurrection scene at the end of Carl Th. Dreyer's *Ordet* (1955): that this was the only instance in cinema where he encountered, not a "filmed miracle," but a "miracle *filmed*," one in which we "can believe."[88] What Reygadas gets at here is cinema's innate ability to mobilize the viewer's envisioning toward moments that are, in Rick Warner's words, "profoundly affirming, not of an already conceived order of things, still less of higher law of understanding, but of a capacity to create something new, something before which our habitual modes of knowing are powerless."[89] In the dissolution of these modes of knowing, the viewer arguably undergoes a "peak experience" common to various aesthetic environments, entailing a loss of individual identity and a merger with what appears as the universe's totality.[90] Such ecstatic transcendence is the stuff, not only of a filmic peak experience, but of the condition of unio mystica present in Kabbalah as in other mystical traditions. And similarly to mystical experiences of unity, these spectatorial unitive states, which operate on faith rather than on reason, are particularly vulnerable to accusations of credulity by a modern perspective (for example, as those leveled against early viewers who, during the foundational 1895 Grand Café screening of Lumiere's *Arrival of the Train at the Station*, ran out terrified of being hit by the oncoming locomotive).[91] Yet can we outline a more favorable definition of these states where on-screen and off-screen are sensed as radically unified? Perhaps an interpretation that lends it, and its resulting knowledge, an aura of incredulity?

Bazin, for one, provides clues as to how this interpretation might look like. Thus, in "Evolution of the Language of Cinema," he famously argued that montage editing distorts reality by imposing on it a certain order—"the *unity* of meaning of the dramatic event."[92] A deep focus-long take realist style, in contrast, was not seen as distorting reality, since it brings "together real time, in which things exist, along with the duration of the action, for which classical editing had insidiously substituted mental and abstract time."[93] Accordingly, by avoiding the unnecessary fragmentation of reality, this form seemed to Bazin more capable of "*reveal*[ing] the hidden meanings in people and things without disturbing the *unity* natural to them."[94] In this formulation, it becomes evident that unity is paramount to Bazin's understanding of the proper image of reality that should be revealed on screen. This is a unity that is largely transcendent to our categorical modes of ordering—that foregrounds "ambiguity," in the sense that when one unravels these modes, the interconnectedness that is exposed between reality's constituents appears incoherent by any traditional coordinates of coherence. To witness with uncertainty such revelation of ambiguous unity, for Bazin, is not merely a "psychological" event; it speaks to a "metaphysical" modality of the cinematic experience and therefore serves as the appropriate "spiritual key"[95] through which we should interpret a realist film. Importantly, while aesthetics occupy a vital role in facilitating this revelation, its foundation seems to reside in "the irrational power of the photograph to bear away our *faith*."[96] Indeed, as articulated in "Ontology of the Photographic Image," Bazin imagines our engagement with photography (and cinema) as always already grounded in irrational faith, which is why he equates it to interactions with religious relics and ritualistic artifacts. It is from this faith-full position that spectators are willing to address the photographic image as transparency rather than representation—as "laying bare the realities" rather than masking them. Once cinema taps into faith, it is able, through proper aesthetic means, to strip "its object of all those ways of seeing it, those piled up preconceptions, that spiritual dust and grime with which my eyes have covered it" and show "the natural image of a world that we neither know nor can see."[97] Concurrently, it also further dissolves the logical separation of real from imaginary, allowing spectators to experience the screen as if they were both part of a unified microcosm, irrationally interconnected.

In Bazin's view, the irrational power of faith has immense positive significance, not only in delineating the proper perspective on photographic ontology but also the correct means of engagement with the life-world. Such investment in faith has subsequently presented the biggest obstacle for film scholars who revisited Bazin's work and critiqued his affinity toward, in Christian Metz's phrasing, "conceptions of the cinema as a mystical revelation, as 'truth' or 'reality' unfolding by right, as the apparition of what is [l'étant], as epiphany."[98] This "idealist" reading, according to Metz, needlessly valorizes the spectator's inner "credulous person," who is "seated *beneath* the incredulous one, or in his heart, [and] continues to believe"[99] in "the reality of an imaginary world."[100] Contrary to Metz's stipulation, which treats cinema's mystical revelations of unity as imaginary, we may also posit the possibility, entertained in Bazin's argumentation, that they are indicative of a certain phenomenological-ontological truth[101]—the existence of an essential order of unity within the phenomenal world that escapes our rational attempts to define it. To even consider such an argument, it becomes necessary to conceptualize it further, using sources external to Bazinian film theory that speak to an underlying phenomenological-ontological order of unity as well as its relationship to (mystical or nonmystical) unitive states and revelatory aesthetics. Drawing on the phenomenology of Maurice Merleau-Ponty and the religious existentialism of Martin Buber, which serve as the theoretical foundation for the previous chapter's concluding discussion, the following is a modest attempt to do just that—an attempt motivated, not by a desire to "authenticate" the Bazinian argument and its premises but by the intention of offering them as a way to open up the terms by which we conventionally define film spectatorship.

Buber's writing provides various descriptions of unitive experience, of which this noted one, articulated in the first person, is particularly evocative:

> I consider a tree.
>
> I can look on it as a picture: stiff column in a shock of light, or splash of green shot with the delicate blue and silver of the background.
>
> I can perceive it as movement: flowing veins on clinging, pressing pith, suck of the root, breathing of the leaves, ceaseless commerce with earth and air and the obscure growth itself.
>
> I can classify it in a species and study it as a type in its structure and mode of life.
>
> I can subdue its actual presence and form so sternly that I recognize it only as an expression of law—of the laws in accordance with which a constant opposition of forces is continually adjusted, or of those in accordance with which the component substances mingle and separate.
>
> I can dissipate it and perpetuate it in number, in pure numerical relation.
>
> In all this the tree remains my object, occupies space and time, and has its nature and constitution.
>
> I can, however, also come about, if I have both will and grace, that in considering the tree I become bound up in relation to it. The tree is now no longer It. I have been seized by the power of exclusiveness.
>
> To effect this it is not necessary for me to give up any of the ways which I consider the tree. There is nothing from which I would have to turn my eyes away in order to see, and no knowledge that I would have to forget. Rather is everything, picture and movement, species and type, law and number, indivisibly united in this event.
>
> Everything belonging to the tree is in this: its form and structure, its colors and chemical composition, its intercourse with the elements and with the stars, are all present in a single whole.

> The tree is no impression, no play of my imagination, no value
> depending on my mood; but it is bodied over against me and has
> to do with me, as I with it—only in a different way.[102]

Drawing on his previously discussed terms, Buber aims to show in
this passage that any object, even one as simple as a tree, is always a
manifold—a Thou—and that our engagement with this object reduces
its multidimensional nature into a particular viewpoint—an It. When
the multitude of different perspectives (or Its) are placed together, certain inconsistencies arise, and a particular ambiguity ensues. For Buber,
however, this ambiguity is not inherent to the object itself but a product
of our objectifying engagement and the reified terms of coherence that
emerge from it. Accordingly, we need to bypass our regular modes of
approaching It, via an attitude of openness and humility, in order to
yield a different vision of the object, a Thou that replaces inconsistency
with totality and ambiguity with mystery. Such a trance vision, in Buber's
mind, does not entail a credulous disavowal of the various definitions of
the object but rather an acknowledgment that in defining it, we necessarily implement analytic separations that fragment its unity. By moving away from such separations, the object thus emerges as "indivisibly
united"—as a mysterious totality where each aspect stands in relation to
each other. This unified vision, though relying on a transformation of
consciousness to manifest itself, is essential rather than experiential in
the sense of not being wholly contingent on a "play of my imagination."
     Crucially, when appearing as "a single whole," the tree is also
revealed as something that "is bodied over against me and has to do with
me, as I with it"; in this sense, the revelatory vision invites the subject to
follow through experientially on an already existing phenomenological-
ontological interconnectedness between them. Such, of course, is the
emblematic expression of Buberian dialogue; yet while a dialogue with
It maintains the distinctions of Cartesian dualism, a dialogue with Thou
goes a long way to dissolve such separations. In this state of rapport, by
Israel Koren's account, there is a "soft unity"[103] that does not fully abolish all differences between I and Thou so much as interweave the two
together in the form of an "embrace."[104] Through embracing, "the true 'I,'
that reason why a human being is called a 'human being,' really extends
beyond itself . . . towards the actual site of Thou. The 'I' of the I-Thou is

therefore comprised of I and Thou; it is an ecstatic being whose point of origin is around its body and its end point extends beyond itself without losing its former grip around its body and without the subject losing its sense of individual self."[105] Following the traditions of Hasidism, embrace of this kind is contextualized through the term "love." Yet for Buber, love is less important as an emotion than as a basic state of relation; loving emotions proper may facilitate an awareness of this relation, but they are only at best its "companions." Dialogical relations between I and Thou, in their purest form, are therefore, in Koren's words, "a clinging of love, but one lacking in the personal feeling of love. In this state, love exists only as being and not as emotion."[106]

It should be stressed again, however, that Buber does not collapse the mysterious totality that is the I-Thou into the relationship between I and eternal Thou, the apprehensible God.[107] In this, the framing of his tree example is also significant. Per his view of a concrete metaphysics, we encounter only the Thou as a particular element of a specific meeting: that is, the totality perceived is always somehow bound to the coordinates of engagement, the circumscribed position of a perceiving consciousness as it relates to an element within the life-world. While this vision exhibits a unity that, in essence, is divine, it does not encapsulate the eternal Thou. Rather, for Buber this eternal Thou acts as "the Centre where the extended lines of relations meet,"[108] not only of a meeting between a particular I and a particular Thou, but of all the meetings that are occurring and may occur between all particular Is and particular Thous. At the same time as interpenetrating these meetings, it also "encompasses" and "includes" them in an embrace, while still preserving their humanity.[109] The eternal Thou's existence, then, subtends all human existence as a unified system, and in this respect is not fully included in each person's particular perspective; yet for Buber, His presence is felt in each meeting, which is also the only context where we may speak of—or rather to—Him.

In light of the previous chapter's conclusion, it may come as no surprise that Buber's description of a vision of mysterious totality parallels similar descriptions in formative phenomenological literature—and in particular, the literature of Merleau-Ponty—that has informed film studies scholarship. Merleau-Ponty's phenomenology, as M. C. Dillon has cogently argued, sought "to liberate phenomena from their traditional restriction to the sphere of immanence, to restore their transcendence, and thereby to lift the curse of mereness from appearance and return to human opinion the measure of truth it has earned."[110] It performs this task, however, without re-erecting the rigid Cartesian dualism of immanence and transcendence, and its attendant conceptual problematic: that, "if the world is completely transcendent, it is completely opaque and cannot be known," but "if the elements of cognition are entirely immanent and transparent, the degree of opacity and givenness needed to give meaning to externality and transcendence is lost, and truth is sacrificed in a quest for certainty that defeats itself."[111] To avoid this deadlock while still maintaining a claim to ontological truth, Merleau-Ponty searched for a middle ground "where immanence and transcendence intersect: that is, in the phenomena manifesting themselves in the perceptual field."[112] Looking at (a phenomenological) ontology through this middle ground, he stipulated that our ontological knowledge is always partial, and an opacity always remains, but did not regard these as justifications for equating partiality with falsity.

If phenomena, as that which is manifested through perception, should be considered real, then for Merleau-Ponty the operation of perception must be given primacy as the key to unlocking the secrets of the life-world. Within phenomenology, perception is meaningful by definition, being an expression of an intentional project that seeks to organize the perceptual field. Following a primordial logic, itself based in what Merleau-Ponty calls the "pre-established harmony"[113] between the look and the world, his organization functions as the extraction of the visible from the invisible, the seen from the unseen.[114] Significantly, by foregrounding a visible figure, perception does not exclude the invisible. Rather, the invisible may be sensed within the visibles, as "the tissue that lines them, sustains them, nourishes them, and which for its part is not a thing, but a possibility, a latency, and a *flesh* of things."[115]

Together, the visibly manifest and the invisibly possible produce a trance vision of, in Dillon's terminology, "a natural or non-arbitrary *unity*"[116]—one that exceeds our normative categories of coherence and that consequently appears in "*ambiguous* richness and determinability."[117] It is this inherent ambiguity that the ego continuously represses through incessant abstractions and reifications, which produce second-order concepts and mistake them for basic truths.[118] The burden of these processes of "sedimentation" is overwhelming, since it permeates all levels of thought, language, and engagement. Accordingly, for Merleau-Ponty, freedom cannot be achieved but through a lifelong "epoché," wherein the layers of sediment are gradually removed.[119] Such work that reveals the unified "flesh of things" is arguably conditioned on a radical and continual departure from our "natural" attitudes—on a series of "active and searching" gazes, which in Vivian Sobchack's phrasing, rest "not on the familiar forms or figures that vision has time and time again constituted, but rather on the latent visibility from which such figures emerge and against which they stand in relation to its latency."[120]

A revelation of this kind abolishes separation between subject and object by experientially intertwining through "the identity of the seer and the visible"—where "he *is* of *it*" and vice versa, as discernible parts belonging to the same flesh.[121] Significantly, like Buber's notion of the embrace, Merleau-Ponty also defines experiential intertwining— the "chiasm"—in corporeal terms, such as that of one hand touching another (the double sensation of touching and being touched). This image allows him to similarly subvert an idea of fusion between subject and object, while still maintaining their interconnectedness as corporeal ingredients of the same flesh. At the same time, it also highlights the affective dimension of Merleau-Ponty's phenomenological ontology. Thus, for him, if individuation brings about a clear-cut separation between subject and object, then it is also the origin of alienation; yet the existence of a primordial experience of our phenomenal reality as one founded on communality, of touching and being touched, ensures the continued presence of a wish for unity with another, in love's intimacies. Such intimacy, which produces a sense of interconnectedness with an ambiguously unified vision, should not be taken, however, as exposing the flesh of the world in its entirety. The source of experience is always a corporeal being that perceives *from somewhere, and toward a particular horizon*. And even if the experience of the thing is informed through intersubjective relations, there is always a limit that denies omniscience. Accordingly, the world is forever something that transcends us, even as we are able to achieve intimacy with its totality. It is the "horizon of all horizons," according to Dillon, which becomes "Merleau-Ponty's name for what others have called God or *Geist* or Being,"[122] and which also parallels Buber's conceptualization of the eternal Thou.

The alleged order of unity of the phenomenal world that both these philosophical stances address is not divulged by intellection but by other means—for example, the aesthetic appreciation of artworks. Buber's advocacy of art, for one, seems at face value to undermine his criticism of a dynamic of objectification, of a dominant I-It relation. Indeed, every act of forming—artistic creation included—places a dangerous limitation on "streaming reality," threatening to turn it into an ossified figure that denies its basic multifarious yet unified nature. Risks such as these are tolerated by Buber, primarily because he acknowledges that the Thou-as-word is, in itself, essentially a form, a framing within the manifold of being. And as an essential form, the Thou is a necessary tool of revelation of that which cannot be fully abstracted, allowing human subjects to relate to the eternal Thou through a finite, albeit ambiguous presence. This capacity of the Thou is diminished, however, as it inevitably turns into an It, its contours hardening into a concept.

The different stages of form evolution are rendered acutely percep-tible for Buber in artistic creation, and in particular that of visual art, mainly because it does not emerge from intellectual processes so much as from one's bodily and affective relationship with the world. When the artist enters into an I-Thou rapport with the world, an ambiguously unified form is disclosed. Because form (a Thou) is contained in the coordinates of the particular meeting, this disclosure necessarily entails a sacrifice: namely, in Buber's words, "the obliteration" of "the endless possibility that is offered up on the altar of the form," the exclusion of all other possible meetings beyond the "exclusiveness" of this meeting, which nevertheless are themselves included in the manifold of being. Yet while this "sacrifice" still maintains the integrity of the I-Thou rela-tion, the act of transporting form into an artform might not. Hence, in shepherding the form into the sphere of *It*, the artist may cause it to be hardened into a "structure" and distance the artwork from the original relation. But since the traces of that relation are never fully banished, and structure always "longs"[123] for its return, the artwork can occasionally reveal itself as Thou, inviting the receptive spectator into a meaningful "embrace."

In *I and Thou* Buber pays little attention to aesthetics, making it seem as if this invitation for revelation is not contingent on particu-lar stylistic choices within the artwork. Yet if one takes his oeuvre as a whole, it is possible to see an abiding interest in style, and especially painting style, that extends as far back as the philosopher's early school days. Taken in this context, Buber's approach to art privileged certain aesthetic strategies as ones that, like the word "Thou," were more proximate to the essential forms and their attendant relations—which, in the words of Margaret Olin, have "discarded the representation of sensory data in favor of a relationship to them."[124] Such, for example, was the case of his study of Jewish artist Lesser Ury (1901). In Buber's mind, Ury does not want to produce an image of reality as the sum of disparate objects but rather wishes to assert the "the reciprocity of things," believing that once you "connect a being to all beings, . . . you tease out its most essential."[125] In pursuing this goal, the painter consequently attempts dissolve the represented being's uniqueness through the nuances of color. Such dissolution is inherent to color as color, since only it "can tell about air and sun, fog and shadows: it puts the thing in context; it awakens the underlying harmony." Accordingly, it seems that the unifying effect of color is mostly existent within the visual presentation of a natural landscape. Thus, in Ury's landscapes, "color is the indisputable sole ruler. Here he can truly communicate the soul of the landscape, which reveals itself in the reciprocal effect of the elements, in the reciprocal shades, musings, clarifications, and deepening. The soul of a tree is the continual transformation of a tree. A moment in which a thousand lifefloods are mixed."[126] It is at these particular renderings that Ury turns into an "ecstatic"—"color becomes God for him, an everpresent God, whom he sees in visions. . . . He does not limit the area of color; he wants to present everything as color. His work is an abstraction of everything that does not have color value."[127] Consequently, the artist also invites his audience members to surrender to the trance vision of unified color and become "ecstatics" themselves.

Merleau-Ponty's interest in aesthetics is most clearly present in his last published essay, "Eye and Mind" (1961). Continuing his lifelong struggle against the dominance of conceptual thought, the French philosopher reasserts in this context that the "profane vision" of scientific mentality denies a primordial "'there is' . . . the soil of the sensible and humanly modified world such as it is in our lives for our bodies."[128] In contrast, he argues, "art, especially painting, draws upon this fabric brute meaning which operationalism would prefer to ignore."[129] In a

description that mirrors Buber's, Merleau-Ponty depicts the act of painting as one in which the painter "practices a magical theory of vision. He
[*sic*] is obliged to admit that objects before him pass into him or else
that . . . the mind goes out through the eyes to wander among objects."
This is not the objectifying gaze of the scientist that reduces an entity
like a mountain into a discrete empirical thing. Rather, the relationship
between subject and object is one of exploratory reciprocity, where
"it is the mountain itself which from out there makes itself seen by
the painter; it is the mountain that he interrogates with his gaze."[130] The
invitation "extended" by the mountain is one that asks the painter "to
unveil the means, visible and not otherwise, by which it makes itself
mountain before our eyes [and which] exist only at the threshold of profane vision."[131] When this invitation is accepted, the resulting artwork
is also capable of bestowing on the viewer a sense of being in intimate
communion with what appears on the canvas.

Though such unitive experiences are grounded in certain
phenomenological-ontological realities, for Merleau-Ponty their realization is nevertheless contingent on a proper use of aesthetics. For
example, in his analysis of both the content and attendant painting
reproductions of the essay's original publication, Galen Johnson points
to the lingering influence Paul Cézanne had on Merleau-Ponty's thinking, which in this context focuses on the artist's late watercolors of Mont
Sainte-Victoire. Much like in Buber's discussion of Ury, Merleau-Ponty
highlights Cézanne's ability to disclose a trance vision of unity through
color's indivisibility. Thus, in his words, "the orchestration of color har-
monies from the transparencies of each color modulates toward more
delicate and less resounding chords. . . . Moreover, the blank spaces of
white paper are not filled in, but are more and less brilliant highlights,
unifying visible with invisible. . . . Without losing the objectivity of his oil
paintings, both these features of Cézanne's watercolors draw our attention to the surface composition of the painter's late work and its sublimity and spirituality rather than the features of mass, monumentality,
and solidity."[132]

In bringing together the philosophies of Merleau-Ponty and Buber,
what therefore becomes apparent is their shared phenomenological-
ontological claims of an order of unity to our life-world that often proves
inaccessible due to the sedimentation of categorical thinking, and of art's

ability to reveal that unity through unitive experiences. Bazin's film theory, it has been argued, works under similar assumptions. Where these thinkers diverge, however, is in the object of their aesthetic interrogation, yet this divergence is not insurmountable when attempting to synthesize the three views. Such synthesis would move away from Bazin's exclusive emphasis on film as a revelatory medium and join Merleau-Ponty's and Buber's proposition that other artforms may have the capacity for revelation. It would also recognize the possibility that Bazin was correct in his assertion that film may have greater success at prompting unitive states because it presents image as reality more forcefully than other visual arts, and as a result, invites us to assume the irrational stance of faith. Beyond questions of medium specificity, the juxtaposition of these theories also highlights a critical necessity to foreground the significant role of style in effecting unitive experiences, and to look at aesthetics broadly rather than narrowly in relation to said objective. This latter point is of particular relevance when considering Bazin's emphasis on "realism" over "abstraction" in reference to photographic media's revelatory role. Such a proposition seems unduly limited in light of the artistic examples provided by Buber and Merleau-Ponty, which point away from strict realism in the context of aesthetic unitive experiences, as well as of subsequent film studies theories that undervalue realism as a way of triggering such "spiritual" epiphanies. Moving past an essentialist prescriptive position, then, we would do well to recognize the existence of a range of potentially "revelatory styles" and to surface historical and cultural contingency as a main factor in the realization of this potential, considering that "revelations" are always already dependent on the participation of a perceiver with a particular "localized" frame of reference. This understanding underlies the attempt of Judaic-themed Israeli cinema to induce experiences of revelation by drawing on the tradition of Jewish mystical thought and expression with which its Israeli audiences are (increasingly) familiar. It is in this framework that a spectrum of aesthetic resources—extending from straightforward presentations of the wondrous to enigmatic images of the everyday—becomes readily available for adaptation through cinematic means, amplifying the medium's inherent capacity to draw out a "faithful" spectatorial response.

The example of Judaic-themed Israeli cinema finally brings us back to the issue of mysticism and its relevance to a model of filmic unitive states. Indeed, though sharing similar assertions, out of the three thinkers discussed, only Buber seems to speak the language of mysticism;[133] Merleau-Ponty does not, and even "the mystic" Bazin prefers to abstain from mystical terminology. In light of film studies' traditional reliance, from Bazin onward, on a "secularized" phenomenology,[134] why then should we consider Buber's brand of existential mysticism helpful for our discussion of these states within a cinematic framework? It is undeniably relevant in relation to experiences of audiences that are culturally predisposed toward mystical traditions. Yet can it not be significant for a generalized model as well? A possible reply to these questions may arrive from confronting the fundamental reason why mystical thought has been excluded from theoretical elaborations on spectatorship in the first place: namely, the belief that a model of "scientific" value cannot incorporate any claims that relate spectatorial "epiphanies" to divine origin. Such a position, from a phenomenological-ontological standpoint, could be countered by asserting that even if an explanatory model for unitive states were to base itself solely on traditional phenomenology, its claims would never yield more than "imperfect knowledge."[135] Thus, to the extent that one accepts an order of unity as a phenomenological-ontological truth, one must also admit that there will always be something transcendent to our finite ability to conceive of it. And if one accepts that, then the issue of whether this unity is of "divine" or "natural" origin becomes moot—or rather, a question of a "localized" frame of reference, of discourse, of belief system (or Faith). Accordingly, since origin fails to act as proper grounds for exclusion, what seems more useful in engaging filmic unitive states is an inclusive approach, which traces experiential similarities across different "localized" frameworks that contextualize these states a posteriori and arguably shape them a priori (in the sense that we can never fully unravel our categories of coherence). With this in mind, Buberian philosophy emerges as an important ingredient in the proposed model of cinematic spectatorship,[136] not only because it speaks, like traditional phenomenology, of a unifying order, but also because it invites us to break free from the confines of traditional phenomenology's "secular" perspective and its influence on film scholarship, so as to consider unitive experiences through the terms of (Jewish) mysticism and their New Age reverberations.

It may be that unitive states that unravel categorical separations are not reflective of any phenomenological-ontological truth; that they *should* be considered naive, if not downright delusional. In light of evidence to their existence in aesthetic engagements, this perspective should not stop film studies scholars from mapping them out and locating the general characteristics of their particular ekstasis; nor should it prevent scholarship from looking at the rich descriptive language of mysticism for ways to speak about these experiences, not only in reference to spectators who are immersed in this language, but in relation to those who are removed from it. Where the proposition that such states expose a certain truth *does* provide us with some added value, however, is in potentially giving credence to the insight they yield within a cinematic setting. By entertaining this possibility, it may become feasible to consider unitive filmic moments, generously and on their own terms, as instances of illumination, revealing a fundamental unity that encompasses the life-world. Under such narrow provisions, the cinema that "bears away our faith" to these ends comes close in its operation to that of the traditional Hasidic tale, which sought to bridge the seemingly disparate notes of our perceived reality through a "melody of faith." And in so doing, this cinema also offers us a new front through which to contemplate the meaning and limits of our own spectatorial credulity.

AFTERWORD

Toward a Global Mystical Society

In Israel of the new millennium, the landscape of Judaism has experienced a significant transformation. Israeli society's secular precincts, once bearers of the national ethos of Zionism and its halfhearted repressions of Judaic life, are now manifesting a veritable "Jewish Renaissance." No longer is Judaism something that must be sublimated and displaced through the parameters of the Zionist "civil religion"; rather, it has become legitimate for this constituency to pursue Jewish religion with fervor through a range of engagements and a variety of emphases. Concurrently, as Israeli dominant culture came to embrace Judaism, Israel's religious sector, once marginalized, has gradually found (implicit or explicit) ways to further integrate within this very culture. Even if not often carried to the extreme of abandoning religion, such adaptive measures are nevertheless unprecedented in Israeli history, divulging a profound recognition by observant Israeli Jews of the dangers of treating Judaism as a static entity that must be protected through fundamentalist scripturalism. This movement toward reconciliation between Israeli secularism and Judaism, however, is accompanied by an opposing movement that is also very much present in Israeli life—one that pulls these sides away from each other, marking the gap between them as unbridgeable. It is in this conjunction of coming together and pulling apart that we are able to best sense a fundamental ambivalence around how to relate to the Judaic in the Israeli setting—a question that has not been broached so forcefully, and with such great urgency, until recent times.

Judaic-themed Israeli films, a novel phenomenon in the young history of Israeli cinema, seem geared toward answering this query, and as a result are marked by its underlying ambivalence. Whether dealing with such topics as the existence and character of God, the nature of gender and sexual relations, the dynamics of communal and personal ritual, or the tensions between Israeli-religious and Israeli-secular social realities, these works rarely provide clear-cut answers. Rather, even when avowedly upholding a one-sided position, they seem particularly unstable as texts, drawing Judaism and secularism away from each other as they are brought in tandem (and vice versa). The resulting uncertainty seems to act as the background, and arguably the catalyst, for an appeal to mystical experience, much as it has always been within Judaic tradition.[1] Inspired by similar appeals in other parts of contemporary Israeli culture, several Judaic-themed films may be said to look toward mysticism for an avenue of liberation—a site where the basic coordinates that govern secular-religious relations and render it (at times cripplingly) ambivalent may be unraveled, and where a greater unity, one of far-reaching mystery rather than synthesis of known terms, may be achieved. This nod takes place on the level of content and form, relying on the capability of its audience (the Israeli-Jewish at least) to pick up on culturally determined mystical cues, amplified by cinema's innate "magical" capacity to induce states that defy our commonsensical understanding of the world. Such states may indeed be deemed (ontologically) false and (psychologically) credulous; in the spirit of ambivalence, the films tend to fluctuate on the validity of these propositions, even within themselves. A common thread of agreement may nevertheless be found through this corpus: the underlying belief that mystical experiences can have some social usefulness within the Israeli—and perhaps even the global—context.

In his insightful volume *The Mystical Society*, Philip Wexler addressed the growing investment in mysticism within the global New Age and attempted to tease out its "emerging social vision." Looking at a variety of mystical practices across diverse contemporary cultural settings, Wexler argues that they coalesce around certain key features: "reorganizing the internal self, through work aimed at transcending time and space; choosing as a goal to create a more flexible ego, even if not dissolving it completely; demonstrating how a person can be simultaneously present in this and other worlds; and adjusting the self so that it would remain more open to relationships and more connected to a greater and more absolute universe, which provides meaning and vitality."[2] These features speak to a different mode of subjectivity than the one commonly found within present-day society, and which stresses stability as a means of self-protection. Instead "of this protected subject, we discover a subject that is without boundaries and a subject that shatters its own boundaries, which evolves from the tradition of worldly mysticism that influences current everyday life."[3] Under the effect of mystical states, personhood is therefore no longer seen as alienated from its surrounding reality, human or otherwise, through conceptual barriers. Rather, it finds itself connected to everything through being part of "a broader and quivering life of energy and the cosmic 'self.'"[4]

For Wexler, this connection lays the groundwork for a new form of social reality. Thus the experience of boundlessness undercuts the conventional separation between inside and outside, consequently prompting the self to be interweaved into social dynamics. The dialogue of sociality that supposedly emerges in this novel context is quite antithetical to the traditional form of dialogue, "for the exchange is not about the trading of words between social subjects, but about the transmission of a meaningful experience between self and environment."[5] As a result, a system of social codification is replaced by a form of "social energy," of tapping into a supposed fluid and integrative level of Being where relations are less about transaction than they are about transformation. To the extent that this form is realized today, it does not conform to any traditional definition of a social movement: it is a movement of personal efforts that are nevertheless cognizant of their relations in the world, a "decentered and diffused"[6] structure that nonetheless attempts to maintain a sense of communality. According to Wexler, the fact that such social behavior is presently thriving serves as an indication that a "mystical society" is not entirely a figment of our imagination. And while it is too soon to determine their greater potential, he nevertheless locates in these humble beginnings a welcomed model for social change.

As far reaching as it is evocative, Wexler's take on contemporary mysticism is not without its blind spots. He argues, for one, that the present postmodern state of diffusion, coupled with the rise of virtual information technology, has already created an experience of boundlessness, which the current appeals to mysticism feed on and expand; an opposing view, however, would see this perception of postmodernism as overstated and would stress the continued presence of principal cultural terms (for example, secularity and religion) within today's "virtual" environment, albeit in a less firmly dialectical and more ambivalent way than before. Furthermore, Wexler's attempt to trace such mystical experiences to New Age spirituality, and through them to imagine this social phenomenon as embodying the revolutionary potential of his "microcosmic model," seems overextended. In contrast, one could also argue that the lingering presence of cultural terms of coherence even in the most extreme of New Age mystical experiences has opened the way for their subsequent co-option into preexisting modes of social relations. Thus envisaged, the less conservative expressions of the New Age still seem too constricted by conventional discursive categories to provide the revolutionary alternative of which Wexler speaks (the dictum "spiritual but not religious," for example, shows how much spirituality continues to rely on religion for its self-definition); while its more conservative variations, on the other hand, follow the traditions of historical mysticism and explicitly use mystical experience to reaffirm orthodox social and belief systems.[7]

Judaic-themed Israeli cinema appears to recognize these difficulties and hence often features mystical experiences, at the very best, as neither easily instigated nor effortlessly sustained, and at the very worst, as doomed from the start in their struggle against the very building blocks that structure our social consciousness and wall it in. Yet while these films may not echo Wexler's optimism, they nevertheless share his lingering commitment to a certain kind of "social vision." Their continuous courting of mysticism seems to hold tentative hope of both cinema's ability to induce mystical experiences in the being of its spectators and of these experiences' ability to institute greater social change. Thus, though mired in the ambivalence of Israel's religious-secular landscape, Judaic-themed cinema's gaze nevertheless reaches toward a radical horizon, "which has a certain Archimedean value, if not utopian"[8]—a beyond of mystical social existence founded on the continuous subversion of discursive systems, including those theologies that undergird mysticism itself. This beyond heralds not a departure from the world as from its limiting conceptual terms, for the purpose of locating a unity within it, illuminated by a flash of a once hidden light.

NOTES

Introduction

1 Tessler, "Here He Comes." In this and all subsequent quotes from Hebrew sources, the translation is mine.

2 In the context of this study, God is referred to in a third person singular masculine form (uppercase). This choice is not made with the intention of affirming the androcentric tendencies of Judaic culture, which the articulation of God as male epitomizes and justifies. Rather, this perception and its attendant language are retained for the sole aim of accurately representing the traditions that are the object of this study. Furthermore, for the purposes of this study I do not affirm the actual existence of "wholly other" beings beyond the realm of reason, whether divine or otherwise. Instead, I follow Tomer Persico's experiential approach, which "questions the ontological reality of metaphysical structures, herein treated only as epistemological entities" operating in the subject's "soul (body and consciousness)" (34). See Persico, *Jewish Meditative*.

3 I hereby subscribe to Nathan Abrams's assertion "that there is a clear distinction between Jewishness, as ethnic identity, and Judaism, as a religion or a set of rites" (209). As a result, this book uses the term "Judaic" to designate the specifically religious elements of "Jewish" identity, experience, and history. See Abrams, "My religion is American."

4 For an overview of Israeli cinema studies' scholarly concerns, and where the Judaic places in them, see Chyutin and Mazor, "Israeli Cinema Studies," especially 182–83. Importantly, the book's focus on

Judaism and occasional conflation of "Israeli-Jewish" with "Israeli" is not meant to dismiss Israel's Arab minorities, but only to streamline an argument on the country's dominant cinema, while avoiding the pitfalls of treating *Palestinian* as *Israeli*.

5 Cf. Peleg, *Directed by God.*

6 Pence, "Cinema of the Sublime," 29.

7 This study reiterates the three-part categorization due to its heuristic clarity and its prevalence within both scholarly and public discourse in Israel. Yet it is important to note that this categorization tends to ignore or marginalize the presence of other clearly defined religious communities in Israeli society, such as Reform Jews, Conservative Jews, and Modern Orthodox. The relative smallness of these constituencies, and their resulting absence from the Israeli screen, serve as the immediate reasons for their exclusion from consideration in this study. Yet their existence, as well as that of variations within the aforementioned main categories, should remind us to always treat essentialist conceptualizations of Israel's religious landscape with a measure of suspicion. For more on this need, see Yonah and Goodman, "Introduction," 9–38; Sagi, *Jewish-Israeli Voyage,* 208–56.

8 See, for example, Auron, *Israeli Identities,* 315–17. A definition based on adherence to a traditional Halakhic lifestyle is undoubtedly not the sole way of relating to the "Judaic," yet its persistence in Israeli cultural history warrants its inclusion here as the principal prism through which religiousness has been imagined by scholars and laypersons alike. With that being said, the following pages nevertheless reveal how Israeli Jews, especially in recent decades, have at times resisted this definition of Judaism and opened it up to multiple interpretations and negotiations. See also Yadgar, *Beyond Secularization,* 12–13; Lahav, *Women, Secularism, and Belief,* 34, 116–70.

9 The close identification of Judaism with Haredi scripturalism has resulted in the creation of a sliding scale of "less" and "more" religious, which in turn allowed for the devaluing and de-legitimization of non-Haredi forms of Judaism in the Israeli public sphere. The following study does not aim to replicate these biases but also does not aim to deny this dominant perspective through which Israeli culture, Israeli cinema included, tends to operate. It therefore refers to the sliding scale, but with recognition that this scale does not differentiate

between more or less religious, but solely between more or less scripturalist. This choice hopefully allows to sustain focus on the main
dilemma through which Judaism is imagined in Israel—that is, between
enclosure from and exposure to secular-liberal culture—while not
succumbing to value judgments that define one answer as better or
purer than the other. It also does not come at the expense of revealing
the challenges to the sliding scale, especially within the contemporary
Israeli religious landscape. See also Yonah and Goodman, "Introduction," 19–20; Yonah and Goodman, "Gordian Knot," 205–6.

10 Zicherman, *Black Blue-White*, 83–98; Leon, *Gentle Ultra-Orthodoxy*, 1–67.
11 Shapira, *Jews*, 95.
12 Auron, *Israeli Identities*, 33.
13 See, for example, Auron, *Israeli Identities*, 289; Barak-Erez, *Laws and
    "Other" Animals*, 153–59.
14 Ravitzky, *Freedom Inscribed*, 275.
15 Evidence of this trend can be found in recent statistical data. For exam-
    ple, a *Haaretz* poll from 2019 determined that "most Jews in Israel,
    65% of them, believe in God, and many also believe in personal prov-
    idence," yet it also showed a majority was against strict observance
    and in favor of opening stores and allowing for public transportation
    on the Sabbath. Similarly, a 2018 study by Camil Fuchs and Shmuel
    Rosner showed that in Israel, "a great majority of Jews believe in God
    (78%)" (41), yet among them many "do not feel committed to follow-
    ing religious edicts to the letter" (12), and often perform activities that
    run counter to religious law. See Pfeffer, "*Haaretz* Poll"; Rosner and
    Fuchs, *#IsraeliJudaism*. See also Sasson, Tabory, and Selinger-Abutbul,
    "Framing Religious Conflict."
16 Cf. Ettinger, "Is Orthodox Judaism"; Sheleg, *New Religious Jews*, 54–93,
    136–69; El-Or and Neria, "Ultraorthodox Flâneur"; Stadler, "Work."
17 Cf. Ettinger, "In Israel;" Klin-Oron and Ruah-Midbar, "Secular by the
    Letter," 59–61.
18 For more on Jewish Renewal, see, for example, Werczberger and
    Azulay, "Jewish Renewal Movement"; Newberg, "Elu v'Elu."
19 Cf. Ruah-Midbar and Zaidman, "Everything Starts Within."
20 Cf. the 2019–20 Tel Aviv Museum exhibition, *A New Age: The Spiri-
    tual in Art*, whose aim was to explore "attitudes to art with a spir-
    itual aspect" in light of "the renewed interest in art that expresses

spiritualism or deals with the metaphysical and supernatural" (134); or the 2022 Eretz Israel Museum exhibition, *Art of Enchantment*, which sought to "bring the magic back to art" by exploring the intersection between ancient ritual and contemporary artistic creation. See Coen-Uzzielli, foreword.

21 See Klin-Oron and Ruah-Midbar, "Secular by the Letter."

22 Persico, *Jewish Meditative*, 282.

23 Ruah-Midbar, "Current Jewish Spiritualities," 104.

24 Ruah-Midbar, "A Channeler," 514–15.

25 Werczberger, "Self, Identity, and Healing."

26 Ruah-Midbar, "Temptation of Legitimacy."

27 Ruah-Midbar and Eshed, "Canaanites and Neo-Pagans," 37, 43.

28 Ruah-Midbar, "A Channeler," 516–18.

29 Sheleg, *Jewish Renaissance*, 132.

30 Ruah-Midbar, "A Channeler," 519–20.

31 Cf. Persico, "Neo-Hasidic Revival."

32 Cf. Cherlow, *Who Moved*.

33 Cf. Leibovitch, "Spiritual Traditionalists."

34 As Boaz Huss explains it, "many [New Age] themes, such as the anticipation of a spiritual cosmic transformation, the use of meditative and healing techniques to achieve such a transformation, psychological renderings of religious notions and the sanctification of the self, as well as the belief in the compatibility of spirituality and science, recur in many contemporary Kabbalistic and Hasidic formations" (111). See Huss, "New Age of Kabbalah."

35 Myers, "Kabbalah," 180–81.

36 Myers, "Kabbalah," 182.

37 Myers, "Kabbalah," 183–84.

38 Myers, "Kabbalah," 185.

39 See, for example, Ohana, "Buber Was a Mysticist"; Horowitz, "Insight into the Life"; Ben-Pazi, "Your Existence"; Leibovitch, "Deconstructing Walter Benjamin."

40 According to Boaz Huss, the definition of Kabbalah as mysticism that so appeals to the postmodern New Age mentality—a phenomenon centered on "a person's ecstatic, direct and unmediated encounter with divinity" (10)—originated in the modern era as a result of efforts by Jewish philosophers like Buber and Scholem. This claim may

serve to explain why these figures are evoked at the present moment together with certain Kabbalists of old (such as Isaac Luria, Nachman of Bratslav, and Abraham Aboulafia), whose teachings are most amenable to Buber and Scholem's idea of what constitutes Kabbalah as mystical practice. See Huss, *The Question*.

41 Sheleg, *New Religious Jews*, 21; Sheleg, *Jewish Renaissance*, 167.

42 Parciack, "Beyond the Fence," 328.

43 Gertz, *Holocaust Survivors*, 16–41.

44 Rivlin, *Mouse That Roared*, 26.

45 Shohat, *Israeli Cinema*, 122.

46 Peleg, "Secularity and Its Discontents," 9–10.

47 Kimchi, *Israeli Shtetls*, 194.

48 Peleg, *Directed by God*, 29.

49 Parciack, "Religious Experience," 84–85.

50 Kimchi, *Israeli Shtetls*, 219–23; Altschuler, *Carnival*, 121–200.

51 Parciack, "Religious Experience," 83; Miri Talmon, "A Touch Away," 58–59.

52 Cf. Efrat, *Return*, 19–32.

53 Parciack, "Religious Experience," 84–86.

54 Loshitzky, *Identity Politics*, 79.

55 Shenkar, "Representations of Disengagement," 187, note 8.

56 Importantly, though Maale is associated with the Religious Zionist community, in 2014 it opened an "ultra-Orthodox track" for training Haredi female filmmakers. See Charitan, "Haredi Women Make Films."

57 Talmon, "A Touch Away," 60.

58 In recent years Judaic themes are arguably even more prominent in Israeli television than in Israeli cinema, following the inter/national successes of such series as *A Touch Away* (Zafrir Kochanovsky, Ron Ninio, and Ronit Weiss-Berkowitz, 2006), *Srugim* (Hava Divon and Eliezer Shapiro, 2008–10), *Shtisel* (Ori Elon and Yehonatan Indursky, 2013–), *The New Black* (*Shababnikim*, Eliran Malka and Danny Paran, 2017–), and *Fire Dance* (Rama Burshtein, 2022–), among others. On Israeli television's Judaic turn, see Dardashti, "Televised Agendas"; Talmon, "A Touch Away"; Weiss, "Frum with Benefits"; Peleg, *Directed by God*, 105–34.

59 While this study focuses on works made by observant and non-observant filmmakers for the broader film market, it is also important to note the existence of Judaic-centered Israeli filmmaking that

caters solely for limited consumption within religious communities. Exemplary of this phenomenon is the Haredi film industry that evolved over the past two decades, and whose films are rarely seen outside of the ultra-Orthodox sector. For more on this industry, see Vinig, *Haredi Cinema*; Vinig, *Their Own Cinema*; Friedman and Hakak, "Jewish Revenge"; Elimelech, "Attitudes to the Other"; Benit, "Fantasy of Other"; Aharoni, *It's Not Cinema*.

60 Shenker, "Representations of Disengagement."

61 See, for example, Harris, "Introduction."

62 Cf. Seigelshifer and Hartman, "Staying and Critiquing"; Seigelshifer and Hartman, "The Emergence."

63 Padva, "Gay Martyrs"; Cohen, *Soldiers*, 189–97.

64 The present argument follows the "national cinema paradigm" due to its dominance within Israeli film studies. This choice is not meant to downplay the importance of transnational dimensions but does denote a desire to work out of the prevalent terms of previous scholarship rather than oppose them completely. This agenda notwithstanding, the included elaborations on Israeli cinema and culture—as is exemplified in the book's afterword—do attempt on some level to contextualize their objects of study transnationally, thereby laying the groundwork for subsequent research of a globalized nature. On the necessity and nature of transnational readings in the study of Israeli cinema, see also Chyutin and Mazor, "Israeli Cinema Studies," 193; Harris and Chyutin, *Casting a Giant Shadow*, and especially its extended introduction.

65 Peleg, *Directed by God*, 1.

66 Yonah and Goodman, "Introduction," 9. Tomer Persico even goes so far as to claim that "since the 1990s, the commonplace division of Israeli society to secular, Masorti, Religious Zionist, and Haredi groups has ceased to be relevant to any educated analysis of social reality in Israel" (282). See Persico, *Jewish Meditative*.

67 Alush-Levron, "Creating a Significant Community," 87.

68 Alush-Levron, "Creating a Significant Community," 91 (italics in the original).

69 Alush-Levron, "Creating a Significant Community," 89.

70 Lahav, "Postsecular Jewish Theology," 190. See also Lahav, *Women, Secularism, and Belief*.

71 This study is particularly indebted to Ronie Parciack's evocation of "ambivalence" within Judaic-themed Israeli films, though her definition of this operative term is understandably incongruent with the one presented here, in light of the fact that she relates exclusively to the period before Israeli cinema's "Judaic turn." See Parciack, "Religious Experience."

72 Katz, Ratzabi, and Yadgar, "Introduction," 1.

73 Garb, *The Chosen*, 11.

74 Garb, *The Chosen*, 13.

75 Cf. Mualem, *Poets of Infinity*; Bar-Yosef, *Mysticism*; Wolfson, "New Jerusalem Glowing"; Maor, *Mysti-Kan*; Omer, *"Tikkun,"* 449–508.

76 Garb, *The Chosen*, 195.

77 Garb, *The Chosen*, 12.

78 Katz, Ratzabi, and Yadgar, "Introduction," 9. See also Garb, *The Chosen*, 13; Elqayam and Mualem, foreword, 7–9.

79 Garb, *The Chosen*, 222.

80 Garb, *The Chosen*, 212.

81 Persico, *Jewish Meditative*, 225.

82 Persico, *Jewish Meditative*, 219.

83 Cf. Persico, *Jewish Meditative*, 206–7; Garb, *The Chosen*, 218–19.

84 Wolfson, *Through a Speculum*, 5.

85 Wolfson, *Through a Speculum*, 58.

86 Wolfson, *Through a Speculum*, 31.

87 Wolfson, *Through a Speculum*, 3 (my italics).

88 Wolfson, *Through a Speculum*, 65.

89 Scholem, *Major Trends*, 55–56 (italics in the original).

90 Idel, *Kabbalah*, 13–14.

91 Idel, *Kabbalah*, 78.

92 Idel, *Kabbalah*, 82.

93 Idel, *Kabbalah*, 84.

94 Idel, *Kabbalah*, 88.

95 See also Idel, *Hasidism*, 158–64; Idel, *Enchanted Chains*, 33–40.

96 In defining "peak experience," sociologist Abraham Maslow stated that this "is a natural, not a supernatural" phenomenon; for that reason, he also "gave up the name 'mystic'" in reference to such experiences (Maslow, "Lessons," 10). Boaz Huss feels similarly resistant to using the term *mysticism* even when applied in the academic and popular

study of Kabbalah, since it presupposes "theological claims" (11) about the existence of God and a universal form of experience that is "the result of a direct and intensive encounter" (12) with Him. For the purposes of the current study, I adopt Tomer Persico's definition of "mystical experience [as] culturally constructed, i.e., as definitely influenced by time and place culture and religion, of the person who undergoes it," while at the same time as being "equally influenced, and even more, by the structure of his or her brain, the physiological structure that is, ultimately, the basis for all human life." Following this, "mysticism" is understood herein as a cultural category with significant symbolic value to Israeli social reality, and specifically to the ideological and experiential functioning of Judaic-themed Israeli cinema. As such, I do not assume a divine origin to those experiences defined as mystical, and indeed I emphasize how this category, when used in a New Age Israeli context, makes itself amenable to perceptions that downplay, dilute, and/or bypass theistic dogmas. Concurrently, I do assume shared phenomenological characteristics between so-called mystical experiences and others that exist outside of the discursive borders of "mysticism," based on the common ground of human physiology. This assumption does not render "mystical" an obsolete and ineffective term but rather highlights its contemporary significance in making spirituality seem relevant to—or even "at home in"—avowedly nonspiritual contexts. See Maslow, "Lessons"; Huss, *The Question*; Persico, *Jewish Meditative*. Also see Daniel Reiser's critique of Huss's argument, with which I tend to concur: Reiser, *Vision as a Mirror*, 71–73.

97 Dillon, *Merleau-Ponty's Ontology*, 156.

98 The relatively young field of "Religion and Film" began to take form in the 1990s and has gained greater prominence over the past two decades. Throughout this history, it has been shaped primarily by scholars from the fields of religious studies and theology rather than those of cinema studies per se. This has led to a disciplinary focus on analyzing the onscreen presence of theological concepts and religious symbols (mainly from Christianity) and a relative lack of engagement with scholarship in film theory.

Chapter 1

1 Heschel, *God in Search of Man*, 138.
2 Bazin, "Cinema and Theology," 402.
3 Bazin, "Cinema and Theology," 393.
4 Bazin, *What Is Cinema?*, 12.
5 Pence, "Cinema of the Sublime," 32.
6 Pence, "Cinema of the Sublime," 52.
7 Pence, "Cinema of the Sublime," 29.
8 My choice of "spiritual" over other operative terms (e.g., "transcendental," "sacramental," "devotional," or "sacred") is meant to foreground the prominent scholarly inclination of moving arguments beyond a particular religious framework (mainly Christian) and toward the broader category of "spirituality," understood as the "enduring and universally acknowledged 'practices' that evidence the presence of 'Spirit' (not the Holy Spirit of the Trinity) in everyday life and are found in all world religions" (Wright, "Religion, Spirituality, Film," 200). This perennialist tendency shows scholarship to be reflecting Hegel's philosophy of *Geist*—and specifically the argument that "underlying the multiplicity of historical and geographically dispersed religions was an ultimately metaphysical transhistorical substratum" (Murphy, *Politics of Spirit*, 4)—while attempting to overcome the biases of his "gradation" argument, in which different levels of spirituality were ascribed to different religious cultures from a perspective that was "manifestly Eurocentric and . . . overtly Christocentric" (Murphy, *Politics of Spirit*, 75). See Wright, "Religion, Spirituality, Film"; Murphy, *Politics of Spirit*.
9 Schrader, "Rethinking Transcendental Style."
10 Nayar, *Sacred and the Cinema*, 47.
11 Bazin, *What Is Cinema?*, 166 (my italics).
12 Bazin, *What Is Cinema?*, 166.
13 Bazin, *What Is Cinema?*, 7.
14 Bazin, *What Is Cinema?*, 12.
15 Cardullo, *André Bazin*, 5.
16 Cardullo, *André Bazin*, 6.
17 Nayar, *Sacred and the Cinema*, 38.
18 It should be noted that not all of these writers were similarly closed-minded. Out of the four, Schrader, the last to contribute, was also

notoriously the most forceful in asserting a single spiritual style. In contrast, Agel, Ayfre, and Sontag were more willing to entertain different approaches to spiritual film aesthetics. Yet their sympathies seemed to be ultimately directed toward the ascetic stylistics that Schrader would later endorse, especially in the works of French film-maker Robert Bresson. See also Nayar, *Sacred and the Cinema*, 35–56; Brian Price, "Sontag, Bresson."

19 Cf. Dorsky, *Devotional Cinema*; Loughlin, "Within the Image"; Pence, "Cinema of the Sublime"; Bird, "Film as Hierophany"; Fraser, "*American Gigolo*"; Knudsen, "Zen and the Art"; Efird, "*Andrei Rublev.*"

20 Ayfre, "Robert Bresson," 20–21.

21 Agel, *Cinema and the Sacred*, 40 (my italics). See also on Agel's use of the operative term "soul" in this context: Cooper, "Cinema of Contemplation."

22 Sontag, "Spiritual Style," 38.

23 Dorsky, *Devotional Cinema*, 18.

24 Quicke, "Phenomenology and Film," 241.

25 Phenomenologists of religion have held particular influence on this scholarship, such as Rudolf Otto (*The Idea of the Holy* [1917]), Gerardus van der Leeuw (*Sacred and Profane Beauty* [1948]), and Mircea Eliade (*The Sacred and the Profane* [1957]). Certain theologians have also found their way into writing on the spiritual style, such as Jacques Maritain ("Religion and Culture" [1931]), Simone Weil (*Gravity and Grace* [1947]), and Paul Tillich (*The Protestant Era* [1948]).

26 The origin of the term "ontotheology" is found in Heidegger's critique of a certain "foundational thinking" that abides by the following conditions: "(a) foundational thinking is thinking that ultimately appeals to a ground; (b) that ground, to be ultimate, must be conceived as *causa sui*; (c) the characterization '*causa sui*' uniquely specifies an absolute, the God of Western monotheism" (51). See Dillon, *Merleau-Ponty's Ontology*.

27 Schrader, *Transcendental Style*, 111.

28 Schrader, *Transcendental Style*, 6.

29 Bird, "Film as Hierophany," 7.

30 Bird, "Film as Hierophany," 8.

31 Ayfre, "Neo-Realism," 185.

32 Ayfre, "Neo-Realism," 186.

33 Ayfre, "Neo-Realism," 185.

34 Schrader, *Transcendental Style*, 89.

35 Godard and Delahaye, "The Question," 25.

36 Ayfre, "Robert Bresson," 15–16.

37 Ayfre, "Robert Bresson," 22.

38 Schrader, *Transcendental Style*, 39.

39 Sontag, "Spiritual Style."

40 Robert Sinnerbrink refers to this as the "transparency thesis," wherein we "'see through' the image and see the object as such" (99). See Sinnerbrink, "Cinematic Belief."

41 Schrader, *Transcendental Style*, 47.

42 Schrader, *Transcendental Style*, 77.

43 While Philip Rosen argues that these terms should not be used interchangeably in interpreting Bazinian terminology, and that belief should be chosen over faith as being more accurate, I believe that the two terms' juxtaposition better represents the openness and fluidity of Bazin's philosophy. It is in the spirit of this openness that I also foreground faith over belief as an operative term in the present study. See Rosen, "Belief in Bazin."

44 Schrader, *Transcendental Style*, 109–47. For a critique of Schrader's position on Dreyer, see Tyberg, "Forms of the Intangible."

45 Cf. Nayar, *Sacred and the Cinema*; Kickasola, *Liminal Image*; Sinnerbrink, "Cinematic Belief"; Davis, "Ozu, the Ineffable"; De Luca, "Carnal Spirituality"; Wilson, *The Strange World*. On the limits of this line of inquiry, see Chyutin, "Transcendental Style Reconsidered."

46 Hadar, "The First Secular Man"; Mochiach, "David Volach."

47 See, for example, Schnitzer, "An Artistic Miracle."

48 Utin, *New Israeli Cinema*, 62–63.

49 Utin, *New Israeli Cinema*, 63.

50 Utin, *New Israeli Cinema*, 68.

51 Marx, *Disability in Jewish Law*, 107–14.

52 Mishnah Avodah Zarah 3,3.

53 Deut. 22:6–7.

54 Babylonian Talmud, Hullin 142a.

55 See also Zanger, "*Beaufort* and *My Father, My Lord*"; Preminger, "Between the Sin of Hubris."

56 Zanger, "*Beaufort* and *My Father, My Lord*," 228–31.

57 Schrader, *Transcendental Style*, 49 (my italics).

58　Dorsky, *Devotional Cinema*, 40.

59　Dorsky, *Devotional Cinema*, 38.

60　Sobchack, *Carnal Thoughts*, 91–92.

61　Sobchack, *Carnal Thoughts*, 96.

62　Sobchack, *Carnal Thoughts*, 98–99.

63　Kickasola, *Liminal Image*, 79.

64　Schrader, *Transcendental Style*.

65　Kickasola, *Liminal Image*, 34.

66　Kickasola, *Liminal Image*, 39.

67　Sivan, "Interview," 6.

68　For example, his experimental short *Returnee*, made in advance of *The Wanderer*, where Sivan plays the part of a religious Jew undergoing a crisis of belief.

69　Sivan, "Directors and Scriptwriters to Watch," 34.

70　For such a reading, see Chyutin, "Judaic Cinecorporeality"; Harris, *Warriors, Witches, Whores*, 101–3.

71　Pedaya, *Walking through Trauma*.

72　Scarry, *Body in Pain*, 193.

73　Scarry, *Body in Pain*, 193.

74　Scarry, *Body in Pain*, 198.

75　Scarry, *Body in Pain*, 201 (my italics).

76　Scarry, *Body in Pain*, 205.

77　Though the Bible remains mute on the topic, the Midrash does include iterations of the Binding story, which describe Yitzhak as taking an active part in his own sacrifice, even to the extent of asking Abraham to tie him well so that the involuntary movements of his wounded body would not somehow interfere with the father's execution of divine will. See Shenhar, *Love and Hate*, 185.

78　Scarry, *Body in Pain*, 237.

79　Scarry, *Body in Pain*, 241.

80　Scarry, *Body in Pain*, 202.

81　Metz, *Imaginary Signifier*, 44.

82　Bazin, "Death," 31.

83　Daney, "Screen of Fantasy," 38–39.

84　Bazin, "Death."

85　Daney, "Screen of Fantasy," 39.

86　Sivan, "Interview," 8.

87 Shaviro, *Cinematic Body*, 251.

88 Shaviro, *Cinematic Body*, 247.

89 Shaviro, *Cinematic Body*, 249.

90 Benjamin, "Work of Art," 233.

91 Sivan, "Interview," 8.

92 Raphael, *Judaism*, 38.

93 Olin, "Graven Images," 18. See also Bland, *Artless Jew*.

94 Raphael, *Judaism*, 2.

95 Nayar, *Sacred and the Cinema*, 35.

96 Savran, *He Came Upon the Place*, 61–104.

97 Kochan, *Beyond the Graven Image*, 62.

98 Raphael, *Judaism*, 38.

99 Reiser, *Vision as a Mirror*, 19–20.

100 Halbertal, "Of Pictures and Words," 12–13.

101 Idel, *Kabbalah*, 116–18. See also Idel, *Enchanted Chains*, 97–102; Persico, *Jewish Meditative*, 64–73.

102 Chajes, "Jewish Art," 446.

103 Atzmon, "Visual Analysis," 110.

104 Tzachi Weiss notes that "the sermonic method which deals with the shape of Jewish font letters . . . received prominent standing in Middle Age Jewish literature through Kabbalistic works of linguistic, theosophical-theurgical, and Hasidic preoccupation" (208). See Weiss, *Letters*.

105 Atzmon, "Visual Analysis," 100.

106 Atzmon, "Visual Analysis," 102–3.

107 Atzmon, "Visual Analysis," 110.

108 Atzmon, "Visual Analysis," 101.

109 Dan, *Kabbalah*, 43.

110 Wolfson, *Through a Speculum*, 280–81.

111 Chajes, "Jewish Art," 446.

112 Atzmon, "Visual Analysis," 104.

113 Atzmon, "Visual Analysis," 108.

114 Chajes and Baumgraten, "About Faces," 78.

115 J. H. Chajes notes that in "what we might call 'the thinking with the diagram,'" the goal "was to move the reader to an understanding of, and even participation in, the living, developmental dynamism of the Godhead" (44). See Chajes, "Imaginative Thinking."

116   Chajes, "Jewish Art," 446.
117   Chajes, "Kabbalistic Tree," 180.
118   Chajes, "Imaginative Thinking," 53–54.
119   Sobchack, "Embodying Transcendence," 199.
120   Of its far-reaching embrace, Gilbert S. Rosenthal notes that "the notion of *tikkun ha-olam*—healing, mending, repairing the world, improving society—has become a popular concept these days. Everyone seems to be invoking the term of the concept: it is a shibboleth in both Jewish and non-Jewish circles; it has captivated the imagination of scholars and theologians, of statespersons and politicians. . . . The term has become synonymous with social activism. In a word, *tikkun ha-olam* has arrived" (214). See Rosenthal, "*Tikkun ha-Olam*."
121   Cf. Chajes, "Kabbalistic Tree," 185; Persico, *Jewish Meditative*, 83–89.

Chapter 2

1   Benjamin, "Theses," 264.
2   Dekel, *Gendered*, 182–210.
3   For more on Judaic feminism in Israel, see, for example, Kehat, *Feminism and Judaism*; Cohen, *A Woman and Her Judaism*; El-Or, *Next Pessach*.
4   Wolosky, "Foucault," 23.
5   Hartman, *Feminism Encounters*, 61.
6   Though this chapter focuses on Israeli cinema, it is worth noting a few televisual texts that share a similar interest in Judaic restrictions on female modesty, such as *A Touch Away*, *Srugim*, and *Shtisel*.
7   The term "devoted resisters" is used by Valeria Seigelshifer and Tova Hartman to describe the position of Orthodox female filmmakers, who share a commitment, not to "religion's status quo but to Judaism and to their Jewish community" (129). While this is not exactly the position of *The Secrets* and *Bruriah*, which are made outside the strict confines of Israel's Judaic sector, there is a kinship there that the term "devoted resisters" helps flesh out. See Seigelshifer and Hartman, "The Emergence." See also Seigelshifer and Hartman, "Staying and Critiquing."
8   Lahav, *Women, Secularism, and Belief*, esp. 116–70.

9   See, for example, Shenhar, *Love and Hate*.
10 2 Sam. 11.2.
11 Exum, *Plotted*, 26.
12 Exum, *Plotted*, 29.
13 Valman, *The Jewess*, 4.
14 Gilman, "Salome."
15 Exum, *Plotted*, 30.
16 Exum, *Plotted*, 33.
17 See, for example: Exum, *Plotted*, 19–53, 175–237; Abrams, *New Jew*, 45–46.
18 Raphael, *Judaism*, 71.
19 Raphael, *Judaism*, 70.
20 Raphael, *Judaism*, 81.
21 Raphael, *Judaism*, 86.
22 Raphael, *Judaism*, 87.
23 Raphael, *Judaism*, 90.
24 Hartman, *Feminism Encounters*, 54.
25 Hartman, *Feminism Encounters*, 51–59.
26 For other examples, see Chyutin, "King's Daughter."
27 Shemer, "Failed Intersectionality," 367.
28 Shemer, "Failed Intersectionality," 373–74.
29 Shemer, "Failed Intersectionality," 374.
30 See Bar-on, "Religious Settlement."
31 Most prominent in this context are Joseph Cedar's first two features, *Time of Favor* (2000) and *Campfire* (2004). See Harris, *Warriors, Witches, Whores*, 108–16; Kaplan, *Projecting the Nation*, 158–64; Kozlovsky-Golan, "The Arrangement."
32 Koren, *Altering the Closet*, 152–56.
33 Cf. Ziv, "Our Virgin Friends."
34 Cf. Foster, "The Representation."
35 Anderman, "Red Cow."
36 Hacohen-Bick and Ronel, "Zelda's Poetics of Poverty," 65.
37 Halperin, "Zelda," 67.
38 Bar-Yosef, "Zelda," 50.
39 Kann, "Zoharic Images," 66.
40 Cf. Raveh, "A Story of Women's Suffering."
41 Munk, "Sacred and Profane," 5.

42 Munk, "Sacred and Profane," 5.

43 Munk, "Sacred and Profane," 6–7.

44 Munk, "Sacred and Profane," 8.

45 Munk, "Sacred and Profane," 7.

46 Bar On, "Born Again."

47 Harris, *Warriors, Witches, Whores*, 116.

48 See, for example, Koren, *Hereby Renewed*, 74; El-Or, *Next Pessach*.

49 A similar position is documented in Hagar Lahav's study of "secular-believer" women, whose Judaic faith "focuses on the emotional, the irrational, the subjective" (117). See Lahav, *Women, Secularism, and Belief*.

50 See also Harris, *Warriors, Witches, Whores*, 117; Zanger, "Between the Sea and the Mikveh," 536. A similar approach is found in Galron's play *Mikveh* (2005).

51 Ruth 1:16–17.

52 Exum, *Plotted*, 138.

53 Alpert, "Finding Our Past," 93.

54 Alpert, "Finding Our Past," 95.

55 Exum, *Plotted*, 75.

56 Harris, *Warriors, Witches, Whores*, 117.

57 Adler, "The Virgin," 29.

58 Harris, *Warriors, Witches, Whores*, 120.

59 Adler, "The Virgin," 103.

60 Riviere, "Womanliness as Masquerade," 37, 38.

61 Doane, "Film and the Masquerade," 139.

62 Butler, *Bodies That Matter*, 86.

63 Rachel Harris supports an interpretation of the scene along these lines, arguing that "the *mikveh* in *Bruriah* connects the married couple [and] erases the tensions that had existed between them" (121; italics in the original). See Harris, *Warriors, Witches, Whores*.

64 Adler, "The Virgin," 104.

65 Scholem, *Messianic Idea*, 3.

66 Scholem, *Messianic Idea*, 4.

67 Scholem, *Messianic Idea*, 6.

68 Dan, *Apocalypse*, 195–96.

69 Scholem, *Messianic Idea*, 42.

70 Scholem, *Messianic Idea*, 38 (italics in the original).

71 Dan, *Apocalypse*, 219.
72 Scholem, *Messianic Idea*, 45.
73 Dan, *Apocalypse*, 219–20.
74 Dan, *Apocalypse*, 219.
75 Scholem, *Messianic Idea*, 47.
76 Scholem, *Messianic Idea*, 14.
77 Dan, *Apocalypse*, 150.
78 Scholem, *Messianic Idea*, 47.
79 Dan, *Apocalypse*, 216.
80 Dan, *Kabbalah*, 80.
81 Dan, *Apocalypse*, 221.
82 Scholem, *Messianic Idea*, 47.
83 Mosès, *Angel of History*, 50.
84 Cf. Rabinbach, "Between Enlightenment and Apocalypse."
85 Mosès, *Angel of History*, 65.
86 Mosès, *Angel of History*, 66.
87 Fenves, *Messianic Reduction*, 16.
88 Mosès, *Angel of History*, 66–67 (my italics).
89 Mosès, *Angel of History*, 68 (italics in the original).
90 Mosès, *Angel of History*, 70.
91 Mosès, *Angel of History*, 72.
92 Benjamin, "Theses," 261.
93 Mosès, *Angel of History*, 114.
94 Benjamin, "Theses," editor comment on p. 261 (italics in the original).
95 Del Novo, "Kabbalistic Heart," 184.
96 Del Novo, "Kabbalistic Heart," 190 (italics in the original). Though the philosopher critiqued Jewish mysticism, several studies have argued for "possible affinities between Levinas and Kabbalistic tradition" (194), including that of Luria. See Wolfson, "Secrecy, Modesty, and Feminine."
97 Morgan, *Emmanuel Levinas*, 221.
98 Levinas, *Existence and Existents*, 36.
99 Levinas, "Enigma and Phenomenon," 75.
100 Levinas, "Enigma and Phenomenon," 77.
101 Levinas, "Enigma and Phenomenon," 69.
102 Levinas, "Enigma and Phenomenon," 72 (italics in the original).
103 Levinas, "Enigma and Phenomenon," 76.

104 Levinas, *Totality and Infinity*, 23.

105 Morgan, *Emmanuel Levinas*, 177.

106 Levinas, *God, Death, and Time*, 139 (my italics).

107 Morgan, *Emmanuel Levinas*, 179.

108 Morgan, *Emmanuel Levinas*, 180–81.

109 Cf. Brereton and Fruze, "Transcendence"; Gangle, "Messianic Media."

110 Cf. Ruah-Midbar, "A Channeler," 503–4.

111 Feldman, "Carnival by Night," 186.

112 Yassif, *Safed Legends*, 105.

113 Girgus, *Cinema of Redemption*, 191.

114 Girgus, *Cinema of Redemption*, 171. Importantly for this discussion, feminist critics such as Irigary have highlighted the ways in which Levinasian philosophy maintains patriarchal stereotypes of femininity as facilitating the ethical transcendence of a male subject. My argument follows Claire Elise Katz's suggestion, that by juxtaposing his philosophical writings with his theological ones, we can see how "Levinas derives his image of the feminine from the women of the Hebrew Bible," and through them, applauds characteristics that "are not the usual, stereotypical traits of women" (57). This juxtaposition, in turn, allows us to locate "a space for appreciating his description of the feminine as positively inflected" (3), and permits us to recover Levinas for feminism with the grain of his own work, rather than against it. See Katz, *Levinas*.

115 Sanhedrin 98a.

116 Triger, "Self-Defeating," 24.

117 Triger, "Self-Defeating," 19.

118 Doane, *Gilda*, 13.

119 Moshe Idel notes how, though the world of Kabbalah was deprived of female mystics (as opposed to that of Christian mysticism, for example), this nevertheless did not engender a disavowal or vilification of female elements within its theology. Quite to the contrary: "it may be possible that the distinctly masculine nature of Kabbalists may explain the appearance of quite a few female characters in the teachings of divinity within many schools of Kabbalah. The rise of the female character of the Shekhinah (starting in late twelfth-century Kabbalah) may turn out to be the result of a search for the feminine complementary by male Kabbalists." And this search ultimately led

"mystics of one gender to project a positive image with the attributes of the other gender unto the metaphysical entity with which they wanted to unite" (145). See Idel, "The Wife and the Mistress."

120   Devine, "How Shekhinah," 81.
121   Scholem, *Messianic Idea*, 23 (my italics).
122   Benjamin, "Theses," 257.

Chapter 3

1   Buber, *I and Thou*, 118.
2   Lederman and Weiser-Ferguson, preface, 167.
3   Nelson, "Transformations," 9.
4   Nelson, "Transformations," 10.
5   Bell, *Ritual Theory*, 19.
6   Nelson, "Transformations," 13 (italics in the original).
7   Plate, *Religion and Film*, vii (italics in the original).
8   Edgar Morin, *The Stars*, 71.
9   Cf. Arthur Green's statement that "prayer is the beating heart of Judaic belief" (97), or Abraham Heschel's claim that Jewish prayer is "the queen of all mitzvahs" (167). See Green, *These Are the Words*; Heschel, "Jewish Prayer."
10   Margolin, *Inner Religion*, 13.
11   Margolin, *Inner Religion*, 14.
12   Margolin, *Inner Religion*, 14.
13   Margolin, *Inner Religion*, 15.
14   Margolin, *Inner Religion*, 31.
15   Margolin, *Inner Religion*, 36.
16   Reif, *Judaism*, 123.
17   Reif, *Judaism*, 128.
18   Steinsaltz, *A Guide*, 14.
19   Steinsaltz, *A Guide*.
20   Steinsaltz, *A Guide*, 24.
21   Cf. Heschel, "Jewish Prayer," 174.
22   Margolin, *Inner Religion*, 36.
23   Margolin, *Inner Religion*, 33. For more on "mystical prayer" in Kabbalah and especially Hasidism, see also Idel, *Hasidism*, 267–315.

24 Jacobson, *Hasidic Thought*, 44.

25 Scholem, *Messianic Idea*, 216.

26 Jacobs, *Hasidic Prayer*, 17.

27 Margolin, *Inner Religion*, 109. See also in the context of the Besht's "ecstatic prayer": Etkes, *Ba'al Hashem*, 100–106.

28 Jacobs, *Hasidic Prayer*, 93.

29 Jacobs, *Hasidic Prayer*, 79.

30 Persico, *Jewish Meditative*, 198.

31 Persico, *Jewish Meditative*, 107.

32 Sagi, *Prayer*.

33 Margolin, *Inner Religion*, 19.

34 Margolin, *Inner Religion*, 373.

35 Koren, *Mystery of the Earth*, 214–16.

36 Heschel, "Jewish Prayer," 164.

37 See, for example, Elior, *Paradoxical Ascent*, 59–60.

38 Guilherme, "God as Thou," 374.

39 Buber, *I and Thou*, 114. This inclination is consistent with Jack Cohen's claim that "Buber was not involved in group worship. He did not attend the synagogue, nor did he seem to be impressed with the liturgical aspects of Jewish tradition. Prayer for him was highly personal, an individual achievement" (216). See Cohen, *Major Philosophers*.

40 Persico, *Jewish Meditative*, 241.

41 Buber, *I and Thou*, 115.

42 Persico, *Jewish Meditative*, 241.

43 Persico, *Jewish Meditative*, 15.

44 Cherlow, *Who Moved*, 71.

45 Cherlow, *Who Moved*, 72.

46 See, for example, Ram, "Why Are the Teachings."

47 Sagi, *Prayer*, 171.

48 Idel, *Hasidism*, 311.

49 Reik, *Ritual*, 257.

50 Heschel, "Jewish Prayer," 165.

51 Heschel, "Jewish Prayer," 162.

52 Buber, *I and Thou*, 39 (italics in the original). In a volume dedicated to Hasidism, Moshe Idel notes that beyond spoken prayer, "there is a superior method, involving mental work, that is non-vocal activity."

Because and in spite of its great mystical power, "this superior prayer is highly unusual" (303). See Idel, *Hasidism*.

53 Sagi, *Prayer*, 73.
54 Barkai, "Deadly Mission."
55 Wiskind-Elper, *Tradition and Fantasy*, 115.
56 Elior, *Paradoxical Ascent*, 14.
57 Wiskind-Elper, *Tradition and Fantasy*, 93.
58 Peleg, "New Holy Community," 79.
59 Alush-Levron, "Creating a Significant Community," 93.
60 Peleg, *Directed by God*, 79.
61 Alush-Levron, "Creating a Significant Community," 100.
62 Peleg, *Directed by God*, 79.
63 Alush-Levron, "Creating a Significant Community," 94.
64 Alush-Levron, "Creating a Significant Community," 100.
65 Weinstock, *Uman*, 313. On the significance of crying in R. Nachman's teachings, see also Mark, *Mysticism and Madness*, 240–47.
66 Sobchack, "Embodying Transcendence," 195 (italics in the original).
67 Sobchack, "Embodying Transcendence," 198.
68 Sobchack, "Embodying Transcendence," 197 (italics in the original).
69 See, for example, Martin and Ostwalt, *Screening the Sacred*; Marsh, *Theology*; Bryant, "Cinema, Religion, and Popular Culture," esp. p. 106; Lyden, *Film as Religion*, esp. p. 47; Fraser, *Images of the Passion*, 2–21; Ayfre, *Cinema and Christian Faith*, 106–12; Mayward, "Cinematic Summoned Self," 481–82; Schrader, "Rethinking Transcendental Style," 20.
70 Plate, *Religion and Film*, vii.
71 Plate, *Religion and Film*, 6.
72 Plate, *Religion and Film*, 9.
73 Plate, *Religion and Film*, 42.
74 Plate, *Religion and Film*, 8–9.
75 Plate, *Religion and Film*, vii (my italics).
76 Plate, introduction, 6.
77 Hoberman and Rosenbaum, "Idolmakers," 48.
78 I use "life-world" in the narrower sense, as detailed in Lee, "Pluralistic Concept."
79 Merleau-Ponty, *Phenomenology of Perception*, ix.
80 Sokolowski, *Introduction to Phenomenology*, 152–53.
81 Merleau-Ponty, *Primacy of Perception*, 117.

82 Sobchack, *Address*, 5 (italics in the original).

83 Sobchack, *Address*, 11.

84 Sobchack, *Address*, 12.

85 Sobchack, *Address*, 133.

86 Sobchack, *Address*, 23.

87 Sobchack, *Address*, 278 (italics in the original).

88 Sobchack, *Address*, 138.

89 Sobchack, *Carnal Thoughts*, 149.

90 Sobchack, *Address*, 54 (my italics).

91 Buber, *I and Thou*, 116.

92 Buber, *I and Thou*, 23.

93 Buber, *I and Thou*, 46.

94 Guilherme, "God as Thou," 367.

95 Buber, *I and Thou*, 11.

96 Buber, *I and Thou*, 27–28.

97 Buber, *I and Thou*, 6.

98 Buber, *Martin Buber–Carl Rogers*, 103–4.

99 This move is performed by Buber himself, who, according to Paul Mendes-Flohr, "interpreted the central concepts of biblical religion—Creation, Revelation, and Redemption—not theologically, but . . . phenomenologically, as concepts that point to the experienced reality of dialogue" (266). See Mendes-Flohr, *Divided Passions*.

100 Sagi, *Prayer*, 187.

101 Plate, introduction, 1.

102 Plate, *Religion and Film*, 13.

103 Buber, *I and Thou*, 118.

104 Sobchack, *Carnal Thoughts*, 298 (italics in the original).

Chapter 4

1 Nachman of Bratslav, *Likkutei Moharan* 64.5, quoted in Wiskind-Elper, *Tradition and Fantasy*, 22.

2 Jacobson, *Hasidic Thought*, 13–14.

3 Kauffman, "Hasidic Story," 102.

4 Yassif, *Hebrew Folktale*, 401.

5 Feiner, *Jewish Enlightenment*, 36–38.

6 Ross, *Beloved-Despised*, 27–37; Ross, *A Pearl Hidden*, 4–9.

7 Mark, foreword, 19–21.

8 Ross, *Beloved-Despised*, 135–37.

9 For example, in the republication of Hasidic tale anthologies, or on the state-supported Zusha Organization website (zusha.org.il), meant "to help all who is interested in knowing, reading, and discovering Hasidic tales."

10 See, for example, Peleg, "New Holy Community," 80; Peleg, *Directed by God*, 40–41; Ginsburg, "Love in Search," 376; Kaplan, *Projecting the Nation*, 178.

11 In this discussion, the term "modern" is used in the framework of what Charles Taylor called the "acultural" discourse of modernity. This discourse positions modernity "not in terms of its specific point of arrival but as a general function that can take any specific culture as its input" (154) and sees it as necessarily "bring[ing] about intellectual and spiritual changes [to] old habits and beliefs—religion or traditional morality" (155). While clearly reductive and even misleading, this discourse has held sway in negotiations of Jewish identity over the past two centuries, including those performed in Israel. As such, it has affected not only the deportment of those who aligned themselves with the avowed values of secular modernity but also those who have sided with religious tradition and fought for its continuation into the era of Enlightenment. See Taylor, "Two Theories."

12 Dan, *Hasidic Story*, 35–36.

13 Mark, foreword, 51; Yassif, *Hebrew Folktale*, 406–7.

14 Piekarz, *Studies*, 17–18.

15 Dan, *Hasidic Story*, 195.

16 Yassif, *Hebrew Folktale*, 405–6.

17 See, for example, Nigal, *The "Other"*, 11; Kauffman, "Hasidic Story," 102; Dan, *Hasidic Story*, 3–7.

18 Yassif, *Hebrew Folktale*, 406.

19 Dvir-Goldberg, *Palace of Leviathan*, 9–10.

20 Yassif, *Hebrew Folktale*, 402–3; Wiskind-Elper, *Tradition and Fantasy*, 13; Piekarz, *Studies*, 106.

21 Dan, *Hasidic Novella*, 11; Yassif, *Hebrew Folktale*, 402.

22 Elstein, *Ecstatic*, 21; Mark, foreword, 65–66; Dan, *Hasidic Novella*, 8.

23 Dan, *Hasidic Novella*, 8; Dan, *Hasidic Story*, 53–58. See also Yassif, *Hebrew Folktale*, 402, 420; Dvir-Goldberg, *Palace of Leviathan*, 22–64.

24 Elstein, *Ecstatic*, 183. See also Yassif, *Hebrew Folktale*, 423–27; Dan, *Hasidic Story*, 86–87.

25 Wiskind-Elper, *Tradition and Fantasy*, 47–48, 80–82.

26 Dvir-Goldberg, *Palace of Leviathan*, 51–64.

27 Yassif, *Hebrew Folktale*, 435–36.

28 Yassif, *Hebrew Folktale*, 108–11.

29 Kauffman, "Hasidic Story," 111.

30 Kauffman, "Hasidic Story," 104.

31 Kauffman, "Hasidic Story," 111.

32 Kauffman, "Hasidic Story," 115.

33 Elstein, *Ecstatic*, 94.

34 Nigal, *The "Other"*, 12–13.

35 Yassif, *Hebrew Folktale*, 434. See also Nigal, *The "Other"*, 19–56.

36 Zeitlin, *In the Grove*, 11–14.

37 Rapoport-Albert, *Studies in Hasidism*, 119. See also Mark, *Mysticism and Madness*, 111–74.

38 Elior, *Paradoxical Ascent*, 180.

39 Elior, *Paradoxical Ascent*, 179 (italics in the original).

40 Wiskind-Elper, *Tradition and Fantasy*, 117.

41 Importantly, the use of mythopoetic imagery did not deny the traditional tale's claim to historical situatedness, as it often referred allegorically to current events and social tensions. See Mark, foreword, 52; Steinsaltz, introduction, 17.

42 On the origins of this role in pre-Hasidic Kabbalah, see Gondos, "Seekers of Love," 25–28.

43 Wiskind-Elper, *Tradition and Fantasy*, 13; Kaufmann, "Two *Tsadikim*," 424, 431–32.

44 Dan, *Hasidic Story*, 90.

45 Dan, *Hasidic Story*, 184–85; Dan, *Hasidic Novella*, 22–23.

46 Ross, *Beloved-Despised*, 300.

47 Ross, *Beloved-Despised*, 135.

48 Ross, *Beloved-Despised*, 93.

49 Persico, "Neo-Hasidic Revival," 301.

50 Ross, *Beloved-Despised*, 78.

51 Mendes-Flohr, *Divided Passions*, 91.

52 Ross, *Beloved-Despised*, 105–7, 125.

53 Ross, *Beloved-Despised*, 116, 342–43.

54 Buber, *Tales of Rabbi Nachman*, 4.

55 See, for example, Caplan, "Baal Sham Tov"; Koet, "Dialoguing with Jewish Tradition"; Shandler, "Serious Talk."

56 Kauffman, "Hasidic Story," 125.

57 Zicherman, *Black Blue-White*, 306.

58 Doron, *Shuttling between Two Worlds*, 54–55, 142–44.

59 Sharabi, "'Soft' Religion and 'Strict' Religion," 434–60. See also Weinstock, *Uman*, 326–31, 337–40.

60 Ross, *Beloved-Despised*, 266.

61 Ross, *Beloved-Despised*, 118.

62 Wiskind-Elper, *Tradition and Fantasy*, 117.

63 Peleg, "New Holy Community," 79.

64 Peleg, "New Holy Community," 80.

65 Peleg, "New Holy Community," 78.

66 Hoffman, "Reparation," 187–88.

67 Interestingly, in one deleted scene, the film shows Moshe haggling with a Hasid boy about the exorbitant price of branches to be used for roofing his Sukkah.

68 Ginsburg, "Love in Search," 374.

69 Peleg, *Directed by God*, 42.

70 Sagi, *Prayer*, 140.

71 Peleg, *Directed by God*, 42.

72 Duvdevani, "A Great Miracle."

73 Dvir-Goldberg, "Besht," 48–49.

74 Kaufmann, "Hasidic Women," 233.

75 Kaufmann, "Hasidic Women," 241.

76 Kaufmann, "Temerl," 99.

77 Cf. Abrams, *Female Body*, 29–45.

78 Kaufmann, "Temerl," 103.

79 Wiskind-Elper, *Tradition and Fantasy*, 103.

80 Kaufmann, "Hasidic Women," 242.

81 Burshtein performs a similar strategy in her debut feature, *Fill the Void* (2012). See Chyutin, "The King's Daughter," 54.

82 Doron, *Shuttling between Two Worlds*, 125–26.

83 Wiskind-Elper, *Tradition and Fantasy*, 196–97.

84 Elior, *Paradoxical Ascent*, 69.

85 Ross, *Beloved-Despised*, 333.

86 Mendes-Flohr, *Progress and Its Discontents*, 40–41.

87 Ross, *Beloved-Despised*, 501–2.

88 Qtd. in Warner, "Filming a Miracle," 62 (italics in the original).

89 Warner, "Filming a Miracle," 67.

90 Cf. Bourque, "Social Correlates."

91 See Gunning, "Aesthetic of Astonishment."

92 Bazin, *What Is Cinema?*, 36 (my italics).

93 Bazin, *What Is Cinema?*, 39.

94 Bazin, *What Is Cinema?*, 38 (my italics).

95 Bazin, *What Is Cinema?*, 36.

96 Bazin, *What Is Cinema?*, 14 (my italics).

97 Bazin, *What Is Cinema?*, 15.

98 Metz, *Imaginary Signifier*, 52 (italics in the original). See also Cardullo, *André Bazin*, 4.

99 Metz, *Imaginary Signifier*, 72 (italics in the original).

100 Metz, *Imaginary Signifier*, 118.

101 In the context of Merleau-Ponty's philosophy, M. C. Dillon defines phenomenological ontology as one where ontological primacy is given to phenomena (i.e., "reality is conceived in terms of phenomenality" [90]). See Dillon, *Merleau-Ponty's Ontology*.

102 Buber, *I and Thou*, 7–8.

103 Koren, *Mystery of the Earth*, 140.

104 Koren, *Mystery of the Earth*, 142.

105 Koren, *Mystery of the Earth*, 147.

106 Koren, *Mystery of the Earth*, 276.

107 In the words of Paul Mendes-Flohr, "Buber does not say that one has an experience of God per se, but rather that one experiences, or, more precisely, apprehends, God as the eternal Thou" (261). See Mendes-Flohr, *Divided Passions*.

108 Buber, *I and Thou*, 100.

109 Koren, *Mystery of the Earth*, 158.

110 Dillon, *Merleau-Ponty's Ontology*, ix.

111 Dillon, *Merleau-Ponty's Ontology*, 34.

112 Dillon, *Merleau-Ponty's Ontology*, 54.

113 Merleau-Ponty, *The Visible*, 133.

114 Sobchack, *Address*, 86 (italics in the original).

115 Merleau-Ponty, *The Visible*, 133.

116 Dillon, *Merleau-Ponty's Ontology*, 67 (my italics).

117 Dillon, *Merleau-Ponty's Ontology*, 68.

118 Dillon, *Merleau-Ponty's Ontology*, 49.

119 Dillon, *Merleau-Ponty's Ontology*, 101.

120 Sobchack, *Address*, 90.

121 Sobchack, *Address*, 134–35.

122 Dillon, *Merleau-Ponty's Ontology*, 79 (italics in the original).

123 Dillon, *Merleau-Ponty's Ontology*, 40.

124 Olin, *Nation*, 126.

125 Buber, "Lesser Ury," 65.

126 Buber, "Lesser Ury," 67–68.

127 Buber, "Lesser Ury," 66.

128 Merleau-Ponty, "Eye and Mind," 122.

129 Merleau-Ponty, "Eye and Mind," 123.

130 Merleau-Ponty, "Eye and Mind," 127–28.

131 Merleau-Ponty, "Eye and Mind," 128.

132 Johnson, "Ontology and Painting," 40.

133 In the mid-1910s, Buber publicly dissociated himself from "mysticism," defining it as oppositional to his developing dialogical philosophy. Nevertheless, this philosophy clearly incorporates mystical tenets into its formulation of I-Thou dialogue. See Koren, *Mystery of the Earth*, 160.

134 See, for example, Andrew, *Major Film Theories*, 142–52; Sobchack, *Address*.

135 Dillon, *Merleau-Ponty's Ontology*, 2.

136 Here Buber's philosophy is more helpful than those of Benjamin and Levinas, previously discussed, because of its emphasis on an experience of unity and its relationship to *unio mystica*. The influence Buber had on these other two thinkers, however, does not invalidate their contribution to further developing the model at hand. On the connections and distinctions between these philosophers, see, for example, Kelly, "Reciprocity."

Afterword

1 For example, according to Ora Wiskind-Elper, R. Nachman of Bratslav viewed "overwhelming uncertainty," within an ontological-mystical context, as "a necessary first step in attaining true understanding of the world," with his reasoning being that "only when one begins to search beyond appearances can one see the glimmering of the divine—indeed among the shadowy forms of one's own world" (70). See Wiskind-Elper, *Tradition and Fantasy*.

2 Wexler, *Mystical Society*, 42.

3 Wexler, *Mystical Society*, 175.

4 Wexler, *Mystical Society*, 166.

5 Wexler, *Mystical Society*, 175.

6 Wexler, *Mystical Society*, 48.

7 See, for example, Zinnbauer et al., "Religion and Spirituality," 561; Persico, "Neo-Hasidic Revival," 296–99; Garb, *The Chosen*, 71–98.

8 Wexler, *Mystical Society*, 153.

BIBLIOGRAPHY

Abrams, Daniel. *The Female Body of God in Kabbalistic Literature: Embodied Forms of Love and Sexuality in the Divine Feminine* [Hebrew]. Jerusalem: Hebrew University Magnes Press, 2004.

Abrams, Nathan. "'My religion is American': A Midrash on Judaism in American Films, 1990 to the Present." In *Religion in the United States*, edited by Jeanne Cortiel et al., 209–25. Heidelberg: Winter Verlag, 2011.

———. *The New Jew in Film: Exploring Jewishness and Judaism in Contemporary Cinema*. London: I. B. Tauris, 2012.

Adler, Rachel. "The Virgin in the Brothel and Other Anomalies: Character and Context in the Legend of Beruriah." *Tikkun* 3, no. 6 (1988): 28–32, 102–5.

Aharoni, Matan. *"It's Not Cinema, It's a Social Gathering": Communal and Social Boundaries in Haredi Leisure Culture* [Hebrew]. Jerusalem: Bialik Institute, 2022.

Alpert, Rebecca. "Finding Our Past: A Lesbian Interpretation of the Book of Ruth." In *Reading Ruth: Contemporary Women Reclaim a Sacred Story*, edited by Judith A. Kates and Gail Twersky Reimer, 91–96. New York: Ballantine Books, 1996.

Altschuler, Nugit. *Carnival and Vice Versa: On Yiddish and Israeli Popular Cinema* [Hebrew]. Tel Aviv: Resling, 2020.

Alush-Levron, Merav. "Creating a Significant Community: Religious Engagements in the Film *Ha-Mashgihim* (God's Neighbors)." *Israel Studies Review* 31, no. 1 (Summer 2016): 86–106.

Anderman, Nirit. "Red Cow: Finally, a Film by a Woman Director at the Jerusalem Film Festival" [Hebrew]. *Haaretz*, July 31, 2018. Accessed November 1, 2021. www.haaretz.co.il/gallery/cinema/jerusalemfilmfestival/.premium -REVIEW-1.6334894.

Andrew, J. Dudley. *The Major Film Theorists: An Introduction*. Oxford: Oxford University Press, 1976.

Atzmon, Leslie. "A Visual Analysis of Anthropomorphism in the Kabbalah: Dissecting the Hebrew Alphabet and Sephirotic Diagram." *Visual Communication* 2 (2003): 97–114.

Auron, Yair. *Israeli Identities—Jews and Arabs Facing the Mirror and the Other* [Hebrew]. Tel Aviv: Resling, 2008.

Ayfre, Amédée. "*The Cinema and the Christian Faith*." Translated by J.-F. Tiffoche. Master's thesis, Regent University, 1988. Originally published as *Le cinéma et la foi chrétienne* (Paris: Editions Fayard, 1960).

———. "Neo-Realism and Phenomenology." In *Cahiers du Cinéma: The 1950s: Neo-Realism, Hollywood, New Wave*, edited by Jim Hillier, 182–91. Cambridge, MA: Harvard University Press, 1985.

———. "The Universe of Robert Bresson." In *The Films of Robert Bresson*, edited by Ian Cameron, 6–24. New York: Praeger, 1970.

Bar-On, Ya'akov. "Born Again with a Passion" [Hebrew]. *News1*, April 2, 2011. Accessed November 17, 2013. www.news1.co.il/Archive/0024-D-58261-00 .html.

———. "Religious Settlement and Coming Out: 'Red Cow'—When Reality Meets the Movie" [Hebrew]. *Maariv Online*, January 30, 2019. Accessed October 31, 2021. www.maariv.co.il/culture/movies/Article-682259.

Bar-Yosef, Hamutal. *Mysticism in Modern Hebrew Poetry* [Hebrew]. Tel Aviv: Miskal-Yedioth Ahronot and Chemed Books, 2008.

———. "Zelda, Malhut" [Hebrew]. *Moznaim* 60, no. 8/9 (February–March 1987): 48–52.

Barak-Erez, Daphne. *Laws and "Other" Animals—The Story of Pigs and Pork Prohibitions in Israel* [Hebrew]. Tel Aviv: Keter, 2015.

Barkai, Tal. "Deadly Mission: A Script about Violence Born Out of Faith" [Hebrew]. *Ynet*, June 20, 2013. Accessed March 11, 2015. www.ynet.co.il/ articles/0,7340,L-4395123,00.html.

Bazin, André. "Cinema and Theology." *South Atlantic Quarterly* 91, no. 2 (Spring 1992): 393–407.

———. "Death Every Afternoon." In *Rites of Realism: Essays on Corporeal Cinema*, edited by Ivone Margulies, 27–31. Durham, NC: Duke University Press, 2003.

———. *What Is Cinema?* Vol. 1. Berkeley: University of California Press, 1968.

Bell, Catherine. *Ritual Theory, Ritual Practice*. Oxford: Oxford University Press, 1992.

Ben-Pazi, Hanoch. "Your Existence, for Better or Worse" [Hebrew]. *Israel Hayom*, November 7, 2019. Accessed January 21, 2022. www.israelhayom.co.il/article/705213.

Benit, Moran. "Fantasy of Other Masculine Existence: Masculine Identities in Ultra-Orthodox Jewish Movies" [Hebrew]. In *Identities in Formation in Israeli Culture*, edited by Sandra Meiri, Yael Munk, Idit Mendelson-Maoz, and Liat Steir Livny, 339–59. Ra'anana, Israel: Open University Press, 2013.

Benjamin, Walter. "Theses on the Philosophy of History." In *Illuminations*, edited by Hannah Arendt, 253–64. New York: Schocken, 1969.

———. "The Work of Art in the Age of Mechanical Reproduction." In *Illuminations*, edited by Hannah Arendt, 217–52. New York: Schocken, 1969.

Bird, Michael. "Film as Hierophany." In *Religion in Film*, edited by John R. May and Michael Bird, 3–22. Knoxville: University of Tennessee Press, 1982.

Bland, Kalman P. *The Artless Jew: Medieval and Modern Affirmations and Denials of the Visual*. Princeton, NJ: Princeton University Press, 2000.

Bourque, Linda Brookover. "Social Correlates of Transcendental Experiences." *Sociological Analysis* 30, no. 3 (Autumn 1969): 151–63.

Brereton, Pat, and Robert Furze. "Transcendence and *The Tree of Life*: Beyond the Face of the Screen with Terrence Malick, Emmanuel Levinas, and Roland Barthes." *Journal for the Study of Religion, Nature and Culture* 8, no. 3 (2014): 329–51.

Bryant, M. Darrol. "Cinema, Religion, and Popular Culture." In *Religion in Film*, edited by John R. May and Michael Bird, 101–14. Knoxville: University of Tennessee Press, 1982.

Buber, Martin. *I and Thou*. 1923. Reprint, Edinburgh: T&T Clark, 1950.

———. "Lesser Ury." In *The First Buber: Youthful Zionist Writings of Martin Buber*, edited by Gilya G. Schmidt, 64–85. Syracuse: Syracuse University Press, 1999.

———. *The Martin Buber–Carl Rogers Dialogue: A New Transcript with Commentary*, edited by Rob Anderson and Kenneth N. Cissna. Albany: State University of New York Press, 1997.

———. *Tales of Rabbi Nachman*. 1906. Reprint, Amherst, NY: Humanity Books, 1988.

Butler, Judith. *Bodies That Matter: On the Discursive Limits of Sex*. London: Routledge, 2011.

Caplan, Jennifer. "Baal Sham Tov: Woody Allen's Hasidic Tale-Telling." *Bulletin for the Study of Religion* 42, no. 3 (September 2013): 11–19.

Caplan, Kimmy, and Nurit Stadler. "Introduction: The Changing Face of Haredi Society in Israel: From Survival to Presence, Strengthening and Self-Assuredness" [Hebrew]. In *From Survival to Consolidation: Changes in Israeli Haredi Society and Its Scholarly Study*, edited by Kimmy Caplan and Nurit Stadler, 11–29. Jerusalem: Van Leer Institute and Hakkibutz Hameuchad, 2012.

Cardullo, Bert. *André Bazin and Italian Neorealism*. London: Continuum, 2011.

Chajes, J. H., and Eliezer Baumgraten, "About Faces: Kabbalistic Visualizations of the Divine Visage in the Gross Family Collection." In *Windows on Jewish Worlds: Essays in Honor of William Gross, Collector of Judaica*, edited by Emile Schrivjer, 73–84. Uitgeverij, Netherlands: Walburg Press, 2019.

Chajes, J. H. "Imaginative Thinking with a Lurianic Diagram." *Jewish Quarterly Review* 110, no. 1 (Winter 2020): 30–63.

———. "Jewish Art." In *Encyclopedia of the Bible and Its Reception* (Vol. 18), 446. Boston: Walter de Gruyter, 2020.

———. "The Kabbalistic Tree as Material Text." *Hen* 43 (1/2021): 162–96.

Charitan, Shifi. "Haredi Women Make Films: This Is How It Looks Like" [Hebrew]. *Behadrei Haredim*, August 30, 2015. Accessed September 1, 2015. http://old.bhol.co.il/article_old.aspx?id=88963.

Cherlow, Semadar. *Who Moved My Judaism? Judaism, Postmodernism, and Contemporary Spiritualities* [Hebrew]. Tel Aviv: Resling, 2016.

Chyutin, Dan. "Judaic Cinecorporeality: Fleshing Out the Haredi Male Body in Avishai Sivan's *The Wanderer*." *Shofar* 33, no. 1 (Fall 2014): 57–82.

———. "'The King's Daughter Is All Glorious Within': Female Modesty in Judaic-Themed Israeli Cinema." *Journal of Jewish Identities* 9, no. 1 (Spring 2016): 39–58.

———. "Transcendental Style Reconsidered: Absence, Presence, and 'a Place which Is Not-a-Place.'" *Journal of Film and Video* 73, no. 3 (Fall 2021): 34–46.

Chyutin, Dan, and Yael Mazor. "Israeli Cinema Studies: Mapping Out a Field." *Shofar* 38, no. 1 (Spring 2020): 167–217.

Coen-Uzzielli, Tania. Foreword to *A New Age: The Spiritual in Art*, edited by Tania Coen-Uzzielli, 132–34. Tel Aviv: Tel Aviv Museum of Art, 2019.

Cohen, Jack C. *Major Philosophers of Jewish Prayer in the Twentieth Century*. New York: Fordham University Press, 2000.

Cohen, Nir. *Soldiers, Rebels, and Drifters: Gay Representation in Israeli Cinema*. Detroit: Wayne State University Press, 2012.

Cohen, Tova, ed. *A Woman and Her Judaism: A Contemporary Religious-Feminist Discourse* [Hebrew]. Jerusalem: Kolech and Rubin Mass, 2013.

Cooper, Sarah. "Henri Agel's Cinema of Contemplation: Renoir and Philosophy." In *A Companion to Jean Renoir*, edited by Alastair Phillips and Ginette
Vincendeau, 313–27. Malden, MA: Wiley Blackwell, 2013.

Dan, Joseph. *Apocalypse Then and Now* [Hebrew]. Tel Aviv: Yediot Acharonot,
2000.

———. *The Hasidic Novella* [Hebrew]. Jerusalem: Bialik Institute, 1966.

———. *The Hasidic Story—Its History and Development* [Hebrew]. Jerusalem:
Keter Publishing, 1975.

———. *Kabbalah: A Very Short Introduction*. Oxford: Oxford University Press,
2005.

Daney, Serge. "The Screen of Fantasy (Bazin and Animals)." In *Rites of Realism:
Essays on Corporeal Cinema*, edited by Ivone Margulies, 32–41. Durham, NC:
Duke University Press, 2003.

Dardashti, Galeet. "Televised Agendas: How Global Funders Make Israeli TV
More 'Jewish.'" *Jewish Film and New Media* 3, no. 1 (Spring 2015): 77–103.

Davis, Darrel W. "Ozu, the Ineffable." In *Reorienting Ozu: A Master and His
Influence*, edited by Jinhee Choi, 33–44. Oxford: Oxford University Press,
2018.

De Luca, Tiago. "Carnal Spirituality: The Films of Carlos Reygadas." *Senses of
Cinema* 55 (July 2010). http://sensesofcinema.com/2010/feature-articles/
carnal-spirituality-the-films-of-carlos-reygadas-2/.

Dekel, Tal. *Gendered: Art and Feminist History* [Hebrew]. Tel Aviv: Hakkibutz
Hameuchad, 2011.

Del Nevo, Matthew. "The Kabbalistic Heart of Levinas." *Culture, Theory, and
Critique* 52, no. 2–3 (2011): 183–98.

Devine, Luke. "How Shekhinah Became the God(dess) of Jewish Feminism."
Feminist Theology 23, no. 1 (2014): 71–91.

Dillon, M. C. *Merleau-Ponty's Ontology*. 2nd ed. Evanston, IL: Northwestern
University Press, 1997.

Doane, Mary Ann. "Film and the Masquerade: Theorising the Female Spectator." In *Feminist Film Theory: A Reader*, edited by Sue Thornham, 131–45.
New York: New York University Press, 1999.

———. "*Gilda*: Striptease as Epistemology." *Camera Obscura* 11 (Fall 1983): 6–27.

Doron, Shlomi. *Shuttling between Two Worlds: Coming to and Defecting from
Ultra-Orthodox Judaism in Israeli Society* [Hebrew]. Tel Aviv: Hakibbutz
Hameuchad, 2013.

Dorsky, Nathaniel. *Devotional Cinema*. Berkeley, CA: Tuumba Press, 2005.

Duvdevani, Shmulik. "A Great Miracle Happened Here" [Hebrew]. *Ynet*, August 5, 2004. Accessed March 17, 2015. www.ynet.co.il/articles/0,7340,L -2958697,00.html.

Dvir-Goldberg, Rivka. "The Besht and 'Mahbarto Hatehora': The Treatment of Women in Hasidic Literature" [Hebrew]. *Masekhet* 3 (2005): 45–62.

———. *The Tsadik and the Palace of Leviathan: A Study of Hassidic Tales Told by Tsadikim* [Hebrew]. Tel Aviv: Hakibbutz Hameuchad, 2003.

Efird, Robert. "*Andrei Rublev*: Transcendental Style and the Creative Vision." *Journal of Popular Film and Television* 35, no. 2 (Summer 2007): 86–93.

Efrat, Gideon. *The Return to the Shteitel* [Hebrew]. Jerusalem: Bialik Institute, 2011.

El-Or, Tamar. *Next Pessach: Literacy and Identity of Young Religious Zionist Women* [Hebrew]. Tel Aviv: Am Oved, 1998.

El-Or, Tamar, and Eran Neria. "The Ultraorthodox Flâneur: Toward the Pleasure Principle. Consuming Time and Space in Contemporary Haredi Population of Jerusalem." In *Consumption and Market Society in Israel*, edited by Yoram S. Carmeli and Kalman Applbaum, 71–94. Oxford: Berg, 2004.

Eliade, Mircea. *The Sacred and the Profane: The Nature of Religion*. 1957. Reprint, Orlando, FL: Harcourt, 1987.

Elimelech, Vered. "Attitudes to the Other in the Haredi Society as Reflected in Haredi Cinema" [Hebrew]. In *From Survival to Consolidation: Changes in Israeli Haredi Society and Its Scholarly Study*, edited by Kimmy Caplan and Nurit Stadler, 116–36. Jerusalem: Van Leer Institute and Hakkibutz Hameuchad, 2012.

Elior, Rachel. *The Paradoxical Ascent to God: The Kabbalistic Theosophy of Habad Hasidism*. Albany: State University of New York Press, 1993.

Elstein, Yoav. *The Ecstatic Story in Hasidic Literature* [Hebrew]. Ramat Gan, Israel: Bar-Ilan University, 1998.

Elqayam, Avi, and Shlomy Mualem. Foreword to *Kabbalah, Mysticism, and Poetry: The Journey to the End of Vision* [Hebrew], edited by Avi Elqayam and Shlomy Mualem, 1–10. Jerusalem: Hebrew University Magnes Press, 2015.

Etkes, Immanuel. *Ba'al Hashem: Besht—Magic, Mysticism, Leadership* [Hebrew]. Jerusalem: Zalman Shazar Center, 2000.

Ettinger, Yair. "In Israel, God Has Almost Nothing to Do with Religion." *Haaretz*, September 14, 2015. Accessed October 2, 2015. haaretz.com/news/ israel/.premium-1.675476.

———. "Is Orthodox Judaism on the Verge of a Historical Schism?" [Hebrew].
    Haaretz, July 27, 2015. Accessed August 2, 2015. www.haaretz.co.il/
    magazine/orthodox/.premium-1.2690140.

Exum, J. Cheryl. *Plotted, Shot, and Painted: Cultural Representations of Biblical
    Women*. Sheffield, UK: Sheffield Academic Press, 1996.

Feiner, Shmuel. *The Jewish Enlightenment in the 19th Century* [Hebrew]. Jerusa-
    lem: Carmel Publishing, 2010.

Feldman, Anat. "Carnival by Night: A New Practice of Modern Tikkun Rituals"
    [Hebrew]. *Democratic Culture* 13 (2011): 181–211.

Fenves, Peter. *The Messianic Reduction: Walter Benjamin and the Shape of Time*.
    Stanford, CA: Stanford University Press, 2011.

Foster, David William. "The Representation of the Body in the Poetry of Ale-
    jandra Pizarnik." *Hispanic Review* 62, no. 3 (Summer 1994): 319.

Fraser, Peter. "*American Gigolo*: Transcendental Style." *Literature/Film Quarterly*
    16, no. 2 (1988): 91–100.

———. *Images of the Passion: The Sacramental Mode in Film*. Westport, CT:
    Praeger, 1998.

Friedman, Yael, and Yohai Hakak. "Jewish Revenge: Haredi Action in the Zion-
    ist Sphere." *Jewish Film and New Media* 3, no. 1 (Spring 2015): 48–76.

Gangle, Rocco. "Messianic Media: Benjamin's Cinema, Badiou's Matheme,
    Negri's Multitude." *Journal of Cultural and Religious Theory* 10, no. 1 (Winter
    2009): 26–40.

Garb, Jonathan. "*The Chosen Will Become Herds*": *Studies in Twentieth Century
    Kabbalah* [Hebrew]. Jerusalem: Carmel Publishing and Shalom Hartman
    Institute, 2005.

Gertz, Nurith. *Holocaust Survivors, Aliens, and Others in Israeli Cinema and
    Literature* [Hebrew]. Tel Aviv: Am Oved and Open University of Israel,
    2009.

Gilman, Sander L. "Salome, Syphilis, Sarah Bernhardt and the 'Modern Jew-
    ess.'" *German Quarterly* 66, no. 2 (Spring 1993): 195–211.

Ginsburg, Shai. "Love in Search of Belief, Belief in Search of Love." In *The
    Modern Jewish Experience in World Cinema*, edited by Lawrence Baron,
    371–76. Waltham, MA: Brandeis University Press, 2011.

Girgus, Sam B. *Levinas and the Cinema of Redemption: Time, Ethics, and the
    Feminine*. New York: Columbia University Press, 2010.

Godard, Jean-Luc, and Michael Delahaye. "The Question: Interview with Rob-
    ert Bresson." *Cahiers du Cinéma in English* 8 (February 1967): 5–27.

Gondos, Andrea. "Seekers of Love: The Phenomenology of Emotion in Jewish, Christian, and Sufi Mystical Sources." In *Esoteric Transfers and Constructions: Judaism, Christianity, and Islam,* edited by Mark Sedgwick and Francesco Piraino, 21–41. London: Palgrave, 2021.

Green, Arthur. *These Are the Words: A Vocabulary of Jewish Spiritual Life* [Hebrew]. 2001. Reprint, Tel Aviv: Yediot Acharonot, 2008.

Guilherme, Alexandre. "God as Thou and Prayer as Dialogue: Martin Buber's Tools for Reconciliation." *Sophia* 51 (2012): 365–78.

Gunning, Tom. "An Aesthetics of Astonishment: Early Film and the (In)Credulous Spectator." 1989. Reprint in *Film Theory and Criticism,* 7th ed., edited by Leo Braudy and Marshall Cohen, 736–50. Oxford: Oxford University Press, 2009.

Hacohen-Bick, Tafat. "'I Want a River/No Small Temple': Poetics and Theology in the Later Poetry of Yona Wallach." *Prooftexts* 38 (2020): 139–78.

Hadar, Alon. "The First Secular Man" [Hebrew]. *Haaretz,* August 22, 2007. Accessed August 11, 2013. www.haaretz.co.il/gallery/cinema/1.1436723.

Halbertal, Moshe. "Of Pictures and Words: Visual and Verbal Representation of God." In *The Divine Image: Depicting God in Jewish and Israeli Art,* edited by Sharon Weiser-Ferguson and Ronit Sorek, 7–13. Jerusalem: The Israel Museum, 2006.

Halperin, Sarah. "Zelda: The Person and Her Poetry—Structures and Motifs" [Hebrew]. *Bitzaron* 23 (1984): 65–70, 81.

Harris, Rachel S., and Dan Chyutin, eds. *Casting a Giant Shadow: The Transnational Shaping of Israeli Cinema.* Bloomington: Indiana University Press, 2021.

Harris, Rachel S. "Introduction: Sex, Violence, Motherhood, and Modesty: Controlling the Jewish Woman and Her Body." *Nashim* 23 (2012): 5–11.

———. *Warriors, Witches, Whores: Women in Israeli Cinema.* Detroit: Wayne State University Press, 2017.

Hartman, Tova. *Feminism Encounters Traditional Judaism: Resistance and Accommodation.* Lebanon, NH: Brandeis University Press, 2007.

Heschel, Abraham Joshua. *God in Search of Man: A Philosophy of Judaism.* London: John Calder, 1956.

———. "The Spirit of Jewish Prayer." *Proceedings of the Rabbinical Assembly of America* 17 (1953): 151–77.

Hoberman, J., and Jonathan Rosenbaum. "Idolmakers." *American Film* (December 1982): 48–55.

Hoffman, Thomas. "Reparation, Forgiveness, and Redemption in a Sukkoth Parable: Movie Review of *Ushpizin*." *International Forum of Psychoanalysis* 19 (2010): 185–90.

Horowitz, Ariel. "Insight into the Inner Life of the Founder of Kabbalah Study" [Hebrew]. *Makor Rishon*, February 18, 2020. Accessed January 21, 2022. www .makorrishon.co.il/culture/204773/.

Huss, Boaz. "The New Age of Kabbalah: Contemporary Kabbalah, the New Age, and Postmodern Spirituality." *Journal of Modern Jewish Studies* 6, no. 2 (July 2007): 107–25.

———. *The Question about the Existence of Jewish Mysticism: The Genealogy of Jewish Mysticism and the Theologies of Kabbalah Research* [Hebrew]. Jerusalem: Van Leer Institute and Hakkibutz Hameuchad, 2016.

Idel, Moshe. *Enchanted Chains: Techniques and Rituals in Jewish Mysticism* [Hebrew]. Jerusalem: Shalom Hartman Institute, 2015.

———. *Hasidism: Between Ecstasy and Magic* [Hebrew]. Tel Aviv: Schocken, 2000.

———. *Kabbalah: New Perspectives* [Hebrew]. Tel Aviv: Schocken, 1993.

———. "The Wife and the Mistress: The Woman in Jewish Mysticism" [Hebrew]. In *Blessed He Who Made Me a Woman? The Woman in Judaism—From the Bible to the Present*, edited by Maya Leibovich, David Yoel Ariel, and Yoram Mazor, 141–62. Tel Aviv: Yediot Acharonot and Chemed Books, 1999.

Jacobs, Louis. *Hasidic Prayer*. 1972. Reprint, Oxford: Littman Library of Jewish Civilization, 1993.

Jacobson, Yoram. *The Hasidic Thought* [Hebrew]. Tel Aviv: Ministry of Defense, 1985.

Johnson, Galen A. "Ontology and Painting: Eye and Mind." In *The Merleau-Ponty Aesthetics Reader: Philosophy and Painting*, edited by Galen A. Johnson, 35–55. Evanston, IL: Northwestern University Press, 1993.

Kaplan, Eran. *Projecting the Nation: History and Ideology on the Israeli Screen*. New Brunswick, NJ: Rutgers University Press, 2020.

Kann, Nitza. "A Boat of Light: Zoharic Images in Zelda's Poetry." *Nashim* 19 (Spring 2010): 64–95.

Katz, Claire Elise. *Levinas, Judaism, and the Feminine: The Silent Footsteps of Rebecca*. Bloomington: Indiana University Press, 2003.

Katz, Gideon, Shalom Ratzabi, and Yaakov Yadgar. "Introduction" [Hebrew].
    In *Beyond Halakha: Secularism, Traditionalism, and "New Age" Culture in
    Israel*, edited by Gideon Katz, Shalom Ratzabi, and Yaakov Yadgar, 1–4. Sede
    Boqer, Israel: Ben Gurion Research Institute, Ben Gurion University of the
    Negev, 2014.
Kauffman, Tsippi. "The Hasidic Story: A Call for Narrative Religiosity." *Journal
    of Jewish Thought and Philosophy* 22 (2014): 101–26.
———. "'Outside the Natural Order': Temerl, the Female Hasid." *Studia Judaica*
    19, no. 1 (2016): 87–109.
———. "Two *Tsadikim*, Two Women in Labor, and One Salvation: Reading Gen-
    der in a Hasidic Story." *Jewish Quarterly Review* 101, no. 3 (Summer 2011): 420–38.
Kehat, Hanah. *Feminism and Judaism: From Collision to Regeneration* [Hebrew].
    Jerusalem: Ministry of Defense, 2008.
Kelly, Andrew. "Reciprocity and the Height of God: A Defense of Buber against
    Levinas." *Sophia* 34, no. 1 (1995): 65–73.
Kickasola, Joseph G. *The Films of Krzysztof Kieślowski: The Liminal Image*. Lon-
    don: Continuum, 2004.
Kimchi, Rami. *The Israeli Shtetls: Bourekas Films and Yiddish Classical Literature*
    [Hebrew]. Tel Aviv: Resling, 2012.
Klin-Oron, Adam, and Marianna Ruah-Midbar. "Secular by the Letter, Reli-
    gious by the Spirit: The Attitudes of the Israeli New Age to Jewish Law"
    [Hebrew]. *Israeli Sociology* 12, no. 1 (2010): 57–80.
Knudsen, Erik. "Zen and the Art of Film Narrative: Towards a Transcendental
    Realism in Film." *Journal of Screenwriting* 1, no. 2 (2010): 343–55.
Kochan, Lionel. *Beyond the Graven Image: A Jewish View*. New York: New York
    University Press, 1997.
Koet, Bart J. "Woody Allen's *Broadway Danny Rose*: Dialoguing with Jewish
    Tradition." *Religions* 12 (2021). Accessed January 31, 2022. www.proquest
    .com/scholarly-journals/woody-allen-s-broadway-danny-rose-dialoguing
    -with/docview/2576402176/se-2.
Koren, Irit. *Altering the Closet* [Hebrew]. Tel Aviv: Yediot Acharonot and
    Chemed Books, 2003.
———. *You Are Hereby Renewed Unto Me: Gender, Religion, and Power Rela-
    tions in the Jewish Wedding Ritual* [Hebrew]. Jerusalem: Hebrew University
    Magnes Press, 2011.
Koren, Israel. *The Mystery of the Earth: Mysticism and Hasidism in Buber's
    Thought* [Hebrew]. Haifa: Haifa University Press, 2005.

Kozlovsky-Golan, Yvonne. "The Arrangement." In *Modern Jewish Experiences in World Cinema*, edited by Lawrence Barron, 377–83. Waltham, MA: Brandeis University Press, 2011.

Lahav, Hagar. "Postsecular Jewish Theology: Reading Gordon and Buber." *Israel Studies* 19, no. 1 (April 2014): 189–213.

———. *Women, Secularism, and Belief: A Sociology of Belief in the Jewish-Israeli Secular Landscape* [Hebrew]. Jerusalem: Van Leer Institute and Hakibbutz Hameuchad, 2021.

Lederman, Eran, and Sharon Weiser-Ferguson. Foreword to *Seated in Seclusion: Bratslav Hasidim and Contemporary Design* [Hebrew], 165–67. Jerusalem: Israel Museum, 2020.

Lee, Nam-In. "The Pluralistic Concept of the Life-World and the Various Fields of the Phenomenology of the Life-World in Husserl." *Husserl Studies* 36 (2020): 47–68.

Leibovitch, Asaf. "Spiritual Traditionalists: A New Social Movement and the Israeli Identity Today" [Hebrew]. In *Beyond Halakha: Secularism, Traditionalism, and "New Age" Culture in Israel*, edited by Gideon Katz, Shalom Ratzabi, and Yaakov Yadgar, 461–497. Sede Boqer, Israel: Ben Gurion Research Institute, Ben Gurion University of the Negev, 2014.

Leibovitch, Nitzan. "Deconstructing Walter Benjamin, the Last European" [Hebrew]. *Haaretz*, November 11, 2014. Accessed January 21, 2022. www .haaretz.co.il/literature/study/.premium-1.2481125.

Leon, Nissim. *Gentle Ultra-Orthodoxy: Religious Renewal in Oriental Jewry in Israel* [Hebrew]. Jerusalem: Yad Ben-Zvi, 2010.

Levinas, Emmanuel. "Enigma and Phenomenon." In *Emmanuel Levinas: Basic Philosophical Writings*, edited by Adriaan T. Peperzak, Simon Critchley, and Robert Bernasconi, 65–78. Bloomington: Indiana University Press, 1995.

———. *Existence and Existents*. 1947. Reprint, Pittsburgh: Duquesne University Press, 2003.

———. *God, Death, and Time*. 1993. Reprint, Stanford, CA: Stanford University Press, 2000.

———. *Totality and Infinity*. 1961. Reprint, Pittsburgh: Duquesne University Press, 1969.

Loshitzky, Yosefa. *Identity Politics on the Israeli Screen*. Austin: University of Texas Press, 2001.

Loughlin, Gerard. "Within the Image: Film as Icon." In *Reframing Theology and Film: New Focus for an Emerging Discipline*, edited by Robert K. Johnston, 287–303. Grand Rapids, MI: Baker Academic, 2007.

Lyden, John C. *Film as Religion: Myths, Morals, and Rituals*. New York: New York University Press, 2003.

Maor, Haim. *Mysti-Kan: Images of Kabbalah, Mysticism, and Spirituality in Contemporary Israeli Art* [Hebrew]. Beer Sheva, Israel: Ben Gurion University Department of the Arts, 2005.

Margolin, Ron. *Inner Religion: The Phenomenology of Inner Religious Life and Its Manifestation in Jewish Sources (from the Bible to Hasidic Texts)* [Hebrew]. Ramat Gan and Jerusalem: Bar Ilan University Press and Shalom Hartman Institute, 2011.

Mark, Zvi. Foreword to *The Complete Stories of Rabbi Nachman of Bratslav* [Hebrew], edited by Zvi Mark, 17–115. Tel Aviv: Miskal and Beit-Hebrew Creation, 2014.

———. *Mysticism and Madness in the Work of Rabbi Nachman of Bratslav* [Hebrew]. Tel Aviv: Am Oved and Shalom Hartman Institute, 2008.

Marsh, Clive. *Theology Goes to the Movies: An Introduction to Critical Christian Thinking*. New York: Routledge, 2007.

Martin, Joel W., and Conrad E. Ostwalt, Jr., eds. *Screening the Sacred: Religion, Myth, and Ideology in Popular American Film*. Boulder, CO: Westview Press, 1995.

Marx, Tzvi C. *Disability in Jewish Law*. New York: Routledge, 2002.

Maslow, Abraham H. "Lessons from Peak Experiences." *Journal of Humanistic Psychology* 2, no. 1 (January 1962): 9–18.

Mayward, Joel. "The Cinematic Summoned Self: The Call of Christ in Martin Scorsese's *Silence*." *Pro Ecclesia* 40, no. 3 (2021): 464–83.

Mendes-Flohr, Paul. *Divided Passions: Jewish Intellectuals and the Experience of Modernity*. Detroit: Wayne State University Press, 1991.

———. *Progress and Its Discontents: The Struggle of Jewish Intellectuals with Modernity* [Hebrew]. Tel Aviv: Am Oved, 2010.

Merleau-Ponty, Maurice. "Eye and Mind." 1961. In *The Merleau-Ponty Aesthetics Reader: Philosophy and Painting*, edited by Galen A. Johnson, 121–48. Evanston, IL: Northwestern University Press, 1993.

———. *The Phenomenology of Perception*. 1945. Reprint, London: Routledge and Kegan Paul, 1962.

———. *The Primacy of Perception*. 1946. Reprint, Evanston, IL: Northwestern University Press, 1964.

——. *The Visible and the Invisible.* 1964. Reprint, Evanston, IL: Northwestern University Press, 1968.

Metz, Christian. *The Imaginary Signifier: Psychoanalysis and the Cinema.* Bloomington: Indiana University Press, 1982.

Mochiach, Nachum. "David Volach: Director Back from Vacation" [Hebrew]. *Habama*, January 21, 2018. Accessed February 15, 2022. www.habama.co.il/ Pages/Description.aspx?Subj=4&Area=1&ArticleID=29496.

Morin, Edgar. *The Stars: An Account of the Star-System in Motion Pictures.* New York: Grove Press, 1961.

Morgan, Michael L. *The Cambridge Introduction to Emmanuel Levinas.* Cambridge: Cambridge University Press, 2011.

Mosès, Stéphan. *The Angel of History: Rosenzweig, Benjamin, Scholem.* 1992. Reprint, Stanford, CA: Stanford University Press, 2009.

Munk, Yael. "Sacred and Profane: Yaelle Kayam Talks about Her Debut Feature *The Mountain*" [Hebrew]. *Cinematheque* 199 (May 2016): 4–9.

Murphy, Tim. *The Politics of Spirit: Phenomenology, Genealogy, Religion.* Albany: State University of New York Press, 2010.

Myers, Jody. "Kabbalah at the Turn of the 21st Century." In *Jewish Mysticism and Kabbalah: New Insights and Scholarship*, edited by Frederick E. Greenspahn, 175–90. New York: New York University Press, 2011.

Nayar, Sheila J. *The Sacred and Cinema: Reconfiguring the "Genuinely" Religious Film.* London: Continuum, 2012.

Nelson, Timothy J. "Transformations: The Social Construction of Religious Ritual." In *Understanding Religious Ritual: Theoretical Approaches and Innovations*, edited by John P. Hoffman, 9–30. New York: Routledge, 2012.

Newberg, Adina. "Elu v'Elu: Towards Integration of Identity and Multiple Narratives in the Jewish Renewal Sector in Israel." *International Journal of Jewish Education Research* 5–6 (2013): 231–78.

Nigal, Gedaliah. *The "Other" in the Hasidic Tale* [Hebrew]. Jerusalem: Institute for the Study of Hasidic Literature, 2007.

Ohana, David. "Buber Was a Mysticist. The Greatest of Mysticists, but the Next Messiah Will Be an Astronomer" [Hebrew]. *Haaretz*, January 4, 2020. Accessed January 21, 2022. www.haaretz.co.il/literature/study/.premium-1 .8399707.

Olin, Margaret. "Graven Images on Video? The Second Commandment and Jewish Identity." *Discourse* 22, no. 1 (Winter 2000): 7–30.

———. *The Nation without Art: Examining Modern Discourses on Jewish Art.* Lincoln: University of Nebraska Press, 2001.

Omer, Mordechai. "*Tikkun*: Shamanism in Art—The Israeli Option." In *Perspectives on Israeli Art of the Seventies: Tikkun*, 449–508. Tel Aviv: Genia Schreiber University Art Gallery, Tel Aviv University, 1998.

Otto, Rudolf. *The Idea of the Holy.* 1917. Reprint, Oxford: Oxford University Press, 1958.

Padva, Gilad. "Gay Martyrs, Jewish Saints, and Infatuated Yeshiva Boys in the New Israeli Religious Queer Cinema." *Journal of Modern Jewish Studies* 10, no. 3 (2011): 421–38.

Parciack, Ronie. "Beyond the Fence: Religious Sentiment in Israeli Cinema" [Hebrew]. In *Fictive Looks: On Israeli Cinema*, edited by Nurith Gertz, Orly Lubin, and Judd Ne'eman, 328–41. Ramat Aviv, Israel: Open University Press, 1998.

———. "The Religious Experience in Israeli Cinema" [Hebrew]. Master's thesis, Hebrew University, 1995.

Pedaya, Haviva. *Walking through Trauma: Rituals of Movement in Jewish Myth, Mysticism, and History* [Hebrew]. Tel Aviv: Resling, 2011.

Peleg, Yaron. *Directed by God: Jewishness in Contemporary Israeli Film and Television.* Austin: University of Texas Press, 2016.

———. "Marking a New Holy Community: *God's Neighbors* and the Ascendancy of a New Religious Hegemony in Israel." *Jewish Film and New Media* 1, no. 1 (Spring 2013): 64–86.

———. "Secularity and Its Discontents: Religiosity in Contemporary Israeli Culture." *Jewish Film and New Media* 3, no. 1 (Spring 2015): 3–24.

Pence, Jeffrey. "Cinema of the Sublime: Theorizing the Ineffable." *Poetics Today* 25, no. 1 (Spring 2004): 29–66.

Persico, Tomer. *The Jewish Meditative Tradition* [Hebrew]. Tel Aviv: Tel Aviv University Press, 2016.

———. "Neo-Hasidic Revival: Expressivist Uses of Traditional Lore." *Modern Judaism* 34, no. 3 (October 2014): 287–308.

Piekarz, Mendel. *Studies in Bratslav Hasidism* [Hebrew]. Jerusalem: Bialik Institute, 1995.

Pfeffer, Anshel. "*Haaretz* Poll: Most Jews in Israel Believe in God, but Support Busses on Saturday" [Hebrew]. *Haaretz*, October 30, 2019. Accessed January 21, 2022. www.haaretz.co.il/news/education/.premium-MAGAZINE-1.8055976.

Plate, S. Brent. Introduction to *Representing Religion in World Cinema: Film-making, Mythmaking, Culture Making*, edited by S. Brent Plate, 1–18. New York: Palgrave, 2003.

———. *Religion and Film: Cinema and the Re-Creation of the World*. Harrow, UK: Wallflower Press, 2009.

Preminger, Aner. "Between the Sin of Hubris in Greek Tragedy and Self-Righteousness and Self-Deprecation in the Binding of Isaac: An Inter-textual Reading of David Volach's *My Father, My Lord* (2007)" [Hebrew]. In *The Curator's Book*, edited by Erez Pery, 81–86. Ashkelon, Israel: Sapir Academic College, 2008.

Price, Brian. "Sontag, Bresson, and the Unfixable." *Postscript* 26, no. 2 (Winter–Spring 2007): 81–90.

Quicke, Andrew. "Phenomenology and Film: An Examination of a Religious Approach to Film Theory by Henri Agel and Amédée Ayfre." *Journal of Media and Religion* 4, no. 4 (2005): 235–50.

Rabinbach, Anson. "Between Enlightenment and Apocalypse: Benjamin, Bloch and Modern German Jewish Messianism." *New German Critique*, no. 34 (1985): 78–124.

Ram, Uri. "Why Are the Teachings of a One-Time Radical Leftist Enjoying a Resurgence in Israel?" *Haaretz*, June 25, 2015. Accessed June 28, 2015. www .haaretz.com/news/features/.premium-1.663086.

Raphael, Melissa. *Judaism and the Visual Image: A Jewish Theology of Art*. London: Continuum, 2009.

Rapoport-Albert, Ada. *Studies in Hasidism, Sabbatianism, and Gender* [Hebrew]. Jerusalem: Zalman Shazar Center, 2015.

Raveh, Inbar. "A Story of Women's Suffering: A Gender Reading of the Story of Judith, Wife of Rabbi Hiyya." *Journal of Ancient Judaism* 3 (2012): 68–76.

Ravitzky, Aviezer. *Freedom Inscribed: Diverse Voices of the Jewish Religious Thought* [Hebrew]. Tel Aviv: Am Oved, 2000.

Reif, Stefan C. *Judaism and Hebrew Prayer: New Perspectives on Jewish Liturgical History*. 1993. Reprint, Tel Aviv: Kineret-Zmora Bitan-Dvir, 2010.

Reik, Theodor. *Ritual: Four Psychoanalytic Studies*. 1946. Reprint, New York: International Universities Press, 1958.

Reiser, Daniel. *Vision as a Mirror: Imagery Techniques in Twentieth Century Jewish Mysticism* [Hebrew]. Los Angeles: Cherub Press, 2014.

Riviere, Joan. "Womanliness as Masquerade." In *Formations of Fantasy*, edited by Victor Burgin, James Donald, and Cora Kaplan, 35–44. London: Methuen, 1986.

Rivlin, Yuval. *The Mouse That Roared: Jewish Identity in American and Israeli Cinema* [Hebrew]. Jerusalem: Toby Press, 2009.

Rosen, Philip. "Belief in Bazin." In *Opening Bazin: Postwar Film Theory and Its Afterlife*, edited by Dudley Andrew and Hervé Joubert-Laurencin, 107–18. Oxford: Oxford University Press, 2011.

Rosenthal, Gilbert S. "*Tikkun ha-Olam*: The Metamorphosis of a Concept." *Journal of Religion* 85, no. 2 (April 2005): 214–40.

Rosner, Shmuel, and Camil Fuchs. *#IsraeliJudaism, A Cultural Revolution* [Hebrew]. Jerusalem: Jewish People Policy Institute and Kinneret, Zmora-Bitan, 2018.

Ross, Nicham. *A Beloved-Despised Tradition: Modern Jewish Identity and Neo-Hasidic Writing at the Beginning of the Twentieth Century* [Hebrew]. Beer Sheva, Israel: Ben Gurion University Press, 2014.

——. *A Pearl Hidden in the Sand: I. L. Peretz and Hasidic Tales* [Hebrew]. Jerusalem: Hebrew University Magnes Press, 2013.

Ruah-Midbar, Marianna. "A Channeler, A Healer, and A Shaman Meet at the Rabbi's: Jewish Israeli Identities in the New Age" [Hebrew]. In *Beyond Halakha: Secularism, Traditionalism, and "New Age" Culture in Israel*, edited by Gideon Katz, Shalom Ratzabi, and Yaakov Yadgar, 498–528. Sede Boqer, Israel: Ben Gurion Research Institute, Ben Gurion University of the Negev, 2014.

——. "Current Jewish Spiritualities in Israeli: A New Age." *Modern Judaism* 32, no. 1 (2012): 102–24.

——. "The Temptation of Legitimacy: Lilith's Adoption and Adaption in Contemporary Feminist Spirituality and Their Meanings." *Modern Judaism* 39, no. 2 (2019): 125–43.

Ruah-Midbar, Marianna, and Eliyahu Eshed. "Canaanites and Neo-Pagans in Canaan: Comparison between Two Israeli Movements of the Last Century" [Hebrew]. *Reshit* 6 (2022): 25–56.

Ruah-Midbar, Marianna, and Nurit Zaidman. "'Everything starts within': New Age Values, Images, and Language in Israeli Advertising." *Journal of Contemporary Religion* 28, no. 3 (2013): 421–36.

Sagi, Avi. *The Jewish-Israeli Voyage: Culture and Identity*. Jerusalem: Shalom Hartman Institute, 2006.

———. *Prayer after "The Death of God": A Phenomenological Study in Hebrew Literature*. Ramat Gan and Jerusalem: Bar Ilan University Press and Shalom Hartman Institute, 2011.

Sasson, Theodore, Ephraim Tabory, and Dana Selinger-Abutbul. "Framing Religious Conflict: Popular Israeli Discourse on Religion and State." *Journal of Church and State* 52, no. 4 (2010): 662–85.

Savran, George. *"He Came Upon the Place": Biblical Theophany Narratives* [Hebrew]. Tel Aviv: Hakibbutz Hameuchad, 2010.

Scarry, Elaine. *The Body in Pain: The Making and Unmaking of the World*. Oxford: Oxford University Press, 1985.

Schnitzer, Meir. "An Artistic Miracle" [Hebrew]. *NRG*, August 24, 2007. Accessed August 11, 2013. www.nrg.co.il/online/47/ART1/626/947.html.

Scholem, Gershom. *Major Trends in Jewish Mysticism*. 1941. Reprint, New York: Schocken Books, 1974.

———. *The Messianic Idea in Judaism and Other Essays on Jewish Spirituality*. New York: Schocken Books, 1995.

Schrader, Paul. "Rethinking Transcendental Style." In *Transcendental Style in Film, with a New Introduction*, 1–33. Berkeley: University of California Press, 2018.

———. *Transcendental Style in Film: Ozu, Bresson, Dreyer*. Berkeley: University of California Press, 1972.

Seigelshifer, Valeria, and Tova Hartman. "The Emergence of Israeli Orthodox Women Filmmakers." *Shofar* 38, no. 2 (Summer 2020): 125–61.

———. "Staying and Critiquing: Israeli Women Orthodox Filmmakers." *Israel Studies Review* 34, no. 1 (2019): 110–30.

Shandler, Jeffrey. "'Serious' Talk." *AJS Review* 35, no. 2 (2011): 349–55.

Shapira, Anita. *Jews, Zionists, and in Between* [Hebrew]. Tel Aviv: Am Oved, 2007.

Sharabi, Asaf. "'Soft' Religion and 'Strict' Religion: The Teshuva Movement in Israel" [Hebrew]. In *Beyond Halakha: Secularism, Traditionalism, and "New Age" Culture in Israel*, edited by Gideon Katz, Shalom Ratzabi, and Yaacov Yadgar, 434–60. Sede Boqer, Israel: Ben Gurion Research Institute, 2014.

Shaviro, Steven. *The Cinematic Body*. Minneapolis: University of Minnesota Press, 1993.

Sheleg, Yair. *The Jewish Renaissance in Israeli Society: The Emergence of a New Jew* [Hebrew]. Jerusalem: Israel Democracy Institute, 2010.

———. *The New Religious Jews: Recent Developments among Observant Jews in Israel* [Hebrew]. Jerusalem: Keter, 2000.

Shemer, Yaron. "Failing Intersectionality: Gender, Ethnicity, and Religious Traditions in Recent Israeli Films." *Quarterly Review of Film and Video* 36, no. 5 (2019): 365–91.

Shenhar, Aliza. *Love and Hate: Biblical Wives, Lovers, and Mistresses* [Hebrew]. Haifa: Pardes, 2011.

Shenker, Yael. "Representations of the Disengagement in Documentary Cinema and Poetry of the National-Religious Community in Israel" [Hebrew]. *Theory and Criticism* 47 (Winter 2016): 181–202.

Shohat, Ella. *Israeli Cinema: East/West and the Politics of Representation*. Rev. ed. London: I. B. Tauris, 2010.

Sinnerbrink, Robert. "Cinematic Belief: Bazinian Cinephilia and Malick's *The Tree of Life*." *Angelaki* 17, no. 4 (2012): 95–117.

Sivan, Avishai. "Directors and Scriptwriters to Watch: Avishai Sivan." In *A Decade in Motion: The New Voice of Israeli Cinema*, edited by Avital Bekerman and Noa Mandel, 34. Tel Aviv: Israeli Film Fund, 2012.

———. Interview. In *The Wanderer—Promotional Booklet for Cannes 2010*. Or Yehuda, Israel: Mouth Agape, 2010.

Sobchack, Vivian. *The Address of the Eye: Phenomenology and Film Experience*. Princeton, NJ: Princeton University Press, 1992.

———. *Carnal Thoughts: Embodiment and Moving Image Culture*. Berkeley: University of California Press, 2004.

———. "Embodying Transcendence: On the Literal, the Material, and the Cinematic Sublime." *Material Religion* 4, no. 2 (2008): 194–203.

Sokolowski, Robert. *Introduction to Phenomenology*. Cambridge: Cambridge University Press, 2000.

Sontag, Susan. "Spiritual Style in the Films of Robert Bresson." In *The Films of Robert Bresson: A Casebook*, edited by Bret Cardullo, 29–44. London: Anthem Press, 2009.

Stadler, Nurit. "Work, Livelihood, and the Miraculous: Defining the Haredi Dilemma in Israel" [Hebrew]. In *Israeli Haredim: Integration without Assimilation?*, edited by Emanuel Sivan and Kimmy Caplan, 88–112. Jerusalem: Van Leer Institute and Hakkibutz Hameuchad, 2003.

Steinsaltz, Adin. *A Guide to Jewish Prayer*. New York: Schocken Books, 2000.

———. Introduction to *Six Stories of Rabbi Nachman of Bratslav* [Hebrew], edited by Adin Steinsaltz, 7–26. Tel Aviv: Dvir Publishing, 1995.

Talmon, Miri. "A Touch Away from Cultural Others: Negotiating Israeli Jewish Identity on Television." *Shofar* 31, no. 2 (2013): 55–72.

Taylor, Charles. "Two Theories of Modernity." *Public Culture* 11, no. 1 (1999): 153–74.

Tessler, Yitzhak. "Here He Comes: The Ultimate Dos in Israeli Cinema" [Hebrew]. *Ynet*, February 26, 2013. Accessed May 31, 2015. www.ynet.co.il/articles/0,7340,L-4348615,00.html.

Triger, Zvi. "The Self-Defeating Nature of 'Modesty'—Based Gender Segregation." *Israel Studies* 18, no. 3 (Fall 2013): 19–28.

Tybjerg, Casper. "Forms of the Intangible: Carl Th. Dreyer and the Concept of 'Transcendental Style.'" *Northern Lights* 6 (2008): 59–73.

Utin, Pablo. *The New Israeli Cinema: Conversations with Filmmakers* [Hebrew]. Tel Aviv: Resling, 2008.

Valman, Nadia. *The Jewess in Nineteenth-Century British Literary Culture*. Cambridge: Cambridge University Press, 2007.

Vinig, Marlyn. *Haredi Cinema* [Hebrew]. Tel Aviv: Resling, 2011.

———. *Their Own Cinema: The New Female Wave of Ultra-Orthodox Cinema* [Hebrew]. Tel Aviv: Resling, 2021.

Warner, Rick. "Filming a Miracle: *Ordet*, *Silent Light*, and the Spirit of Contemplative Cinema." *Critical Quarterly* 57, no. 2 (2015): 46–71.

Weinstock, Moshe. *Uman: The Israeli Journey to the Grave of Rabbi Nachman of Bratslav* [Hebrew]. Tel Aviv: Yediot Acharonot and Chemed Books, 2011.

Weiss, Shayna, "Frum with Benefits: Israeli Television, Globalization, and *Srugim*'s American Appeal." *Jewish Film and New Media* 4, no. 1 (2016): 68–89.

Weiss, Tzahi. *Letters by Which Heaven and Earth Were Created: The Origins and the Meanings of the Perceptions of Alphabetic Letters as Independent Units in Jewish Sources of Late Antiquity* [Hebrew]. Jerusalem: Bialik Institute, 2014.

Werczberger, Rachel. "Self, Identity, and Healing in the Ritual of Jewish Spiritual Renewal in Israel." In *Kabbalah and Contemporary Spiritual Revival*, edited by Boaz Huss, 75–100. Beer Sheva, Israel: Ben-Gurion University Press, 2011.

Werczberger, Rachel, and Na'ama Azulay. "The Jewish Renewal Movement in Israeli Secular Society." *Contemporary Jewry* 31 (2011): 107–28.

Wexler, Philip. *The Mystical Society: An Emerging Social Vision* [Hebrew]. Jerusalem: Carmel Publishing, 2007.

Wilson, Eric G. *The Strange World of David Lynch: Transcendental Irony from Eraserhead to Mulholland Dr.* New York: Continuum, 2007.

Wiskind-Elper, Ora. *Tradition and Fantasy in the Tales of Reb Nahman of Bratslav*. Albany: State University of New York Press, 1998.

Wolfson, Elliot R. "New Jerusalem Glowing: Songs and Poems of Leonard Cohen in a Kabbalistic Key." *Kabbalah: Journal for the Study of Jewish Mystical Texts* 15 (2006): 103–53.

———. "Secrecy, Modesty, and the Feminine: Kabbalistic Traces in the Thought of Levinas." *Journal of Jewish Thought and Philosophy* 14, no. 1–2 (2006): 193–224.

———. *Through a Speculum That Shines: Vision and Imagination in Medieval Jewish Mysticism.* Princeton, NJ: Princeton University Press, 1994.

Wolosky, Shira. "Foucault and Jewish Feminism: The Mehitzah as Dividing Practice." *Nashim* 17 (2009): 9–32.

Wright, Wendy M. "Religion, Spirituality, and Film." In *The Continuum Companion to Religion and Film*, edited by William L. Blizek, 198–208. London: Continuum, 2009.

Yadgar, Yaacov. *Beyond Secularization: Traditionalism and the Critique of Israeli Secularism* [Hebrew]. Jerusalem: Van Leer Institute and Hakkibutz Hameuchad, 2012.

Yassif, Eli. *The Hebrew Folktale: History, Genre, Meaning* [Hebrew]. Jerusalem: Bialik Institute, 1994.

———. *Safed Legends: Life and Fantasy in the City of Kabbalah* [Hebrew]. Haifa: University of Haifa Press, Yediot Acharonot, and Chemed Books, 2011.

Yonah, Yossi, and Yehuda Goodman. "The Gordian Knot between Religiousness and Secularity in Israel: Inclusion, Exclusion, and Transformation" [Hebrew]. In *Secularization and Secularism: Interdisciplinary Perspectives*, edited by Yochi Fischer, 197–221. Jerusalem: Van Leer Institute and Hakkibutz Hameuchad, 2015.

———. "Introduction: Religiousness and Secularity in Israel—Other Possible Perspectives" [Hebrew]. In *Maelstrom of Identities: A Critical Look at Religion and Secularity in Israel*, edited by Yossi Yonah and Yehuda Goodman, 9–45. Jerusalem: Van Leer Institute and Hakkibutz Hameuchad, 2004.

Zanger, Anat. "*Beaufort* and *My Father, My Lord*: Traces of the Binding Myth and the Mother's Voice." In *Israeli Cinema: Identities in Motion*, edited by Miri Talmon and Yaron Peleg, 225–38. Austin: University of Texas Press, 2011.

———. "Between the Sea and the Mikveh: The Siren's Voice in Contemporary Israeli Cinema" [Hebrew]. In *Gender in Israel: New Studies on Gender in the Yishuv and State*, edited by Margalit Shilo and Gideon Katz, 521–42. Beer Sheva, Israel: Ben Gurion University Press, 2011.

Zeitlin, Hillel. *In the Grove of Hasidism and Kabbalah* [Hebrew]. 1965. Reprint, Tel Aviv: Yavne Publishing, 2003.

Zicherman, Haim. *Black Blue-White: A Journey into the Haredi Society in Israel* [Hebrew]. Tel Aviv: Yediot Acharonot and Chemed Books, 2014.

Zinnbauer, Brian J., Kenneth I. Pargament, Brenda Cole, Mark S. Rye, Eric M. Butter, Timothy G. Belavich, Kathleen M. Hipp, Allie B. Scott, and Jill L. Kadar. "Religion and Spirituality: Unfuzzying the Fuzzy." *Journal for the Scientific Study of Religion* 36, no. 4 (December 1997): 549–64.

Ziv, Amalia. "'Our Virgin Friends and Wives'? Female Sexual Subjectivity in Yona Wallach's Poetry." *Hebrew Studies* 56, no. 1 (2015): 333–56.

INDEX

Note: Page numbers appearing in italics refer to photographs.

Printed in the USA
CPSIA information can be obtained
at www.ICGtesting.com
BVHW030152230823
668800BV00001B/127